TUCSON

FIRST EDITION

Tucson

Great Destinations

Kim Westerman

The Countryman Press
Woodstock, Vermont

To my darling CC and his Oliness

ISBN 978-1-58157-046-5

Interior photos by the author unless otherwise specified
Book design by Bodenweber Design
Page composition by Chelsea Cloeter
Maps by Mapping Specialists Ltd., Madison, WI, © The Countryman Press

Published by The Countryman Press, P.O. Box 748, Woodstock, Vermont 05091

Distributed by W. W. Norton & Company, Inc., 500 Fifth Avenue, New York, NY 10110

Printed in the United States of America

10 9 8 7 6 5 4 3 2 1

Recommended by *National Geographic Traveler* and *Travel + Leisure* magazines

A crisp and critical approach, for travelers who want to live like locals.
—*USA Today*

Great Destinations™ guidebooks are known for their comprehensive, critical coverage of regions of extraordinary cultural interest and natural beauty. Each title in this series is continuously updated with each printing to ensure accurate and timely information. All the books contain more than one hundred photographs and maps.

Current titles available:

THE ADIRONDACK BOOK

THE ALASKA PANHANDLE

ATLANTA

AUSTIN, SAN ANTONIO
& THE TEXAS HILL COUNTRY

BALTIMORE, ANNAPOLIS & THE CHESAPEAKE BAY

THE BERKSHIRE BOOK

BIG SUR, MONTEREY BAY
& GOLD COAST WINE COUNTRY

CAPE CANAVERAL, COCOA BEACH
& FLORIDA'S SPACE COAST

THE CHARLESTON, SAVANNAH
& COASTAL ISLANDS BOOK

THE COAST OF MAINE BOOK

COLORADO'S CLASSIC MOUNTAIN TOWNS

COSTA RICA

DOMINICAN REPUBLIC

THE ERIE CANAL

THE FINGER LAKES BOOK

THE FOUR CORNERS REGION

GALVESTON, SOUTH PADRE ISLAND
& THE TEXAS GULF COAST

GLACIER NATIONAL PARK & THE CANADIAN ROCKIES

GUATEMALA

THE HAMPTONS BOOK

HAWAII'S BIG ISLAND

HONOLULU & OAHU

THE JERSEY SHORE: ATLANTIC CITY TO CAPE MAY

KAUAI

LAKE TAHOE & RENO

LAS VEGAS

LOS CABOS & BAJA CALIFORNIA SUR

MAUI

MEMPHIS AND THE DELTA BLUES TRAIL

MEXICO CITY, PUEBLA & CUERNAVACA

MICHIGAN'S UPPER PENINSULA

MONTREAL & QUEBEC CITY

THE NANTUCKET BOOK

THE NAPA & SONOMA BOOK

NORTH CAROLINA'S OUTER BANKS
& THE CRYSTAL COAST

NOVA SCOTIA & PRINCE EDWARD ISLAND

OAXACA

OREGON WINE COUNTRY

PALM BEACH, FORT LAUDERDALE, MIAMI
& THE FLORIDA KEYS

PALM SPRINGS & DESERT RESORTS

PHILADELPHIA, BRANDYWINE VALLEY
& BUCKS COUNTY

PHOENIX, SCOTTSDALE, SEDONA
& CENTRAL ARIZONA

PLAYA DEL CARMEN, TULUM & THE RIVIERA MAYA

SALT LAKE CITY, PARK CITY, PROVO
& UTAH'S HIGH COUNTRY RESORTS

SAN DIEGO & TIJUANA

SAN JUAN, VIEQUES & CULEBRA

SAN MIGUEL DE ALLENDE & GUANAJUATO

THE SANTA FE & TAOS BOOK

SANTA BARBARA AND CALIFORNIA'S CENTRAL COAST

THE SARASOTA, SANIBEL ISLAND & NAPLES BOOK

THE SEATTLE & VANCOUVER BOOK

THE SHENANDOAH VALLEY BOOK

TOURING EAST COAST WINE COUNTRY

TUCSON

VIRGINIA BEACH, RICHMOND & TIDEWATER VIRGINIA

WASHINGTON, D.C., AND NORTHERN VIRGINIA

YELLOWSTONE & GRAND TETON NATIONAL PARKS
& JACKSON HOLE

YOSEMITE & THE SOUTHERN SIERRA NEVADA

The authors in this series are professional travel writers who have lived for many years in the regions they describe. Honest and painstakingly critical, full of information only a local can provide, Great Destinations guidebooks give you all the practical knowledge you need to enjoy the best of each region.

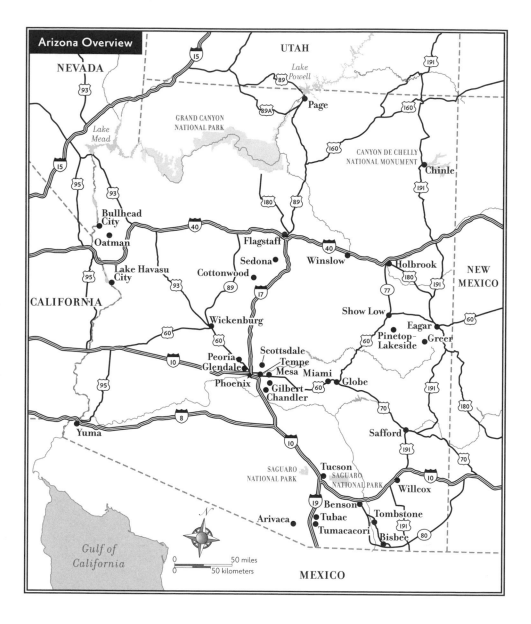

Arizona Overview

UTAH

NEVADA

Lake
Powell

Page

GRAND CANYON
NATIONAL PARK

Lake
Mead

CANYON DE CHELLY
NATIONAL MONUMENT

Chinle

Bullhead
City

Oatman

Flagstaff

Winslow

Holbrook

NEW
MEXICO

Sedona

Lake Havasu
City

Cottonwood

Show Low

Eagar

CALIFORNIA

Wickenburg

Pinetop-
Lakeside

Greer

Peoria
Glendale

Scottsdale
Tempe
Mesa

Miami

Phoenix

Globe

Gilbert
Chandler

Safford

Yuma

SAGUARO
NATIONAL PARK

Tucson

SAGUARO
NATIONAL PARK

Willcox

Benson

Tombstone

Arivaca

Tubac

Tumacacori

Bisbee

Gulf of
California

N

0   50 miles
0   50 kilometers

MEXICO

CONTENTS

ACKNOWLEDGMENTS   8

INTRODUCTION   8

THE WAY THIS BOOK WORKS   9

1 HISTORY: *From Cow Town to Urban Center*   11
Natural History 12
  Basic Topography 12 · Origin of the Basin and Range 12 · More Recent Geological Activity 15 ·
  Fossil Record 15
Social History 16
  Early People 16 · The Hohokam 16 · The Akimel O'odham and Tohono O'odham 18 ·
  The Establishment of Tucson 20 · Tucson Today 22

2 TRANSPORTATION: *Getting There & Getting Around*   27

3 LODGING: *The Best Places for Any Budget*   35

4 CULTURE: *Multicultural Convergence*   61

5 RESTAURANTS & FOOD PURVEYORS: *Salud!*   111

6 RECREATION: *Indoor & Outdoor Fun*   151

7 SHOPPING: *Fab Finds*   185

8 INFORMATION: *Practical Matters*   203

9 IF TIME IS SHORT: *Best of Tucson*   217

GENERAL INDEX   219

LODGING BY PRICE   229   DINING BY PRICE   230   DINING BY CUISINE   231

MAPS
  Arizona 6 · Tucson Metropolitan Area 28 · Downtown Tucson 62 · University of Arizona 67

Acknowledgments

Thanks first to my editor, Kim Grant, who gave me the time and space I needed to write this book. Thanks to the fabulous writers, researchers, and fact-checkers who contributed to various chapters: Morgan Schuldt (Transportation, Lodging, Restaurants & Food Purveyors, and Shopping), Lisa O'Neill (Culture), Aisha Sloan (Recreation, Information), and Christine Bell (History). And thanks to all of my Tucson friends who continue to help me keep up with this ever-changing city.

Thanks to my parents for always encouraging my fascination with travel and always giving me the freedom to go. Thanks to my sister, who has put up with me since the day she was born. And thanks to my dear MaMa, who taught me to know my heart, which has led me to the most beautiful places.

Thanks to Carol for eating her way through Tucson with me and for all the unknown journeys we have yet to take.

To the readers of this book: I'd love to hear about your travels in Tucson, so drop me a line at kwesterm@aol.com.

Introduction

This book is for visitors and residents alike who appreciate expert advice on how to make the most of their time in Tucson. *Great Destinations Tucson* not only recommends the best hotels, restaurants, and activities, but it will also guide you through the logistics of navigating in and around the city, as well as provide useful lessons in the history and culture of Tucson and its surroundings.

A fast 90-mile freeway drive from Phoenix, Arizona's capital and largest urban center, Tucson is, comparatively, a laid-back place: part college town, part winter getaway, and part serene desertscape. Travelers unfamiliar with the Sonoran Desert will be happy to find that it's the greenest desert on earth. This notwithstanding, its lunar contours make it a strange place for newcomers, and its strangeness turns out to be one of its most compelling features.

Tucson appeals to naturalists, especially hikers and birdwatchers. Its world-class resorts and spas, along with top-rated golf courses, make it one of the best relaxation destinations in the country. And there's no better Sonoran food north of the Mexican border than here in the Old Pueblo.

There is no shortage of diverse culture, either. Tucson is home to an international photography center, a center for integrative medicine, and a large Native American reservation. Nightlife is especially vibrant around the University of Arizona, and farther afield there is an award-winning local opera company, a popular chamber music series, and several highly regarded dance and theater troupes.

Contrary to popular belief, Tucson has four distinct seasons, and temperatures routinely drop below freezing on winter evenings. Spring brings stunning wildflower displays, and many native plants bloom a second time in the fall. Summer is an extreme experience. High temperatures can remain above 100 degrees for weeks at a time, but that's when dramatic monsoons grace the desert and cool things down, leaving behind the sweet smell of creosote.

Whether you are planning a short visit, a long trip, or a permanent move, this book is designed to help you have a wonderful journey.

The Way This Book Works

This book is divided into nine chapters and further divided into subcategories, depending on what makes the most sense for each chapter. For example, restaurants are categorized by cuisine and lodgings are broken down by type (resort, B&B, etc.).

Entries include as much specific information as possible—phone numbers, addresses, Web sites—so that you can contact the venue in any way you choose. All information was checked for accuracy as close as possible to the book's publication date, but it is always wise to call ahead.

The book utilizes price ranges rather than specific prices, as costs change with great frequency. Lodging price ranges are based on a per-room rate with double occupancy in high season. (Off-season rates are often lower than listed here.) Restaurant price ranges represent the cost of one meal, including appetizer, main course, and dessert, but not cocktails, wine, or beer.

Price Codes

Code	Lodging	Dining
Inexpensive	Up to $100	Up to $15
Moderate	$100–200	$15–30
Expensive	$200–300	$30–65
Very Expensive	Over $300	$65 or more

The following abbreviations are used for credit card information:

AE: American Express
CB: Carte Blanche
D: Discover Card
DC: Diner's Club
MC: MasterCard
V: Visa

Pottery exhibit at Arizona State Museum Metropolitan Tucson Convention & Visitors Bureau

1

HISTORY

From Cow Town to Urban Center

Tucson and its environs have rich natural and social history. The desert and surrounding foothills and mountains are not only scenic, but provide opportunities for hiking and for appreciating the rich animal and plant life. There are also the geological landforms that shaped this terrain millions of years ago. Life here, both animal and human, has had to adapt in order to occupy such a hostile, if majestic, region.

The land was created in a dramatic geological event that began some 40 million years ago, ripping apart the earth and creating the barriers and ranges that would give the Sonoran Desert the hot, arid environment it enjoys today. It has been home to mammoths, giant ground sloths, giant beavers, lions, camels, and more.

The Hohokam people, who vanished from this valley more than six hundred years ago, made the most of their desert environment, using native flora (such as the agave and the saguaro cactus) for construction purposes and building complex and advanced canal systems from the rivers to irrigate their crops and provide their villages with water. Later, early in the 20th century, the newly created federal Reclamation Service joined the farmers of the Salt River Valley to build the Roosevelt Dam, taming the river that had tormented farmers in the region for more than two thousand years and providing much of Arizona with hydroelectric power.

In the 1930s, with the advent of swamp coolers (evaporative coolers that work with water), it became more practical (and more comfortable) to live in the desert. Tucson and the surrounding cities grew explosively, and even more so when air conditioners became available in the middle of the century. As of July 1, 2008, the population of Metropolitan Tucson has been estimated at 1,023,320. People come to Tucson for health reasons, especially asthmatics, as the hot, dry, clean air carries fewer allergens that can irritate the lungs and bronchial tubes. Veterans who had been gassed in World War I were sent to Tucson for respiratory treatments at the new veterans hospital, as well as for the air. The heat is even good for those who suffer from arthritis.

Artists also flock to Tucson. The city is home to dozens of writers, painters, and jewelry makers, among others. Perhaps it's the sunshine, or the mountains and succulents, but something about this oasis appeals to them.

Once, these lands were occupied by the Hohokam. They were followed by the Tohono O'odham and Akimel O'odham, or Pima. For years the Spanish held the area, and for a time, when Mexico became independent from Spain, Tucson was part of Mexico. This land included some of southern Arizona and southwestern New Mexico, and today it is all part of the United States. There are even towns in Arizona that are still a part of both countries, such as the border town of Nogales. Cultures have mixed and clashed here, and each has left its imprint upon the present community.

NATURAL HISTORY

Basic Topography

The Sonoran Desert is unique in its topography, which ranges from deserts at sea level to mountains that rise to 9,500 feet (2,900 m). This is characteristic of the geological province it occupies, the Basin and Range, which is marked by wide, low valleys that are bordered by long, narrow mountain ranges. Each of these valleys has streams that normally run dry but connect to a major river, such as the Salt or Gila river.

The desert's topography has a strong influence upon the region's peculiar climate. Mountains, depressions, and other topographic features serve as barriers, and these barriers direct the movement of air masses. Where the region would normally receive moist air from the Pacific Ocean, there is a barrier known as a confinement, which, as the name implies, confines the moist air from the Pacific. As a result, moisture that would have created rain in the desert is absorbed. Not all of the moisture is absorbed, however; the desert does get some rain, especially during the summer monsoon season, when the region gets most of its annual rainfall and is subjected to some truly violent and spectacular storms. Still, the Tucson area averages only about 12 inches of rain a year.

The topography of the areas bordering the Sonoran Desert further contributes to the region's climate. West of the desert are Baja California's Sierra San Pedro Martir and Southern California's Laguna Mountains, which run into the Sierra Nevada farther north, near Palm Springs. Here, the rocks range from 140 to 80 million years old.

To the northeast lies an immense cliff called the Mogollon Rim, which marks the edge of the Colorado Plateau, another geological province. This region stretches across Utah and Colorado.

The eastern edge of the Sonoran Desert is primarily made up of mountains and high valleys. Here, the vertical relief can be startling: Elevations range from 3,000 feet (915 m) to 10,000 feet (3,050 m). The valleys here range from sea level near Yuma to 5,000 feet (1,525 m) in southeastern Arizona. Because rising air cools, the climate is more temperate in the areas of higher elevation. The deserts give way to grassland valleys because of greater rainfall and colder winters.

Finally, on the southeastern edge of the Sonoran Desert is the Sierra Madre Occidental, a mountainous set of relatively young (geologically speaking) volcanic rocks.

All of these landforms contribute to the climate of the Sonoran Desert, from its arid nature to its hot summers and mild, pleasant winters. They also come into play when people first enter the region, deciding where and how they will make a living in this hostile, but beautiful, environment.

Origin of the Basin and Range

The Sonoran Desert was created by an event that literally ripped North America apart. It has been dubbed the "Basin and Range disturbance" and was the end result of a sequence of events that stretch back over the last 40 million years. There is evidence that strongly sug-

Natural stone spires at Chiricahua National Monument L.S. Warhol

gests that before this, the province was a smooth upland, devoid of the numerous mountain ranges so distinctive of its modern-day landscape.

About 40 million years ago, there was a great deal of volcanism in the area. Much of this activity took place deep within the earth, but there were surface volcanoes. Some of these collapsed into themselves and formed calderas, or large, circular basins. These can be seen in today's Superstition and Chiricahua mountains. The heat from all this activity melted portions of the lower continental crust, making it far more malleable. At roughly the same time, the Pacific Coast became attached to the edge of the Pacific Ocean tectonic plate. Here is where the ripping begins.

Earth's surface is made up of enormous plates of rock that rest upon a thick, molten layer called the mantle. The mantle is fluid, but not fluid in the way we would normally think of it. Rather, it's like Silly Putty: thick, viscous, and extremely slow to move. But move it does.

Beneath the mantle is a fluid outer core. Again, *fluid* is relative. The outer core is a thicker layer of molten rock that surrounds the even denser, but solid, inner core.

The mantle subjects the plates riding it to intense heat and stress. Although the Pacific Ocean tectonic plate was now attached to the Pacific Coast, it was still on its way northwest, now carrying part of the North American tectonic plate away with it. The lower crust of this region, because of the intense heat of volcanism, had partially melted and began to stretch

Manzanita and rock formations at Chiricahua National Monument L.S. Warhol

with the pull of the Pacific plate. Softened as it was, the crust had no real chance of withstanding the strain and began to pull apart.

The result was an enormous fault zone. To the west of this fractured area, the land was being pulled away. By 12 million years ago, the entire area was caught up in the stretching, expanding in some areas by as much as 80 percent of their original size.

While the lower portion of the crust had melted, the upper part of the crust remained brittle and solid. When subjected to the stress of what was essentially a tug-of-war, the upper crust shattered into a multitude of long, narrow pieces. After breaking, the narrower fragments of crust sank into the molten lower crust while the wider fragments retained more of their former elevation, creating the basins and ranges for which this province is named. Over time, the basins filled with dirt and sand, creating the shape we see today. Nearly all of these formations were born simultaneously in this way. Because of the origin of the stresses, nearly all of the mountains and valleys of this province run perpendicular to the trend of stretching.

The pulling ceased about 8 million years ago. The lower portions of the crust cooled, and though there have been other geologic processes active in the region, the primary one has been erosion.

There is no place quite like the Basin and Range in all the world. From its climate to its parallel mountain ranges, it is a unique environment.

More Recent Geological Activity

When the northwest motion of the Pacific tectonic plate began to pull a portion of the North American tectonic plate with it, it opened up fissures in the earth's crust. This allowed basaltic magma from the mantle to well up and flood areas of the surface. There are three places where this happened in the Sonoran Desert, and all of these have occurred in the last 4 million years. The most notable of these is the Pinacate field, which is located north of Rocky Point, Sonora. The field is home to a 4,000-foot-tall volcano made up of multiple lava flow and ash layers. It lies at the center of the field, surrounded by an alien environment of single-eruption cinder cones, more flows, and craters formed by steam explosions, called diatremes. Some of the latter are more than a mile in diameter.

There is some quiet seismic activity in the Sonoran Desert, but it's mostly activity created by the great influence of California's San Andreas fault. The last major earthquake felt in Tucson was at 2:15 PM on May 3, 1887. It is estimated to have had a magnitude of 7.2 on the Richter scale. Residents of Tucson were startled when they saw smoke rising from the Santa Catalina Mountains. The smoke was the result of fires caused by falling boulders crashing together, creating sparks, and igniting the dry hillside vegetation. The earthquake killed 51 people in Mexico and stopped large pendulum clocks as far away as Phoenix. The earthquake also affected sources of water in the region: Some streams and springs either began flowing or stopped flowing entirely.

Fossil Record

The Sonoran Desert has just as complex a biological history as it does a geological one. The oldest rocks of the Sonoran Desert are approximately 1,200 million years old, dating from the Precambrian era, and hold fossils of algae colonies, evidence that the region was once under a sea. Relatively younger rocks from the Paleozoic era, dating from 570 million years old to 240 million years old, have preserved a rich fauna, including creatures such as trilobites; sharks; corals; crinoids, animals that are often referred to as sea lilies; clams; oysters; a variety of cephalopods; bryozoans, or moss animals; and conodonts, early eel-like creatures. These animals would have inhabited a warm, shallow ocean with lagoons and coral reefs.

Later deposits, those dating from the Mesozoic era, contain fossils of a more terrestrial nature, revealing that the land was rising and draining. Paleontologists have found deposits from this period with the imprints of lizard tracks and petrified wood. There was water present, as evidenced by ancient floodplain and river deposits, with the fossils of clams, sharks, turtles, and even some animals from marine environments, such as the mosasaur. Fossils taken from Cretaceous beds contain the remains of coniferous forests full of ginkos and cycads. Rocks dating from the same period include the fossils of sauropods, duckbill and horned dinosaurs, and a few of Arizona's earliest mammals.

Cenozoic-era deposits paint a portrait of a land similar to a lush savanna, dominated by mammals. These include early horses, oreodonts (ancestors of camels and peccaries), as well as the titanothere, a huge, rhinolike animal.

By 10 million years ago, grass and, as a result, grazing animals, became prevalent. Fossils from the last 2 million years include bison and nearly modern horses, mastodons, camels, mammoths, huge ground sloths, wolves, giant beavers, short-faced bears, and even lions. Some of these fossils even contain traces of dart wounds, left by North America's first people, the Paleo-Indians.

SOCIAL HISTORY

Early People

The earliest people in North America, Paleo-Indians, left behind only a fragmentary history, despite having inhabited the Americas anywhere from ten thousand to forty thousand years. It is thought that they dwelt in this region as nomads, their location dependent upon the seasons, the availability of resources, and the movements of the animals upon which they depended. They are believed to have traveled in family groups including in-laws, grandparents, children, and so on, taking shelter where they could find it or making small structures from animal skins and plants. They used the same materials for clothing.

Evidence suggests that before fifteen thousand years ago, they did not use spears to hunt. Instead, these early people survived by hunting and foraging, preying on young and/or weak animals, taking from fresh kills, and gathering edible seeds and plants. They made tools by flint knapping, or shaping raw stone into tools for cutting, chopping, hammering, and scraping, tools used more for the processing of animals than the acquiring. Some tools were made from bones, the tusks of mammoths and mastodons, wood, and other plant materials. They even used stones to grind different varieties of seeds into flour.

About fifteen thousand years ago, the Paleo-Indians began using spears with flint-knapped points to hunt. They became formidable hunters, preying upon mammoths, mastodons, camels, horses, and giant sloths. Flint knapping became a new art, and the spear point their signature artifact. Today, these spear points have been labeled as Folsom and Clovis and are among the best known of Paleo-Indian artifacts. Clovis points range from 2 to 5 inches long and are lance shaped with fluted sides. The name comes from the site where these spear points were first discovered, a little south of the city of Clovis, New Mexico, at the famous Blackwater Draw site. These spear points have been found all over the Northern Hemisphere. Folsom points were first found in Folsom, New Mexico, in 1927, inside the remains of an Ice Age bison. These points are smaller, symmetrical, leaf shaped, and wide, with shallow grooves running their length.

Despite their longevity, little is known about these early people. We may never know how they raised children or their celebrations and superstitions. We are left with some art, but not enough to really establish an idea of a tradition. They were the first people in the Southwest and the rest of North America, and in many cases they are our ancestors. Still, they remain enveloped in a great deal of mystery.

The Hohokam

A culture that was active from the beginning of the current era to about the mid-15th century A.D., the Hohokam (the name is pronounced ho-ho-KAHM and is borrowed from the Akimel O'odham, or Pima) are believed to have belonged to the Mesoamerican cultures (the Aztecs and Mayans) and came north to this valley around 300 B.C. They lived primarily around the Gila, Salt, and Verde river drainages, an area known as the Phoenix Basin, as well as in villages around the bases of the Tucson Mountains. The Hohokam were neighbors to the Patayan, ancestors of the modern-day Yuma. The Patayan lived along the Colorado River and in Southern California. The Hohokam also were neighbors to the Trincheras of Sonora, Mexico; the Mogollon of eastern Arizona, northwest Chihuahua, Mexico, and southwest New Mexico; and the Anasazi in northern Arizona, northern New Mexico, and parts of Utah and Colorado. Based on oral tradition, it is thought that the Hohokam are the

A roadrunner crossing the street David Jewell © Metropolitan Tucson Convention & Visitors Bureau

ancestors of the Akimel O'odham and Tohono O'odham peoples.

These people made the most of their environs. Sticks of ironwood were used to dig tubers. A day's hike would take hunters into bighorn sheep country, or into the territory of deer. They collected prickly pear fruits and pounded mesquite beans into flour. They gathered the ribs from dead saguaros, chopped down mesquite trees, and cut poles from ocotillos when they needed to construct housing.

The Hohokam were primarily farmers, developing their own system of irrigation in order to cultivate tobacco, maize, squash, beans, cotton, and agave. Around A.D. 1150 the Hohokam began to grow agave far more extensively. Agave is a type of succulent that is often called the Century Plant because of how long it takes to flower, which it does only once in its lifetime. The Hohokam would eat the hearts, or bases, of the plant roasted, and they scraped the cooked plant's leaves to get to its long fibers, which were used to make yarn for cloth or were twisted into twine and rope. Considered a decorative plant, agave is still used today and was introduced to Europe for this purpose in the middle of the 16th century.

Every available space was used for cultivation, the farmers going so far as to build terraces for this purpose. Sometimes, check dams were built on slopes to collect rainwater and steer it toward their crops. Their strategy was based on the canal and was important in the later establishment of urban centers in this desert. These canals were built using relatively simple tools. One of their most complex and accomplished system of canals was built on the Salt River, and it was able to carry water up to 16 miles away.

By the time the culture vanished in the 16th century, they had built more than 600 miles of canals. The canals nearer the river were larger (around 64 feet across), and they grew smaller as they ran through villages and finally to the fields (about 6 feet across).

Researchers have estimated that it would have taken at least 900,000 cubic meters of earth to be moved to build the canals constructed during the Hohokam Classic Period alone.

The time line archaeologists have established for the Hohokam is called the Hohokam Chronological Sequence (HCS), which is divided into larger periods and smaller phases. It was designed to create a narrative following the rise and fall of the civilization. The Classic Period is the last in the HCS and marks when their influence began to weaken and finally vanish.

In addition to canals, the Hohokam are known for their pottery. Pots were usually used for storage and cooking, but some also had ceremonial and religious significance. Their pieces have been broken down into three traditions: Plain, Decorated, and Red Ware. No matter the tradition, Hohokam ceramics tended to be crafted in the same way, a small clay base attached to a set of coils that were shaped and thinned.

The Hohokam tradition thrived until the 16th century. After that, the culture declined and vanished for reasons that still remain unknown. Oddly enough, it has been hypothesized that the canals that made these people so successful were also the reason for their decline. Irrigation made it possible for people to live closer together in greater and greater numbers. They had to go farther and farther out to hunt and gather food, and so they became more dependent on crops. To accommodate their growing reliance on crops, the canals systems were enlarged, destabilizing the river systems. Studies point to the destruction of the major canal heads by at least two catastrophic floods on the Salt River.

The most advanced civilization of the early American Southwest, the Hohokam truly left their mark on this region. We inherited from them the canals, which were so integral to establishing urban centers in the Sonoran Desert. They were the first to try, and succeed, in making the desert hospitable for human beings, including their descendents, the Akimel O'odham (or Pima) and the Tohono O'odham, and the Anglo American settlers that came later on.

The Akimel O'odham and Tohono O'odham

The Akimel O'odham ("people of the river"), also known as the Pima, lived around the Salt, Yaqui, Sonora, and Gila rivers in extended family groups. They subsisted by farming and foraging but did a fair amount of trading as well. Like their ancestors, the Hohokam, the Akimel O'odham built extensive canal systems, but they were also known for their textiles and baskets. Before clashes with the Europeans in the 1500s, their main rivals were the Apache, who would sometimes raid their villages when times were hard.

In 1539, the Akimel O'odham first encountered the Europeans. The first reported contact was with Spanish missionary Marcos de Niza. Shortly after his arrival, more of the Spanish arrived and began to establish mines, ranches, and forts. There were rebellions between 1695 and 1751; however, these proved unsuccessful, and by the mid-19th century, the Akimel O'odham had been restricted to a tiny corner of the land they had previously roamed.

Today most of the Akimel O'odham inhabit the Gila River Indian Community, which is involved in many economic ventures, including but not limited to golf courses, a luxury resort, an amusement park, three casinos, landfills, industrial parks, and construction supply.

The Tohono O'odham, or "people of the desert," are also believed to be descendents of the Hohokam. There are other claims that the group came north as recently as three hundred years ago.

San Xavier del Bac is the parish church for the Tohono O'odham tribe, but it is open to all. L.S. Warhol

For much of their history, the Tohono O'odham were at war with the Apaches, at least from the late 17th century until the beginning of the 20th, when clashes with European settlers caused the two groups to join forces.

In 1700, Jesuit explorer and missionary Eusebio Kino founded Mission San Xavier del Bac, or the "White Dove of the Desert," in the Santa Cruz Valley. The small settlement of Tucson was located about 7 miles (12 km) upstream. Today the mission is on the San Xavier Indian Reservation, a smaller section of the larger Tohono O'odham Reservation.

Construction on the mission—a joint effort between the Franciscan priests and the Tohono O'odham—began in 1699, and it wasn't completed until 1797. Despite the construction of the mission and many others like it across the Southwest, the Tohono O'odham did not take kindly to the Spanish's attempts to assimilate them. In the mid-1600s and 1700s

San Xavier del Bac Mission as seen from the walking trail through the hills around it L.S. Warhol

there were two rebellions comparable in size to the well-known Pueblo Rebellion of 1680. Their resistance was somewhat successful: The Spanish retreated for a time, and much of the Tohono O'odham culture remained whole for a few more generations. This went on until after the Revolutionary War and Americans began to push west. Native American boarding schools were introduced, as was the U.S. Federal Indian policy, the goal of which was to make the Native Americans as "American" as they possibly could, but without the full privileges of "real" Americans.

Today the Tohono O'odham Nation owns three Desert Diamond Casinos and makes much of its money from them. Unfortunately, the profits are not enough to cover the basic needs of tribal members.

The Establishment of Tucson

The Tucson area has been continuously settled for more than twelve thousand years, but August 20, 1775, is considered to be the town's birthday. This is the day when an Irishman in the Spanish military named Hugh O'Connor first established the Presidio of San Augustin de Tucson. The name Tucson comes from the city's earlier name, "Chuk-son," or "water at the foot of the black mountain."

The settlement was controlled by the Spanish until it became a part of Mexico in 1821, when Mexico gained its independence from Spain. In 1853, the United States purchased a 29,670-square-mile (76,800-square-km) area from Mexico in the Gadsden Purchase, a treaty with Mexico that set aside land needed in order to build a southern transcontinental railroad and attempted to resolve conflicts that lingered after the Mexican-American War.

Until 1863, Arizona was a part of the New Mexico Territory. Before this, Tucson was briefly the capital of the Confederate Arizona Territory, from August 1861 until mid-1862.

For 12 years, from 1867 to 1879, Tucson served as the capital of Arizona. Until the 1930s, Tucson was the largest city and commercial area in Arizona, while Phoenix was actually the place for agriculture and government. When Tucson built the municipal airport, it became even more important. But eventually Phoenix outgrew Tucson and continues to expand. Tucson also continues to grow, but at a more stately pace.

Initially, Tucson's population was primarily made up of soldiers and missionaries. But after the establishment of the presidio, many of the soldiers' families came to the settlement. More people were drawn to Arizona's rich natural resources and the money that could be made from them. Still others saw the potential for cultivating cotton and raising cattle.

With the extension of the Southern Pacific Railroad in the 1880s, even more people were able to come to Tucson. The railroad extension, which was intended to connect California with the rest of the states, revolutionized transport in the area and sparked the real influx of people. If not for this leg of the railroad, the ranchers would not have really made a profit when selling their cattle, because they wouldn't have been able to sell to California or the Midwest. Likewise, the miners and farmers wouldn't have made as much of a profit when selling their copper ore and cotton. These became the three Cs of Arizona: cattle, copper, and cotton. Without the railroad, communities like Ajo, Hayden, San Manuel, and Superior would never have existed, as they were mining towns.

The effect on the desert's environment was catastrophic. Woodcutters stripped hillsides and river valleys of oak and mesquite for wood to run the ore-crushing mills. More than a million sheep and nearly 2 million cattle were set loose to graze and cropped the ranges down to the bare dirt. Hunters were hired to feed the miners and exterminate grizzlies and wolves, and they decimated the populations of bighorn sheep and deer.

In 1885, the University of Arizona was founded. Around the turn of the 20th century, the U.S. Veterans Administration began building Tucson's veterans hospital. After the World War I, many veterans who had been gassed were sent to Tucson because of the positive effect of clean, dry air on their damaged lungs.

By 1900, 7,531 people were living in Tucson, and by 1920 the population swelled to more than 20,000. (In 2006, Pima County, where Tucson is located, passed the 1 million mark, with more than half of those people living within Tucson.) Fortunately, the new century brought with it new concerns. It was around this same time that President Teddy Roosevelt incorporated southern Arizona's mountain islands into the national forest system, then the forest reserve system. Dude ranches began to pop up on the outskirts of Phoenix and Tucson, and these attracted droves of tourists interested in the desert and nostalgic for the lifestyle of the Wild West.

With the construction of the Roosevelt Dam in the early 1900s, life in the area boomed. For some two thousand years, flood surges on the Salt River had terrorized Hohokam, O'odham, Mexican, and Anglo American farmers, and now it was tamed, turning the valley into the largest region of commercial agriculture in the southwestern United States. Between 1916 and 1920, the cultivation of cotton in the Salt River Valley rose from 7,300 acres to 180,000 acres. Other industries also boomed at this time. Since Egypt and the Sudan were embargoed by Britain during World War I, it was easier for companies such as Goodyear and Firestone to turn to Arizona to fill their contracts for cotton used in tires.

The Roosevelt Dam also fueled Arizona with hydroelectric power, which contributed to the explosive growth of Phoenix, developing it into a metropolitan center of close to 2.5 million people. Today, Arizona is completing its shift from an overwhelmingly rural state to one dominated by urban centers.

Tucson Today

Tucson is a place as culturally rich as it is environmentally. The desert is home to countless valuable minerals and a diversity of unusual plants and animals. More so than most other regions of the United States, the climate dictates how one must live here. While water and shelter are vital to survival, they were available even to the first humans who came to this desert. The Paleo-Indians, and later the Hohokam and their descendents, learned how to exploit the land in order to live upon it and thrive. They created the technology to manipulate the little water they had to water their crops and support their villages. Then and now, water remains precious.

Today the same exploitation is happening, but often to the detriment of the environment. Still, there have been significant moves made to protect the desert and to preserve its past. The Arizona-Sonora Desert Museum documents Arizona's history and provides visitors with the chance to see some of the desert fauna in its native habitat, and the 91,446-acre Saguaro National Park is nearby, host to thousands of cacti and other flora. It is illegal to harm or remove a saguaro.

All of this comes together to make Tucson what it is today: a mix of cultures, of urban and rural, of small town and big city. A vivid example of this cultural mix can be seen in the All Souls Procession, which takes place on the first Sunday in November. This event is one of Tucson's largest festivals and is modeled on the Mexican holiday of the Day of the Dead (Dia de los Muertos). It pulls from Latin, African, Celtic, and Anglo American culture. The costumes are usually of dead figures or of the deceased. Thousands of people show up in costume at sundown to mourn, acknowledge, and celebrate dead loved ones and the mystery that surrounds death.

Efforts have been made to preserve historic buildings and locations from Tucson's rich

Tucson Barrios

Spanish speakers might wonder what's so special about a barrio—any city has them; they are quite literally neighborhoods. But Tucson prides itself on the historic barrios specifically located near the city's downtown, with names like Barrio Anita, Barrio Hollywood, and Barrio Santa Rosa. These residential areas, especially the aptly named Barrio Viejo, boast buildings more than 150 years old. Visitors will know they've reached a historic barrio once the streets narrow and they are surrounded by short, adobe row houses with bright pink, purple, and orange exteriors. Some homes and businesses even bear the remnants of writing from old grocery storefronts, providing a glimpse of what life may have looked like when Tucson was still part of Mexico. If you'd like to see the interior of a historic Barrio Viejo building, visit 198 West Cushing Street, where you can sip on a mojito and enjoy dinner at the **Cushing Street Bar and Restaurant** (520-622-7984). Due to a massive development project that expanded downtown's government sector in the 1960s, this section of the city has experienced some gentrification, but it still remains largely Hispanic. Evidence of the area's ties to Mexican culture can be seen by strolling past windows with ornate shrines to Our Lady of Guadalupe. One shrine in particular has attracted curious observers to 420 South Main Avenue for years and has been recognized by the National Register of Historic Places: **El Tiradito**. This grotto is the only shrine in the country dedicated to a sinner, as it was built to honor a man whose transgressions with a married woman left him dead. Visitors often come to light candles and leave written wishes in the holes in the wall to honor this unlikely folk hero.

Deer among the prickly pear cactus   Fred Hood © Metropolitan Tucson Convention & Visitors Bureau

social history, and these sites can be seen in Tucson's historic districts and neighborhoods, such as El Presidio, with its mansionlike houses built during Tucson's youth. Everywhere one goes in Tucson, one can see traces of the past, with 19th-century buildings alongside structures put up in the last 20 years or so. The past is inescapable in Tucson, but it does not hold back progress. The city has made great strides in becoming a modern urban center, but that does not mean that it must give up its roots.

NEIGHBORS ALL AROUND

The communities around Tucson offer endless recreational and sightseeing opportunities. The following suggestions are just a few of the things to do and places to see around the area. (For a more detailed look at things to do in and around Tucson, see the Recreation chapter later in this book.)

To the North

Standing at 9,175 feet, **Mount Lemmon** is the highest peak in the Santa Catalina Mountains and is one of Tucson's great escapes, especially in the summer when the cooler mountain temperatures of Coronado National Forest offer respite from the city's heat. Start in the foothills east of town where the Catalina Highway wends 25 miles up the Santa Catalina Mountains to Summerhaven, a small village of about 100 full-time residents where, if it's between mid-December and April, you'll want to check out the slopes of **Mount Lemmon's Ski Valley** (the southernmost ski destination in the United States) before grabbing a piece of fresh-fruit pie at the **Mount Lemmon Café.** Less than an hour's drive west on I-10 is **Picacho Peak State Park.** Four times older (22 million years) than the Grand Canyon and the site of the Civil War's westernmost battle, the peak itself is quite a sight, standing nearly 3,500 feet on a vast lava field accessible by hiking paths. Roughly 35 miles north of town, just off AZ 77, is the town of Oracle, home to **Oracle State Park** and the 250-acre campus of **Biosphere 2,** where guided tours offer visitors the chance to explore an array of closed, man-made ecosystems, including a tropical rain forest, an ocean, and a savanna.

To the South

There's no shortage of destinations south of Tucson. Just 10 minutes from downtown on the Tohono O'odham San Xavier Indian Reservation is **Mission San Xavier del Bac,** one of the great cultural landmarks of southern Arizona. Founded in 1699 by Catholic missionary Father Eusebio Francisco Kino, the mission's art and architecture exemplify the fusion of New Spanish and Native American design. About an hour away (56 miles southwest along Ajo Way) in the Quinlan Mountains is **Kitt Peak National Observatory.** Open to the public for daily tours (and by reservation nightly for those looking to do some stargazing), the observatory boasts the largest, most diverse collection of optical telescopes in the world. If it's a touch of regional art and craft you're after, the galleries and studios of the artists colony at **Tubac** are less than an hour south on I-19. Or stay on I-19 and head toward **Nogales,** Arizona's largest international border town, where Mexican and American cultures flourish together.

To the East

A number of historic mining towns surround Tucson, and two of the most fabled are less than two hours away. Just 70 miles southeast of Tucson (off AZ 80) is **Tombstone.** Founded in the late 1800s, Tombstone is best known for the infamous shootout at the O.K. Corral, the history of which still invigorates local culture and preservation efforts. Once the site of the most productive copper deposits in all of Arizona, the town of **Bisbee** (40 miles southeast of Tombstone) offers guided tours of the old **Copper Queen Mine.** Or if it's a walk you're after, explore the boutiques and galleries along Bisbee's hilly Main Street as it climbs the hills of the Mule Mountains, and then sip a drink in Arizona's oldest continuously running hotel, the **Copper Queen.** Two hours out of town on I-10 east, 36 miles southeast of Wilcox off AZ 186 (the "Apache Trail"), you'll find **Chiricahua National Monument,** whose stone spires and columns are the remains of a volcanic eruption 27 million years ago.

To the West

Just 8 miles west of downtown, where Speedway Boulevard ends at North Camino de Oeste, **Gates Pass** begins. Originally built in 1883 as a shortcut through the Tucson Mountains, Gates Pass's scenic overlooks now are part of the much larger **Tucson Mountain Park,** site of trailheads, hiking paths, and recreation areas. Reach the top of the pass before sunset and join the many locals who gather daily to watch the sun set over **Saguaro National Park.** If it's a day trip you're planning, consider staying on Gates Pass Road as it wends west over the Tucson Mountains to Kinney Road. There, on the western side of the Tucsons, off South Kinney Road, you'll find **Old Tucson Studios.** Dubbed the "Hollywood of the West" for the more than 60 films shot there since 1939, this film studio and theme park offers Western-movie buffs guided tours and live staged gunfights. Turn north onto Kinney Road, and in a few miles you'll come to one of the most popular attractions in all of Arizona, the **Arizona-Sonora Desert Museum.** Situated on 15 acres of prime Sonoran Desert, the museum is both a botanical garden and an animal habitat, showcasing the diversity of the low desert's flora and fauna.

2

Transportation

Getting There & Getting Around

Located just 60 miles north of the U.S.–Mexico border and 120 miles southeast of Phoenix on the northeastern edge of the Sonoran Desert, and surrounded by five mountain ranges—the Santa Catalina and Tortolita mountains to the north, the Santa Ritas to the south, the Rincons to the east, and the Tucson Mountains to the west—Tucson's unique geography has long made it a gateway city of the Southwest.

One of the oldest continuously inhabited settlements in the New World, the area of present-day Tucson was settled first by the Hohokam people who emigrated on foot to the Santa Cruz valley nearly nearly 1,400 years ago. Several hundred years later, in the 1700s, Spanish missionaries and soldiers arrived by mule and horse to establish churches and presidios. America began its vast expansion west in the 1800s, and it wasn't long before wagons, stagecoaches, and locomotives began crisscrossing the desert landscape, connecting what was then a sleepy desert outpost to the rest of the world. Whatever the times and by whatever the means, it seems Tucson has always been a place worth getting to. Whether by plane, train, or automobile, visitors to Tucson today can expect to come and go with all the ease and comfort modern travel affords.

And so to keep you in the know and on the move, the following chapter offers some of the best options for travel to, from, and around the Old Pueblo.

GETTING TO TUCSON

By Car
Skirted on its west side by I-10, the major east–west corridor connecting Florida with California, and intersected from the south by I-19, which runs north from the border town of Nogales to I-10 on Tucson's south side, the Old Pueblo is within a day's drive from any number of southwestern cities.

From Phoenix
The most direct route from Phoenix to Tucson is the two-hour straight shot southeast on I-10. If, however, you're looking for a more leisurely drive, take your time along old AZ 79. Built before I-10 and at roughly the same mileage, this little-traveled back road through pristine Sonoran Desert passes a number of smaller Arizona towns and includes the Pinal Pioneer Parkway, a 42-mile stretch of road beginning in the desert uplands on the north

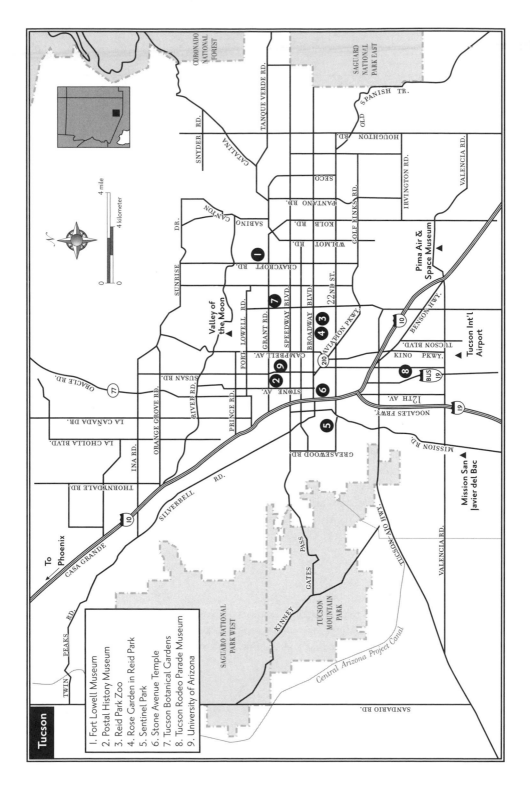

Tucson

1. Fort Lowell Museum
2. Postal History Museum
3. Reid Park Zoo
4. Rose Garden in Reid Park
5. Sentinel Park
6. Stone Avenue Temple
7. Tucson Botanical Gardens
8. Tucson Rodeo Parade Museum
9. University of Arizona

slope of the Santa Catalina Mountains and wending northward to just above the town of Florence. In winter, expect to see the desert blooming Mexican poppies and desert verbena. With any number of small-town diversions along the way, you'll want to have a map handy. Distance: 118 miles.

From Albuquerque
Like most car travel through the Southwest, the drive from Albuquerque to Tucson is a scenic one. Take I-25 south through the sandstone bluffs around Truth or Consequences to the village of Hatch. In Hatch pick up some of New Mexico's best chile peppers before picking up NM 26 south to I-10 west. Once on I-10, you're just three hours to Tucson. Distance: 448 miles.

From Flagstaff
Another straight shot, but one with the potential for stunning desert vistas, owing not only to the number of exits offering pull-offs with scenic views, but to the 6,000-foot drop in elevation that occurs over the 147-mile stretch of I-17 south between Flagstaff and Phoenix. Once you hit Phoenix, look for I-10 east to Tucson. Distance: 265 miles.

From San Diego
At about six hours, San Diego is roughly half a day's drive to Tucson. Take CA 94 east to I-8 east toward the Casa Grande junction, where you'll pick up I-10 east to Tucson. This is one of the more beautiful drives out of California, taking you over the Laguna Mountains, across In-Ko-Pah Gorge, through the farmland of Imperial Valley, past Imperial dunes, and over the rolling hills of the Sonoran Desert. Distance: 409 miles.

From Las Vegas
The most direct route to Tucson from Las Vegas also offers a quintessentially Western driving experience. Take US 95 south from Las Vegas to I-515 south to US 93. If you've got time to spare, take a few minutes to admire the spectacular views of the Colorado River from atop Hoover Dam. Once you're back on the road, take I-40 east to US 93. At just two lanes and with few roadside attractions, US 93 south to Wickenburg (also known as Arizona Joshua Parkway because of the spiny Joshua trees that flourish in every direction) takes you through one of the most alien landscapes in the country. From Wickenburg it's another 50 miles to Phoenix, where you will pick up I-10 east to Tucson. Distance: 418 miles.

From Los Angeles
Aside from 55 miles on the San Bernardino Freeway that takes you out of Los Angeles to I-10 east, you'll be crossing the sun-blasted Mojave Desert, where extreme summer temperatures hover near 120 degrees. If you're driving in June, July, or August, make sure to gas up, bring plenty of water, and observe signs warning you to limit your use of air-conditioning or risk overheating. Distance: 487 miles.

From El Paso
As drives go, the trip from El Paso to Arizona is as uncomplicated as it gets—five hours, one highway. Jump on I-10 west and stay on it through New Mexico to Tucson. Distance: 316 miles.

By Bus

Greyhound Lines, Inc. (1-800-231-2222; www.greyhound.com) serves Tucson and any number of points north, south, east, and west of the city. The newly renovated Tucson Greyhound Station (471 West Congress Street) is just off I-10 and a short walk from downtown accommodations and attractions. (For bus or other transportation services around Tucson, see *Getting Around Tucson* later in this chapter.)

From Phoenix

Greyhound Lines (602-389-4200) provides eight buses daily to Tucson from its downtown station at 2115 East Buckeye Road. Travel time: two to two and a half hours.

From Flagstaff

Greyhound Lines (928-774-4573) buses run five times daily to Tucson from its station at 399 South Malpais Lane. Travel time: six to eight hours.

From San Diego

Greyhound Lines (619-515-1100) coaches depart four times daily for Tucson from its downtown station at 120 West Broadway. Travel time: 11–15 hours.

From Las Cruces

Greyhound Lines (575-524-8518) has three buses departing daily for Tucson from its station at 901 South Valley Drive. Travel time: five to five and a half hours.

From Las Vegas

Greyhound Lines (702-384-9561) buses run three times daily to Tucson from its station at 200 South Main Street. Travel time: 12–16 hours.

Cesar Chavez mural

From Los Angeles

Greyhound Lines (213-629-8401) has five coaches running daily for Tucson from its station at 1716 East Seventh Street. Travel time: 8–12 hours.

From El Paso

Greyhound Lines (915-542-1355) buses depart five times daily for Tucson from its station at 200 West San Antonio Avenue. Travel time: four to six hours.

By Train

Originally constructed in 1907, renovated in 1941, and restored to its former glory in 2004, **Tucson's Southern Pacific Depot** is once again a full-service, fully staffed station served three times a week by **AMTRAK**'s (1-800-USA-RAIL; www.amtrak.com) Sunset Limited and Texas Eagle lines. Located in the heart of the city's revitalized downtown district, the depot (520-623-4442) at 400 East Toole Avenue is within easy walking distance of the famed Hotel Congress, site of the 1934 capture of the gangster John Dillinger and his infamous gang; the newly restored Rialto Theatre, stage to some of the best musical acts in the country; and the Ronstadt Transit Center, downtown's major public transportation hub. In addition to a gift shop, offices, and a restaurant, the depot also houses the Southern Arizona Transportation Museum (520-623-2223) and is the home of Southern Pacific Engine #1673, the starring locomotive in the screen version of the classic Rodgers and Hammerstein musical *Oklahoma.*

By Plane

If you're traveling to Tucson from afar, chances are you're flying, and if you're flying, you're landing at **Tucson International Airport.** Served by nine major airlines with more than 65 flights departing daily to dozens of cities, both foreign and domestic, TIA (520-573-8000; www.tucsonairport.org) is the nation's oldest municipal airport, and now, after a multimillion-dollar renovation and expansion of its main terminal, is also one of the most modern. As of 2007, Tucson's airport boasts not only free Wi-Fi access and new flight view monitors, but an additional 80,000 square feet of terminal space, including newly expanded baggage claim and rental car areas capable of handling the ever-growing influx of visitors. Now, more than ever, TIA also reflects the rich ethnic and cultural diversity of the Old Pueblo. In addition to four small galleries throughout the airport, major concourses showcase the paintings, sculpture, and photography of local and regional artists, while outside, russet sandstone facades complement the warm browns and violet shadows of the desert landscape just beyond the terminal doors.

GETTING AROUND TUCSON

Tucson, like most western cities, was developed on a grid system, with any number of separate and distinct neighborhoods clustered all around town, making travel by car your best option for getting a feel for all that Tucson has to offer. However, there are other options.

By Bus

Sun Tran (520-792-9222; www.suntran.com), operating 38 routes with a fleet of 206 alternatively fueled coaches, is Tucson's award-winning public transportation system. Buses depart daily (weekdays 6 AM–6:15 PM, weekends 8:30–4:45) from three transit hubs: the Roy Laos Transit Center in south Tucson, the Ronstadt Transit Center downtown, and the Tohono Transit Center in the northwest part of the city. Buses make more than 2,200 stops across Tucson and the greater Pima County area, and all are lift-equipped for wheelchairs and include a bike rack capable of holding two bicycles at a time. Fares are $1 for adults; children under five ride free. For more information about routes and schedules, visit the Sun Tran Web site.

The **T.I.C.E.T.** (Tucson Inner City Express Transit) shuttle system is free and has three routes around downtown, with service weekdays 6:30 AM–7:00 PM. Buses run every 10 minutes on the Yellow and Blue routes.

By Taxi

Given its geographic spread (200 square miles and growing) and the absence of a quick cross-city expressway connecting Tucson's east and west sides, a taxi driver who knows his way around town might be your best bet.

Keep in mind that taxis from the airport (located about 6 miles from downtown) contract at slightly higher prices than do cabs you'll catch around town. AAA Airport Taxi, Allstate Cab, Checker Cab, and Yellow Cab offer the following rates: a $4.50 flag drop, $2.50 each mile, and $22 per hour waiting time, with no extra charges for baggage or shared rides to the same location.

AAA Airport Taxi: 520-207-4790
Allstate Cab: 520-798-1111
Checker Cab: 520-623-1133
Yellow Cab: 520-624-6611

By Rental Car

If you've flown to Tucson and you're spending more than a few days, you'll want to rent a car. Seven major rental car agencies are located at Tucson International Airport and throughout the city. For each of the following, the national reservations number is listed first, then the local number.

Alamo: 1-800-327-9633; 520-573-4740
Avis: 1-800-331-1212; 520-294-1494
Budget: 1-800-527-0700; 520-573-8475
Enterprise: 1-800-736-8222; 520-325-7909
Hertz: 1-800-654-3131; 520-573-5201
National: 1-800-227-7368; 520-573-8050
Thrifty: 1-800-847-4389; 520-807-2467

By Trolley

Older than the state of Arizona itself, Tucson's trolley system began operating in 1906 as a replacement for the horse- and mule-drawn streetcars that once serviced the city center. After the reinstitution of trolley service in the mid-1980s and more recent efforts to renew Tucson's downtown, **Old Pueblo Trolley** (520-792-1802) has now expanded its line from the western gates of the University of Arizona, past the boutiques, bars, and eateries that make up the Fourth Avenue business district, to downtown, the city's arts and culture epi-

On the road in the area around Tucson

center. At $1 each way for adults (50 cents for children on Friday nights and all day Satur-
day) and 25 cents for all passengers all day Sunday, the streetcar is the next best thing to
walking the historic West University neighborhood. Jump on the trolley at any point along
its route on Friday 6–10 PM, Saturday noon–midnight, and Sunday noon–6.

By Bicycle

Whether you're looking to cover distances great or small, Tucson is a cyclist's town. Biking
offers visitors one of the most intimate and leisurely ways of getting to know the historic
neighborhoods and barrios of the Old Pueblo. And with efforts always ongoing to improve
and expand commuter bicycle routes around town, those hoping to go green will be pleased
to find most major cross-town streets include designated bike lanes. If it's recreation
you're after, Tucson offers that, too. Take advantage of the **Rillito River Bike Trail,** which
stretches 18 miles along the Rillito wash, from Craycroft Road in the north to I-10 in the
south. Don't have a bike? Not a problem. BICAS (520-628-7950), a local community-run
bike shop, will outfit you with a cruiser that does the job. For more information, see *Bicycling* in chapter 6.

3

LODGING

The Best Places for Any Budget

Whether you're looking for a world-class health spa, a family-friendly guest ranch, a romantic B&B, an all-inclusive luxury resort, or simply a restful night's stay at a quality hotel, Tucson can accommodate any traveler. This chapter describes and highlights the best in each category. In doing so, the listings cover everything from the modestly appointed to the pinnacles of opulence. All evaluations take into consideration a number of factors, including history, architecture, amenities, ambience, and, when appropriate, sustainability. Potential visitors should keep in mind that rates are seasonal and subject to change. Therefore, calling ahead is the best way to ensure the most accurate estimate for planning your getaway. This is particularly true during the peak season of winter, when Tucson's warm, sunny climate attracts vacationers and retirees in droves.

Lodging Price Codes

Inexpensive	Up to $100
Moderate	$100–200
Expensive	$200–300
Very Expensive	Over $300

The following abbreviations are used for credit card information:

AE: American Express
CB: Carte Blanche
D: Discover Card
DC: Diner's Club
MC: MasterCard
V: Visa

Bed & Breakfasts

CASA TIERRA ADOBE

520-578-3058, 1-866-254-0006
www.casatierratucson.com
11155 W. Calle Pima, Tucson, AZ 85743

Price: Moderate–Very Expensive
Credit Cards: AE, D, MC, V
Handicapped Access: Limited
Pets: No

If your vision of a Tucson B&B conjures thoughts of sun-baked adobe brick archways, vaulted viga ceilings, and colorful Talavera tile work, then this four-bedroom hacienda-style home is for you. Situated west of the Tucson Mountains amid 5 acres of gorgeous Sonoran Desert just 30 minutes from downtown, Casa Tierra ("Earth House") features three charming guest rooms and one spacious, two-bedroom suite, all of which open onto a private patio or deck with its own chiminea fireplace. An interior patio surrounds a garden courtyard with stone fountains, and there is a separate patio set away from the home where guests can soak in a whirlpool under the stars or

A courtyard at Casa Tierra Adobe Courtesy Casa Tierra Adobe

take in the night sky with the owner's high-powered telescope. An ample vegetarian breakfast is served every morning in the dining room and includes fresh ground coffee, granola, yogurt, fruit, and eggs.

CATALINA PARK INN

520-792-4541, 1-800-792-4885
www.catalinaparkinn.com
309 E. First St., Tucson, AZ 85705
Price: Moderate
Credit Cards: AE, D, MC, V
Handicapped Access: No
Pets: No

Built in 1927, this stately, two-story adobe mansion situated in the West University Historic District (just minutes from the Old Pueblo Trolley line, which runs from Fourth Avenue, down University Boulevard, to the western gates of the University of Arizona)

is a testament to old-world craftsmanship. Mexican mahogany doors, crown moldings, and polished oak floors lend refinement to the inn, which also features luxurious gardens brimming with succulents, cacti, desert flowers, and herbs. In all, there are six guest rooms: four elegantly appointed rooms in the main residence, and two rooms located in a cottage set off from the main residence that open onto the inn's walled courtyard. Breakfast (which can be taken in the dining room or in bed with the day's paper) includes freshly brewed coffee and gourmet fare such as savory papaya lime scones or lemon ricotta pancakes. Amenities here are higher-tech than other B&Bs and include an in-room stereo with iPod dock, cable television with DVD player, and free wireless high-speed Internet. Service is gracious without being intrusive.

EL PRESIDIO B&B

520-623-6151, 1-800-349-6151
www.bbonline.com/az/elpresidio
297 N. Main Ave., Tucson, AZ 85701
Price: Moderate
Credit Cards: AE, MC, V
Handicapped Access: Limited
Pets: No

Situated in one of Tucson's oldest barrios, El Presidio Historic District, this painstakingly restored Victorian-era adobe mansion dates back to 1886 and is a local architectural marvel, listed on the National Register of Historic Places for its curious mixture of Territorial, Spanish Colonial, and Mission Revival styles. Guest rooms, of which there are only four—two in the main building and two accessible via the inn's courtyard—are richly appointed with antique furniture (collected over a lifetime by owners Patti and Jerry Toci), fresh cut flowers, kitchenettes, private baths, and high-speed wireless Internet connections. A full gourmet breakfast is served every morning in the Veranda Room, overlooking a cobblestone garden courtyard graced year-round with date palms and pomegranate trees. The inn's downtown setting puts it within easy walking distance of galleries, museums, restaurants, and bars.

HACIENDA DEL DESIERTO

520-298-1764, 1-800-982-1795
www.tucson-bed-breakfast.com
11770 E. Rambling Trail, Tucson, AZ 85747
Price: Moderate–Expensive
Credit Cards: AE, D, MC, V
Handicapped Access: No
Pets: No

With a Spanish-style garden courtyard at the center of its 16 secluded acres, Hacienda del Desierto offers a variety of accommodations, from a private casita (featuring two bedrooms, a full kitchen, saguaro ribbed

Guest room at Casa Tierra Adobe Courtesy Casa Tierra Adobe

ceiling, Saltillo tile floors, an antique wood-burning stove, and artisan-style furnishings) to a two-room patio suite (with full private bath, a kitchenette, antique gas-burning stove, and courtyard views) to two smaller guest rooms, La Rose and The Galleria. A continental-plus breakfast (including juice, cereal, eggs, baked goods, and coffee) is offered every morning in the guest dining room or outside in the courtyard, where views of the Rincon Mountains and surrounding Sonoran Desert invite bird-watching or hiking on the inn's private nature trail.

LA POSADA DEL VALLE

520-885-0883
www.mytucsonbnb.com
1640 N. Campbell Ave., Tucson, AZ 85719
Price: Inexpensive–Moderate
Credit Cards: AE, D, MC, V

Handicapped Access: Yes
Pets: Yes (on a case-by-case basis)

Designed in the 1920s, making it one of the earliest examples of Santa Fe–style architecture in Tucson, La Posada del Valle also prides itself on being Tucson's first B&B. True to style, La Posada features rounded pink adobe walls, Spanish tile overhangs, brick breezeways, and a large garden courtyard surrounded by 80-year-old date palms and vibrant bougainvillea. Rooms here include a private casita for longer stays and five themed rooms, each with fine Southwest furnishings and regional art. All rooms open onto either a small private courtyard or a garden. Guests gather each morning on the covered porch for a large country breakfast. In-room spa services—massage, reflexology, and naturopathy—are available for an extra charge.

Hacienda del Desierto entrance Courtesy Hacienda del Desierto

Mountain views from the patio at Hacienda del Desierto   Courtesy Hacienda del Desierto

PACA DE PAJA B&B

520-822-2065, 1-888-326-4588
www.pacadepaja.com
16242 Pinacate, Tucson, AZ 85736
Price: Moderate
Credit Cards: None
Handicapped Access: Yes
Pets: No

If you're looking to experience Arizona the way it used to be, Paca de Paja is the place. This small, Santa Fe–style B&B tucked away in the desert west of Tucson exudes Southwest ambience while also marking a return to sustainable living. The house itself is made from straw bale, an energy-efficient, low-impact building method that also incorporates eco-architectural touches such as passive solar design, radiant floor heating, water harvesting systems, pollinator gardens, and wildlife watering holes. It's this harmony with the surrounding desert landscape that has made Paca de Paja the first Arizona B&B to be listed in the *National Green Pages* and one of only 20 Tucson homes selected for the Solar Alliance's Innovative Home Tour. For all its practicality, no expense has been spared for ambience and comfort. The sole guest suite and its adjacent sitting room feature Mexican hand-carved antiques, Navajo rugs, Antiguo and Talavera tiles, kilims, Native American baskets, and Southwestern artwork. Other amenities include mountain bikes, a natural history library, and a short nature trail just off the guest suite's flagstone porch. Breakfasts feature homemade quiche, burritos, fresh baked breads, fruit, coffee, and juice.

THE ROYAL ELIZABETH B&B

520-670-9022, 1-877-670-9022
www.royalelizabeth.com
204 S. Scott Ave., Tucson, AZ 85701
Price: Moderate–Expensive
Credit Cards: AE, D, MC, V
Handicapped Access: Limited
Pets: No

The Blenman House, an 1878 adobe Victorian mansion on the National Register of Historic Places, is home to one of the poshest B&Bs anywhere in town, The Royal Elizabeth. Common rooms feature fir columns, palatial hardwood floors, and lofty 17-foot ceilings, while private rooms (of which there are six, varying in size and decor) are elegantly appointed with period antiques and stellar in-room amenities such as flat-screen televisions, MP3 players, ambient white noise machines, high-speed wireless Internet, and a full line of complimentary Neutrogena bath products. The secluded backyard courtyard is portioned for both shade and sun and includes a heated swimming pool and hot tub that, like the rest of the B&B, are surrounded by brightly blooming bougainvillea and cactus gardens. Other amenities include a complimentary self-serve cocktail and wine bar, a gourmet two-course breakfast (that changes daily and features locally grown, seasonal ingredients), on-call spa services (including licensed massage therapy, shiatsu, and cranial sacral therapy), and a home theater lounge (complete with HDTV, satellite cable, surround sound, and DVD player). *USA Today* has ranked The Royal Elizabeth as one of the top five urban B&Bs in the nation.

SAM HUGHES INN

520-861-2191
www.samhughesinn.com
2020 E. Seventh St., Tucson, AZ 85719
Price: Inexpensive–Moderate
Credit Cards: AE, D, DC, MC, V
Handicapped Access: No
Pets: Yes (on a case-by-case basis)

Taking its name from the Sam Hughes Historic District, a quiet residential neighborhood just east of the University of Arizona, this 1931 Spanish Colonial B&B with Art Deco accents features three guest rooms (each with its own private bathroom and free wireless Internet) and a separate adobe casita that opens onto a walled garden patio. Antique Southwestern furnishings, Mexican hide chairs, exposed vigas, custom tile work—all of it lends the inn a touch of Old-World charm. A breakfast of eggs, baked goods, and fresh fruit can be taken in the dining room, under the ramada-covered patio, or in the courtyard, fountainside in the sunken garden surrounded by shade trees. Despite its proximity to the university, this is one of the more tranquil B&Bs you're likely to find anywhere in town.

Guest Ranches

HACIENDA DEL SOL GUEST RANCH RESORT

520-299-1501, 1-800-728-6541
www.haciendadelsol.com
5601 N. Hacienda del Sol Rd., Tucson, AZ 85718
Price: Moderate–Very Expensive
Credit Cards: AE, CB, D, DC, MC, V
Handicapped Access: Yes
Pets: No

Consistently named one of the top inns in the country by *Travel + Leisure* for its impeccable service, stunning 34-acre foothills setting, and world-class amenities (including hot stone massage), the Hacienda del Sol Guest Ranch Resort has been a getaway for the rich and famous since it first opened its doors in the 1930s to legends of the screen like Clark Gable, John Wayne, and Katharine Hepburn. The inn's elegant Spanish Colonial architecture and lush garden courtyards add a touch of understated elegance to a resort that also features one of

Tucson's most popular fine-dining restaurants, The Grill, and Terraza del Sol, its more casual counterpart (see chapter 5). Accommodations are select (there are only 20 rooms in the whole place) and range from smaller courtyard guest rooms to suites to private casitas, each a blend of Old West elegance (hand-carved wood-beam ceilings, authentic Native American rugs and throws, artisanal furniture) and modern-day convenience (satellite TV, high-speed Internet access, complimentary terry-cloth robes). Other amenities include use of a heated outdoor pool, a hot tub, riding stables, and spa services like seaweed wraps, mud masks, and salt glow treatments.

TANQUE VERDE RANCH

520-296-6275, 1-888-574-3833
www.tanqueverderanch.com
14301 E. Speedway Blvd., Tucson, AZ 85748
Price: Expensive–Very Expensive
Credit Cards: AE, D, DC, MC, V
Handicapped Access: Yes
Pets: No

A *Condé Nast Traveler* Top 5 Ranch and a Travel Channel Top 10 Family Vacation Destination, Tanque Verde Ranch combines all the thrills of a dude ranch with all the luxuries of a world-class resort. Located just east of Tucson, in the foothills of the Rincon Mountains and between Coronado National Forest and Saguaro National Park, this working 60-acre ranch (the largest of its kind in North America) features a stable of 108 horses, all of which are available for guided and private trail rides, overnight pack trips, trailside breakfast rides, horsemanship and roping lessons, and team penning competitions. Accommodations at the ranch range from Redington Rooms (smaller rooms accommodating up to four), Coronada Casitas (medium-sized rooms featuring a sitting area and a private patio), and the most luxurious of all, the Sonoran

The pool at Tanque Verde Ranch

Suites (complete with separate bedrooms, fireplaces, and private patios). All rooms offer stunning views of the Sonoran Desert, as well as full use of saunas, indoor and outdoor pools, hot tubs, and a state-of-the-art fitness room. The ranch also offers hiking and nature tours, off-site mountain biking trips, catch-and-release fishing on Lake Corchran, dance instruction, tennis (on five courts), and morning yoga.

WHITE STALLION RANCH

520-297-0252, 1-888-977-2624
www.wsranch.com
9251 W. Twin Peaks Rd., Tucson, AZ 85743
Price: Moderate–Very Expensive
Credit Cards: AE, D, MC, V

Handicapped Access: Yes
Pets: No

At the foot of the rolling Tucson Mountains and bordering Saguaro National Park, White Stallion Ranch offers Old West hospitality in a working ranch setting, complete with a Longhorn cattle herd and a rodeo grounds. In addition to The Hacienda, a private, four-bedroom, white-brick house available for more extended stays, the ranch grounds feature 41 guest rooms, ranging in size from deluxe, multibedroom suites to economy singles. Whatever your accommodations, expect expansive, picturesque desert views and a familial atmosphere that is delightfully unpretentious. There's no shortage of activities, either. The ranch features horseback riding, hayrides, a Saturday rodeo (including steer wrestling, team roping, and barrel racing), a petting zoo, a fitness center, saunas, massage, tennis courts, a heated pool and redwood hot tub, and a 27-seat movie theater.

Hotels & Motels

A ROADRUNNER'S HOSTEL
520-628-4709
www.roadrunnerhostel.com
346 E. 12th St., Tucson, AZ 85701
Price: Inexpensive
Credit Cards: None
Handicapped Access: Yes
Pets: No

For younger travelers on a budget, this pink, adobe-style house has all the feeling of a home away from home. Located at the edge of the historic Armory Park neighborhood and within easy walking distance of downtown art galleries, theaters, concert venues, and bars (see chapter 6), the house itself is divided accordingly: three separate dorm rooms (male, female, coed), each with six dorm-style bunk beds; four private rooms sparely furnished with a double bed and a dresser; a spacious common area with a large-screen cable TV, movie collection, and leather couches; a communal kitchen with two refrigerators and a large stainless-steel stove; and two Mac computer terminals, each with 24-hour high-speed Internet access. Free downtown shuttle service picks up and drops off just feet from the front door. This is breezy living that's easy on the pocketbook.

BEST WESTERN INN SUITES
520-297-8111, 1-800-554-4535
www.bwsuite.com
6201 N. Oracle Rd., Tucson, AZ 85704
Price: Moderate–Expensive
Credit Cards: AE, CB, D, DC, MC, V
Handicapped Access: Yes
Pets: Yes

Set amid the Catalina Foothills, this Best Western is within convenient proximity to several of Tucson's premier shopping plazas, among them the Tucson Mall (Tucson's largest mall, featuring more than two hundred vendors and six major department stores), the Foothills Outlet Mall (a high-end factory-outlet mall and shopping center of more than 90 retailers), and La Encantada (an open-air shopping plaza mixing upscale boutiques and fine-dining restaurants). Standard room amenities include high-speed Internet access, flat-screen TVs, and in-room refrigerators and microwaves. Guests can also expect full use of the hotel's heated pool, hot tub, tennis and basketball courts, and a fitness center. Complimentary breakfast is served every morning.

BEST WESTERN LAS BRISAS HOTEL—TUCSON AIRPORT
520-746-0271, 1-866-217-2140
www.bwlasbrisas.com
7060 S. Tucson Blvd., Tucson, AZ 85706
Price: Inexpensive–Moderate
Credit Cards: AE, CB, D, DC, MC, V
Handicapped Access: Yes
Pets: Yes

Set amid 5 acres of well-manicured desert garden landscape, the Best Western Las Brisas is conveniently located less than half a mile from Tucson International Airport via the hotel's complimentary 24-hour shuttle service. All 150 rooms feature free high-speed wireless Internet, cable television, and in-room refrigerators. Other amenities include a heated year-round outdoor pool, a hot tub, and a fitness center featuring a universal gym, free weights, treadmills, and stationary bikes. The hotel's Sirocco Restaurant offers an affordable grazing menu and happy hour. A complimentary continental breakfast is offered daily.

CLARION HOTEL—TUCSON AIRPORT

520-746-3932, 1-800-526-0550
www.clariontucsonairport.com
6801 S. Tucson Blvd., Tucson, AZ 85706
Price: Inexpensive
Credit Cards: AE, D, MC, V
Handicapped Access: Yes
Pets: No

Three blocks from Tucson International Airport and less than 10 minutes from popular downtown attractions (including the Arizona State Museum, the historic Rialto Theatre, and the Tucson Convention Center), the Clarion offers tastefully appointed rooms, as well as full use of a heated outdoor pool, hot tubs, and in-room high-speed Internet. A breakfast buffet is served every morning 6–10 AM, and Morgan's Food and Spirits, the Clarion's on-site restaurant, features simple American dining 6 AM–11 PM daily and two complimentary cocktails 5–7 PM. Free shuttle service to and from the airport is available 24 hours a day.

COMFORT SUITES
AT SABINO CANYON

520-298-2300
www.choicehotels.com
7007 E. Tanque Verde Rd., Tucson, AZ 85715

Price: Moderate
Credit Cards: AE, D, MC, V
Handicapped Access: Yes
Pets: Yes

Just 4 miles from Sabino Canyon Recreation Area, Arizona National Golf Course, and Hi Corbett Field (Arizona's oldest spring training site), Comfort Suites features 90 tastefully decorated rooms and suites on two levels that surround a beautiful, hacienda-style courtyard, site of a heated pool, hot tub, and shading palm trees. In-room amenities include free wireless Internet, a microwave, a coffeemaker, a small refrigerator, cable television (including HBO), and a free daily newspaper. Comfort Suites is also 100 percent smoke-free and offers a full complimentary breakfast.

COMFORT SUITES TUCSON MALL

520-888-6676
www.comfortsuites.com/hotel/az127
515 W. Auto Mall Dr., Tucson, AZ 85705
Price: Moderate
Credit Cards: AE, D, MC, V
Handicapped Access: Yes
Pets: Yes

Located within walking distance of the Tucson Mall (the city's largest) and within easy driving distance of Tohono Chul Natural Park and downtown Tucson, this Comfort Suites has rooms that are clean, spacious, and include free wireless Internet, a coffeemaker, a refrigerator, and cable television. Breakfast here is free (and includes eggs, sausage, waffles, pastries, cereals, juices, and fresh fruit), as is use of an outdoor pool, a hot tub, a sundeck, and a small, all-cardio exercise room.

COURTYARD BY MARRIOTT—
TUCSON AIRPORT

520-573-0000
www.marriott.com
2505 E. Executive Dr., Tucson, AZ 85706
Price: Moderate

Credit Cards: AE, D, MC, V
Handicapped Access: Yes
Pets: No

One of the classier hotels just blocks from the airport is this Courtyard, featuring 150 elegantly appointed rooms, ranging from King suites to double guest rooms. Standout amenities include a 24-hour market featuring salads, sandwiches, soups, cookies, chips, ice cream, beer, soda, and juice; a full-service café serving a breakfast buffet of made-to-order eggs, sausage, bacon, waffles, yogurt, and fresh fruit; a lounge area with flat-screen TVs; a courtyard pool, hot tub, and sunning patio; a fitness center complete with state-of-the-art treadmills, stationary bikes, and free weights; a business center with computers, printers, and high speed Internet; and free shuttle service to and from the airport.

COURTYARD BY MARRIOTT— WILLIAMS CENTRE

520-745-6000, 1-800-321-2211
www.marriott.com/tusce
201 S. Williams Blvd., Tucson, AZ 85711
Price: Moderate
Credit Cards: AE, D, MC, V
Handicapped Access: Yes
Pets: No

Centrally located in midtown, just miles from the University of Arizona, the downtown arts scene, and several premier golf courses, the Courtyard at Williams Centre is also within easy walking distance of Tucson's Park Place Mall, site of any number of restaurants, department stores, and a 20-screen movie theater. The focal point of the hotel itself is the lush garden courtyard, featuring towering palm trees, fountains, a heated pool and whirlpool, shaded stone benches, and a gazebo. The 147 guest rooms and 6 suites include such amenities as high-speed Internet access, valet dry cleaning, cable television, complimentary copies of *USA Today*, and use of the hotel's fitness

room. The hotel's café serves a daily buffet-style breakfast. Despite its close proximity to the airport, this Courtyard does not offer shuttle service.

DESERT DIAMOND CASINO RESORT HOTEL

520-342-3000, 1-877-777-4212
www.desertdiamondcasino.com
7350 S. Nogales Hwy., Tucson, AZ 85756
Price: Moderate–Expensive
Credit Cards: AE, D, MC, V
Handicapped Access: Yes
Pets: No

Among the newer hotels in the area, the Desert Diamond Casino Hotel offers a range of rooms and suites, though whatever your accommodations, all feature 32-inch flat-panel HD television, granite bathrooms, rainfall shower heads, and complimentary wireless and hard line Internet access. In addition to three bars, the Desert Diamond offers a range of on-site dining options, from casual to fine dining to daily themed buffets to a coffee shop. Other amenities include dry cleaning and laundry service, an outdoor fire pit, a jetted hydro spa and outdoor pool, and a fitness center. The 170,000-square-foot casino features 25 poker tables, 24 blackjack tables, more than 1,000 slot machines, and a nightclub. The Diamond Center, the casino's event space, regularly features concerts, boxing, and other live entertainment.

DOUBLETREE HOTEL—REID PARK

520-881-4200, 1-800-222-8733
www.dtreidpark.com
445 S. Alvernon Way, Tucson, AZ 85711
Price: Moderate
Credit Cards: AE, D, MC, V
Handicapped Access: Yes
Pets: Yes

Located across from Tucson's Reid Park (itself the site of jogging paths, racquetball and tennis courts, a zoo, and two LPGAsanctioned golf courses), this resort-style hotel is situated on 14 acres of lush desert landscape and features garden courtyards, a heated outdoor pool and whirlpool, three lighted tennis courts, and a 24-hour fitness room (featuring cardio equipment, free weights, and massage therapy rooms). Each of Doubletree's 295 rooms include high-speed Internet access, 42-inch plasma televisions, and a complimentary line of Neutrogena bath products. On-site restaurants include the Cactus Rose Steak House (featuring patio and fireside dining) and its more casual counterpart, Javelina Cantina.

EMBASSY SUITES—TUCSON PALOMA VILLAGE

520-352-4000
http://embassysuites.hilton.com
3110 E. Skyline Dr., Tucson, AZ 85718
Price: Moderate
Credit Cards: AE, D, MC, V
Handicapped Access: No
Pets: No

Perched in the foothills of the Santa Catalina Mountains with lofty views of the city and the Tucson Valley, this Embassy Suites features 120 suites, each with a separate living space and bedroom. All suites feature two 32-inch flat-screen televisions (one in each room), high-speed Internet access, refrigerators, microwaves, and coffeemakers. A complimentary cooked-to-order breakfast is included with every stay, as is the use of the hotel's heated outdoor pool and fitness center. Also on-site: a newsstand, laundry services, and a convenience store.

EMBASSY SUITES—WILLIAMS CENTRE

1-800-362-2779
http://embassysuites.hilton.com
5335 E. Broadway Blvd., Tucson, AZ 85711
Price: Moderate–Expensive
Credit Cards: AE, D, MC, V
Handicapped Access: Yes
Pets: No

Centrally located in midtown, just minutes from Reid Park, the University of Arizona, and Tucson Electric Park, Embassy Suites at Williams Centre features two-room suites, each with high-speed wireless Internet access, microwave, fridge, wet bar, and coffeemaker. There is also a pool and hot tub, a cocktail lounge with garden atriums, fitness and business centers, and a complimentary breakfast featuring made-to-order omelets, fresh fruit, baked goods, and juices.

FAIRFIELD INN BY MARRIOTT— I-10/BUTTERFIELD BUSINESS PARK

520-747-7474, 1-800-228-2800
www.marriott.com/hotels/travel/tussf
4850 S. Hotel Dr., Tucson, AZ 85714
Price: Inexpensive–Moderate
Credit Cards: AE, D, MC, V
Handicapped Access: Yes
Pets: No

Just off I-10 and 4 miles from Tucson International Airport, this Fairfield Inn (newly renovated in 2006) offers nothing if not convenience, including free high-speed Internet access, an exercise room, a heated pool and Jacuzzi, cable television, and free continental breakfast. Fax and copier services are available at the front desk.

FOUR POINTS BY SHERATON— UNIVERSITY PLAZA

520-327-7341
www.fourpoints.com/tucsonuniversityplaza
1900 E. Speedway Blvd., Tucson, AZ 85719
Price: Moderate–Expensive
Credit Cards: AE, D, MC, V
Handicapped Access: Yes
Pets: No

The Four Points by Sheraton is within easy walking distance of the University of Arizona campus and is less than five minutes by car from Tucson's downtown and Fourth Avenue Business District. Guest amenities include an outdoor heated pool and whirlpool, a fitness room, an on-site restaurant (serving breakfast and lunch), and a cocktail lounge. All 150 guest rooms feature cable television and a complimentary newspaper on weekdays. Free high-speed Internet is available by request, and in-room refrigerators are available for a small charge.

HILTON TUCSON EAST
520-721-5600, 1-800-445-8667
www.hiltontucsoneast.com
7600 E. Broadway Blvd., Tucson, AZ 85710
Price: Moderate–Expensive
Credit Cards: AE, D, MC, V
Handicapped Access: Yes
Pets: No

One of the more impressive features of this Hilton on Tucson's northeast side is the seven-story lobby atrium that invites stunning views of the Catalina Mountains. No less impressive are the hotel's many amenities, including a state-of-the-art fitness room (with free weights and cardio equipment), a scenic outdoor walking track, an enormous outdoor heated pool, a sunning area, and a casual full-service bar and grill on the premises. Accommodations range from standard guest rooms to terrace suites to summit-level executive suites, and all feature flat-panel TVs, high-speed Internet access, and complimentary copies of *USA Today*. Business travelers take note: This Hilton offers complimentary printing services, an on-site notary republic, secretarial services, and audiovisual equipment rental.

HOLIDAY INN EXPRESS HOTEL AND SUITES—TUCSON AIRPORT
520-889-6600
www.ichotelsgroup.com/h/d/ex/1/en/hd/tu smr
2548 E. Medina Rd., Tucson, AZ 85706
Price: Moderate–Expensive
Credit Cards: AE, CB, D, DC, MC, V
Handicapped Access: Yes
Pets: Yes

Minutes from Tucson International Airport via the hotel's free 24-hour shuttle service, this south-side hotel features free high-speed Internet access, complimentary hot breakfast, complimentary happy hour (every Wednesday evening), an outdoor heated pool and whirlpool, on-site business center, and a 24-hour, all-cardio exercise room.

HOLIDAY INN AND SUITES— TUCSON AIRPORT NORTH
520-746-1161
www.hitucsonairport.com
4550 S. Palo Verde Blvd., Tucson, AZ 85714
Price: Moderate–Expensive
Credit Cards: AE, CB, D, DC, MC, V
Handicapped Access: Yes
Pets: No

Located near the Tucson International Airport and the I-10 freeway, the Holiday Inn and Suites is a convenient place to stay for those interested in visiting the Pima Air & Space Museum or Tucson Electric Park (home to the Arizona Diamondbacks's spring training—see chapter 4). The heated pool here is open 24 hours a day, as is the hotel's hot tub. All rooms include free wireless Internet, morning newspaper, and cable television. An on-site restaurant, the Falling Water Grille, serves lunch and dinner daily in an atrium setting, while a sports bar serves up late-night cocktails. Complimentary shuttle service makes getting to the airport quick and easy.

THE HOTEL ARIZONA
520-624-8711, 1-800-845-4596
www.thehotelarizona.com
181 W. Broadway Blvd., Tucson, AZ 85701
Price: Moderate
Credit Cards: AE, D, DC, MC, V
Handicapped Access: Yes
Pets: Yes

Adjacent to the Tucson Convention Center in the heart of downtown, the Hotel Arizona offers 307 spacious, newly renovated rooms on 12 floors, all of which feature tasteful Southwestern decor, wireless Internet access, and separate work space. Also on-site: a heated outdoor pool and sundeck; a business center equipped with computer stations, fax machines, and printers; a restaurant (the Coyote Café and Bistro, serving breakfast, lunch, and dinner); and 40,000 square feet of flexible meeting space.

HOTEL CONGRESS

520-622-8848, 1-800-722-8848
www.hotelcongress.com
311 E. Congress St., Tucson, AZ 85701
Price: Inexpensive–Moderate
Credit Cards: AE, D, MC, V
Handicapped Access: No
Pets: Yes

Since it was built in 1919, Hotel Congress has long been the heart of Tucson's downtown arts and culture scene, as it is just steps away from the historic train depot, the Rialto and Fox theaters, and gallery spaces. All 40 rooms on the second floor feature private baths and retro decor like antique iron-framed beds, vintage radios, and Crosley desk phones connecting to a 1930s switchboard that, legend has it, was used to call in the capture of the infamous gangster John Dillinger and his gang. What the hotel lacks in luxury amenities (there are no pool or spa services here), it more than makes up as one of the trendier spots in town, a place to see and be seen. On the first floor, guests can sip cocktails at the lobby bar or at one of three others around the hotel; enjoy a meal at the Cup Café (among Tucson's hipper restaurants—see chapter 5); or take in a

Hotel Congress   Courtesy Hotel Congress

concert as a VIP (always your status as a guest) at Club Congress, one of the country's best venues for up-and-coming rock acts. In the morning, take your coffee and newspaper on the hotel's patio.

HOTEL TUCSON CITY CENTER CONFERENCE SUITE RESORT

520-622-3000, 1-800-842-4242
www.hoteltucsoncitycenter.com
475 N. Granada Ave., Tucson, AZ 85701
Price: Moderate–Expensive
Credit Cards: AE, D, MC, V
Handicapped Access: Yes
Pets: No

Centrally located in the heart of Tucson's historic downtown Presidio district, this Inn Suites hotel is set on 11 tranquil acres of lush desert landscaping and features 250 guest rooms (including deluxe two-room Jacuzzi suites), a large garden courtyard with heated Olympic-sized swimming pool and hot tub, a separate children's pool and playground, a game room, complimentary evening cocktails, and free airport shuttle services. All rooms come with wireless Internet access, refrigerators, microwaves, and signature toiletries.

HYATT PLACE TUCSON AIRPORT

520-295-0405, 1-800-833-1516
www.tucsonairport.place.hyatt.com
6885 S. Tucson Blvd., Tucson, AZ 85706
Price: Moderate–Expensive
Credit Cards: AE, D, MC, V
Handicapped Access: No
Pets: Yes

All stays at this Hyatt, just a half mile south of the airport, include as standard 42-inch flat-panel high-definition cable television, Wi-Fi Internet access, minifridge, and wet bar. Also available: a coffee and wine café, a 24-hour guest kitchen, a fitness center with state-of-the-art touch-screen cardio and strength equipment, an outdoor heated pool, free continental breakfast, and complimentary 24-hour shuttle service to and from the airport (as well as other locations within a 5-mile radius of the hotel).

LODGE ON THE DESERT

520-325-3366, 1-800-978-3598
www.lodgeonthedesert.com
306 N. Alvernon Way, Tucson, AZ 85711
Price: Moderate–Very Expensive
Credit Cards: AE, D, MC, V
Handicapped Access: Yes
Pets: Yes

Originally a private midtown residence with seven bedrooms when it opened in 1936, Lodge on the Desert underwent major renovations in mid-2009 and expanded to 103 guest rooms (including 13 suites) and 4 spa treatment rooms. Hacienda-style accommodations include Mexican-style tile patios and fireplaces, traditional Southwestern furnishings and decor, custom bath products, plush robes, and free high-speed wireless Internet. Other hotel amenities include an outdoor fireplace, a gorgeous heated outdoor pool, a covered hot tub, and lush courtyards. Those with pets will thrill at the lodge's Very Important Pet program, which includes luxuries like special bedding, turndown service, gourmet baked treats, and room service. Two championship golf courses—the Dell Urich and Randolph—are less than a mile away (see chapter 6).

MARRIOTT UNIVERSITY PARK

520-792-4100, 1-800-228-9290
www.tucsonmarriotthotel.com
880 E. Second St., Tucson, AZ 85719
Price: Expensive
Credit Cards: AE, D, MC, V
Handicapped Access: Yes
Pets: No

The Marriott at University Park, located in Main Gate Square just 2 blocks from the western edge of the University of Arizona, offers 9 floors, 233 rooms, and 17 suites in a hotel that is one of the closest to the university campus. Guests here not only have access to hotel amenities such as an outdoor heated pool, whirlpool, sauna, and fitness room (featuring cardio machines and free weights), but also to the multitude of restaurants, museums, bars, and shops along University Boulevard and Tucson's historic Fourth Avenue. While parking can sometimes be challenging (and pricey), those who can overlook this inconvenience will find themselves in the heart of Tucson's bustling West University neighborhood and just steps away from the Arizona Museum of Art and the Center for Creative Photography (see chapter 4).

RADISSON SUITES

520-721-7100
www.radissontucson.com
6555 E. Speedway Blvd., Tucson, AZ 85710
Price: Moderate
Credit Cards: AE, D, MC, V
Handicapped Access: Yes
Pets: Yes

Radisson Suites Tucson offers 299 suites, each elegantly appointed with clean, modern furnishings, courtyard views, balconies, separate living and sleeping areas, as well as spacious bathrooms featuring two vanities. Guest amenities include a heated pool and hydro spa, a cardio-only fitness room (with complimentary passes and transportation to an off-site, full-service gym), complimentary loaner laptops for use in the hotel's café, a full-service on-site restaurant and lounge offering poolside service, and free high-speed wireless Internet access anywhere in the hotel.

RAMADA INN AND SUITES FOOTHILLS RESORT

520-886-9595, 1-888-666-7934
www.ramadafoothillstucson.com
6944 E. Tanque Verde Rd., Tucson, AZ 85715

Price: Moderate
Credit Cards: AE, D, MC, V
Handicapped Access: No
Pets: Yes

Ranked the number one Ramada in all of Arizona, this foothills resort is located on Tucson's east side and features 115 deluxe guest rooms and two-room suites, all of which surround a garden courtyard that features an outdoor heated pool, a spa, saunas, and a spacious tanning deck. Rooms include free high-speed Internet access, microwaves, refrigerators, and a complimentary weekday newspaper. A breakfast buffet is served every morning, and the hotel hosts poolside socials in the evening.

RANDOLPH PARK HOTEL AND SUITES

520-795-0330, 1-800-227-6086
www.randolphparkhotelandsuites.com
102 N. Alvernon Way, Tucson, AZ 85711
Price: Moderate
Credit Cards: AE, D, MC, V
Handicapped Access: Yes
Pets: Yes

The Randolph Park Hotel is centrally located in midtown Tucson, within close proximity to area attractions like Tucson's Reid Park Zoo, El Con and Park Place malls, Hi Corbett Field, and the Randolph Golf Course. Hotel amenities include a junior Olympic-sized swimming pool, fitness room, and hot tub. Rooms are equipped with a minifridge, microwave, and coffeemaker. Internet access is available in common areas as well as the hotel's business center. Both breakfast and a daily newspaper are complimentary.

RESIDENCE INN BY MARRIOTT

520-721-0991, 1-800-331-3131
www.marriott.com/tusaz
6477 E. Speedway Blvd., Tucson, AZ 85710
Price: Expensive
Credit Cards: AE, D, MC, V

Handicapped Access: Yes
Pets: Yes

Set back from Speedway Boulevard, one of Tucson's main east–west drags, this Residence Inn offers 128 suites, each with separate living and sleeping areas, as well as fully equipped kitchens with stainless-steel appliances. Hotel amenities include free high-speed Internet, an outdoor heated pool and hot tub, a sports court, an on-site fitness center (with cardio equipment and free weights), complimentary passes to an off-site gym, a business center (with computers, printers, and audiovisual equipment), and both a free hot breakfast buffet and cocktail hour in the evenings.

RESIDENCE INN BY MARRIOTT—TUCSON AIRPORT

520-294-5522
www.marriott.com/tusap
2660 E. Medina Rd., Tucson, AZ 85756
Price: Moderate–Expensive
Credit Cards: AE, D, MC, V
Handicapped Access: Yes
Pets: Yes

This Residence Inn, just seconds from Tucson International Airport, features 124 spacious suites, each with separate areas for sleeping and working, as well as a full kitchen and living area. All rooms are outfitted for both hard wire and Wi-Fi Internet access. Other hotel amenities include a hot buffet breakfast served daily, a social hour with complimentary cocktails, grocery shopping services, free daily newspaper, a grilling and picnicking area, heated outdoor swimming pool and whirlpool, and a fitness center offering free weights, stair climbers, stationary bikes, and treadmills.

RESIDENCE INN BY MARRIOTT—WILLIAMS CENTER

520-790-6100, 1-800-331-3131
www.marriott.com/tusri
5400 E. Williams Circle, Tucson, AZ 85711

Price: Expensive–Very Expensive
Credit Cards: AE, D, MC, V
Handicapped Access: No
Pets: Yes

Located near many of Tucson's midtown attractions (including the University of Arizona, Tucson Electrical Park, and the Reid Park Zoo), this four-floor Residence Inn features 120 suites, all of which feature a fully equipped kitchen (with refrigerator, microwave, and coffeemaker), free high-speed Internet access, as well as full use of a state-of-the-art fitness center and both a heated pool and spa. Rates also include a free hot breakfast and evening cocktail hour.

RIVERPARK INN

520-239-2300
www.theriverparkinn.com
350 S. Freeway, Tucson, AZ 85745
Price: Moderate–Expensive
Credit Cards: AE, D, DC, MC, V
Handicapped Access: Yes
Pets: Yes

The Riverpark Inn is a full-service hotel featuring 174 rooms (including 5 suites) in a resortlike setting located within easy walking distance of downtown attractions like the Tucson Convention Center, the Rialto and Fox theaters, and the historic Hotel Congress. All rooms feature free high-speed Internet access, DIRECTV, microwave, and refrigerator. The Riverpark Inn also offers outdoor recreation areas for tennis, shuffleboard, badminton, bocce ball, and croquet; a heated outdoor pool, Jacuzzi, and fitness center; a complimentary full breakfast (including eggs, breakfast meats, fruits, and baked goods); a manager's reception in the evening with complimentary cocktails and light hors d'oeuvres; and an on-site restaurant, the Terrace Café and Bar. Set on 8 acres adjacent to a number of walking trails and jogging paths, the Riverpark Inn also prides itself on being one of the more pet-friendly hotels in Tucson.

RIVERSIDE SUITES

520-202-2210, 520-405-3084
www.riversidesuitestucson.com
1725 E. Limberlost Dr., Tucson, AZ 85719
Price: Moderate–Very Expensive
Credit Cards: AE, D, MC, V
Handicapped Access: No
Pets: No

Riverside Suites is a resort-style gated community with accommodations available at daily, weekly, and monthly rates for 33 full-furnished studios and 1-, 2-, and 3-bedroom suites. All properties are richly appointed with 32-inch flat-panel televisions, wireless Internet access, leather couches, fine linens, enclosed private patios, and fully equipped kitchens. Riverside Suites also boasts amenities like private tennis courts, a state-of-the-art fitness facility, a nine-hole practice putting green, garden courtyards with a heated pool and whirlpool spa, and on-site business conference facilities. Riverside Suites is just seconds from St. Philip's Plaza (see chapter 7) and several exquisite fine-dining restaurants.

SHERATON TUCSON HOTEL AND SUITES

520-323-6262
www.sheraton.com/tucson
5151 E. Grant Rd., Tucson, AZ 85712
Price: Moderate–Expensive
Credit Cards: AE, CB, D, DC, MC, V
Handicapped Access: Yes
Pets: Yes

From its vibrant lobby to its elegantly appointed on-site dining room to its cleanly decorated guest rooms (of which there are 216), this Sheraton offers all the ambience of the Southwest in a quiet midtown setting. All rooms and suites here are newly renovated with modern furnishings

and feature high-speed Internet access. Other amenities include a secluded outdoor courtyard with heated pool, an exercise room, saunas, and a Jacuzzi. The Fire + Spice grill offers full food and drink menus daily.

VARSITY CLUBS OF AMERICA SUITES HOTEL

520-327-0110, 1-800-521-3131
www.ilxresorts.com
3855 E. Speedway Blvd., Tucson, AZ 85716
Price: Moderate–Expensive
Credit Cards: AE, D, MC, V
Handicapped Access: Yes
Pets: No

Aimed at the traveling Pac-10 Conference college sports fan, this 60-suite, two-floor hotel 2 miles from the University of Arizona offers two spacious floor plans (one at 600 square feet, another at 1,000 square feet), both of which include in-room amenities like refrigerators, cable television, and whirlpool bathtubs. The hotel itself features a heated outdoor swimming pool and hot tub, a fitness center, a putting green, billiards, and an on-site sports grill.

VISCOUNT SUITES HOTEL

520-745-6500, 1-800-527-9666
www.viscountsuite.com
4855 E. Broadway Blvd., Tucson, AZ 85711
Price: Inexpensive–Moderate
Credit Cards: AE, DC, MC, V
Handicapped Access: Yes
Pets: Yes

Tucson's only locally owned and operated all-suite hotel with a four-story indoor garden atrium, the Viscount offers 216 two-room suites, all with separate living and sleeping areas, and in-room amenities like free wireless Internet access, microwaves, refrigerators, and coffeemakers. Hotel services include a cocktail lounge, a fitness center, and a heated outdoor pool.

VOYAGER INN AT VOYAGER RV RESORT

520-574-5000, 1-800-424-9191
www.voyagerrv.com/home.html
8701 S. Kolb Rd., Tucson, AZ 85756
Price: Moderate
Credit Cards: AE, D, MC, V
Handicapped Access: Yes
Pets: No

Located on the grounds of the Voyager Resort, this inn features 36 guest rooms, 13 extended-stay casitas, and 3 minisuites, all of which come equipped with efficiency kitchens, high-speed Internet connections, and cable television. The resort itself features a nine-hole golf course with pro shop, miniature golf, sport courts (for tennis, volleyball, bocce, and shuffleboard), horseshoe pits, heated indoor and outdoor pools, hot tubs and saunas, a fully equipped fitness center, a wellness center, a day spa, and an on-site restaurant and bar.

WINDMILL SUITES AT ST. PHILIP'S PLAZA

520-577-0007, 1-800-547-4747
www.windmillinns.com
4250 N. Campbell Ave., Tucson, AZ 85718
Price: Moderate
Credit Cards: AE, D, DC, MC, V
Handicapped Access: Yes
Pets: Yes

At the foot of the Santa Catalinas and adjacent to the fine-dining restaurants and upscale boutiques of St. Philip's Plaza, Windmill Suites features two-room suites, all of which come equipped with a wet bar, a microwave, and free wireless Internet access. Guests here have full access to bicycles, a heated outdoor pool, a whirlpool spa, a cardio fitness room, and complimentary in-room breakfast with newspaper.

Resorts & Spas

ARIZONA INN

520-325-1541, 1-800-933-1093
www.arizonainn.com
2200 E. Elm St., Tucson, AZ 85719
Price: Very Expensive
Credit Cards: AE, D, MC, V
Handicapped Access: Yes
Pets: No

Remarkably quiet for its location in the center of town, the Arizona Inn is a lovingly maintained property nearly one hundred years old. There are 86 individually designed rooms and suites, each minimalist in its approach to contemporary Southwest style. Guest quarters punctuate mature desert landscaping that encompasses 14 pristine acres, ensuring privacy. Service is impeccably Old World formal. Star chef Odell Baskerville heads the main dining room, whose menu is refined retro: think lobster thermidor, truffle-roasted chicken, and venison noisettes with wild huckleberry sauce. And all menu items are available for room service.

CANYON RANCH

520-749-9000, 1-800-749-9000
www.canyonranch.com
8600 E. Rockcliff Rd., Tucson, AZ 85750
Price: Very Expensive
Credit Cards: AE, D, DC, MC, V
Handicapped Access: Yes
Pets: Yes

One part desert retreat, one part luxury spa, Canyon Ranch offers holistic healing for both mind and body in a rural foothills setting. Accommodations at Canyon Ranch harmonize with the surrounding desert landscape and range from modest "deluxe" rooms to more exclusive master suites to the poshest of the posh, the 2,700-square-foot Casa Grande residences, which come richly appointed with one, two, or three bedrooms; full living, kitchen, and dining areas; washer and dryer; computer with high-speed Internet access; and private patio. Whatever your accommodations, expect complimentary terry-cloth robes, an exclusive assortment of signature bath

The pool at the Arizona Inn Courtesy Arizona Inn

products, and gourmet spa fare as part of the ranch's all-inclusive packages. Canyon Ranch also offers on-site health consultations (with physicians, nutritionists, acupuncturists, and exercise physiologists), a 12,000-square-foot indoor aquatic center (featuring five specialty swimming pools), a golf performance center (with PGA-level instruction), state-of-the-art exercise facilities, a beauty salon, and body treatment rooms. If you're considering a stay here, you'll have to relax without a drink. Alcohol is not permitted on the grounds.

HILTON TUCSON EL CONQUISTADOR GOLF & TENNIS RESORT

520-544-5000, 1-800-325-7832
www.hiltonelconquistador.com
10000 N. Oracle Rd., Tucson, AZ 85704
Price: Moderate–Very Expensive
Credit Cards: AE, D, MC, V
Handicapped Access: Yes
Pets: Yes

Honored with the prestigious AAA Four Diamond rating 20 years in a row, the Hilton Tucson El Conquistador is a world-class resort situated at the base of the Catalina foothills on 500 acres of high Sonoran Desert. This Hilton boasts 45 holes of championship golf on 3 distinct courses designed by Greg Nash, 31 lighted tennis courts, luxury spa services (including reiki, sea wraps, and massage), on-site riding stables, a water park, 5 restaurants (ranging from casual poolside dining to lighter café fare to finer Nuevo Latino cuisine), and more than 100,000 square feet of indoor/outdoor meeting space. Accommodations, replete with all the rustic charm of the Southwest, include 428 guest rooms and suites, each with either a private patio or balcony, and all with a minibar, complimentary terry-cloth robes, and wireless high-speed Internet access.

JW MARRIOTT STARR PASS RESORT & SPA

520-792-3500, 1-800-690-8419
www.jwmarriottstarrpass.com
3800 W. Starr Pass Blvd., Tucson, AZ 85745
Price: Very Expensive
Credit Cards: AE, CB, D, DC, MC, V

Handicapped Access: Yes
Pets: No

The only resort of its kind west of downtown Tucson, the Marriott Starr Pass prides itself on its harmonious relationship with the surrounding desert landscape. When it first opened its doors in 2005, the resort donated 150 acres of its pristine land to Tucson Mountain Park. Since that time, nearly 200 additional acres have been preserved, ensuring that all of this Marriott's 575 guest rooms—from its spacious single rooms to its four enormous hospitality suites—feature magnificent views of downtown Tucson and the surrounding desert. All rooms are richly appointed with hand-made artisanal furniture, Mexican Saltillo tile, and authentic Southwestern touches. The Hashani Spa offers 18 different massage packages (including shiatsu, cranial sacral, and hot stone), 14 kinds of facials, 11 body treatments, hair and nail salons, a fitness center, and mountain biking on 13 desert trails. The newly redesigned golf course (an Arnold Palmer Signature facility) features 27 holes of championship golf

Hilton Tucson El Conquistador Courtesy Hilton Tucson El Conquistador

Loews Ventana Canyon Resort's adult pool Courtesy Loews Ventana Canyon Resort

on three 9-hole courses, each of which plays to over 3,200 yards. Like many restaurants across the city, those at Starr Pass are committed to using only locally grown organic ingredients, a commitment that in the coming years will put this Tucson resort in the range of 95 percent sustainability.

THE LODGE AT VENTANA CANYON

520-577-1400, 1-800-828-5701
www.thelodgeatventanacanyon.com
6200 N. Clubhouse Lane, Tucson, AZ 85750
Price: Moderate—Expensive
Credit Cards: AE, D, DC, MC, V
Handicapped Access: Yes
Pets: No

Featuring just 50 guest suites (some with spiral staircases, loft bedrooms, and claw-footed bathtubs), the Lodge at Ventana Canyon is one of the smaller resorts and spas, but it has consistently received a AAA Four Diamond rating and was recently placed on *Condé Nast Traveler*'s gold list for World's Best Places to Stay. The twin jewels of this resort are the two Tom Fazio—designed 18-hole golf courses situated on 600 acres of verdant Sonoran Desert and surrounded on every side by canyons and arroyos. The lodge also features a world-class tennis program managed by Peter Burwash (featuring 12 lighted courts and a full-service pro shop), a spa (recognized as among the best in North America and the Caribbean by *Condé Nast Traveler*'s 2008 Readers' Poll), a 24-hour fitness center, and two pools—a spacious 25-yard competitive swimming pool and a heated baby pool. Two fine-dining restaurants and a poolside snack bar ensure you never have to set one foot off the property.

LOEWS VENTANA CANYON RESORT

520-299-2020, 1-800-234-5117
www.loewshotels.com
7000 N. Resort Dr., Tucson, AZ 85750
Price: Moderate–Very Expensive
Credit Cards: AE, D, DC, MC, V
Handicapped Access: Yes
Pets: Yes

Tucked into the foothills of the Catalina Mountains, Loews Ventana Canyon Resort is Tucson's best overall accommodation in its category. Set on 93 acres, the property never feels crowded, even in high season. Guests scatter amid two pools, two Tom Fazio–designed golf courses (among the best in Arizona), eight tennis courts, and a private-access hiking trail. Rooms and

suites are outfitted in standard Loews fashion with oversized tubs, signature toiletries, and Frette linens. Service staff number one for every three guests, and yet they accomplish their work almost invisibly. There's also a world-class spa and one of Tucson's best fine-dining restaurants, the Ventana Room (see chapter 5).

MIRAVAL TUCSON

520-825-4000, 1-800-232-3969
www.miravalresorts.com
5000 E. Via Estancia Miraval, Tucson, AZ 85739
Price: Very Expensive
Credit Cards: AE, D, DC, MC, V
Handicapped Access: No
Pets: No

Lauded year after year as the number one spa in the world by no lesser authorities than *Travel + Leisure,* SpaFinder, and *Condé*

Loews Ventana Canyon Resort Courtesy Loews Ventana Canyon Resort

A view of the Catalina Mountains from the Westin La Paloma Courtesy Westin La Paloma

Nast Traveler, the 400-acre Miraval spa sits at the base of the Catalina Mountains in the heart of the Sonoran Desert. Luxury accommodations include 118 newly renovated casita-style rooms grouped in six "villages," and the spa itself features more than 70 rejuvenation treatments, everything from prickly pear sugar scrubs to thermal detoxifying mud wraps. Miraval features every conceivable therapy for body and mind, including custom yoga and yogalates, desert running trails, personal training and tennis consultation, a "challenge course" (complete with a climbing wall, tightropes, and elevated balance beam), Zen sand gardens, a desert labyrinth, drumming, hypnotherapy, and gourmet spa cuisine, among many others.

OMNI NATIONAL TUCSON RESORT

520-297-2271, 1-800-528-4856
www.omnitucsonnational.com
2727 W. Club Dr., Tucson, AZ 85742
Price: Expensive–Very Expensive
Credit Cards: AE, D, DC, MC, V
Handicapped Access: Yes
Pets: No

This 650-acre resort in the Catalina foothills is home to two 18-hole championship golf courses: the Catalina Course

Aerial view of the Westin La Paloma   Courtesy Westin La Paloma

(host to more than 30 PGA events and selected as one of *Golf Digest*'s 75 Best Golf Resorts in North America) and the newer Sonoran Course designed by Ryder Cup captain Tom Lehman. Accommodations include the newly remodeled Mountain Vista Collection, 79 short-stay guest rooms nestled in the Catalina fairways (featuring private terraces, balconies, tile floors, chic Southwestern decor, flat-panel televisions, and Wi-Fi), as well as 50 adobe casitas and hacienda suites for longer stays. Also featured at the Omni are long- and short-game practice areas, a comprehensive spa (Tucson's only four star Mobil-rated facility), a 4,500-square-foot fitness center, as well as both fine- and casual-dining options.

WESTIN LA PALOMA RESORT & SPA

520-742-6000, 1-800-937-8461
www.westinlapalomaresort.com
3800 E. Sunrise Dr., Tucson, AZ 85718
Price: Expensive–Very Expensive
Credit Cards: AE, CB, D, DC, MC, V
Handicapped Access: Yes
Pets: No

This foothills resort, a AAA Four Diamond award winner, features 27 holes of golf (including an 18-hole course designed by the Golden Bear himself, Jack Nicklaus, that, according to *Golf Digest,* ranks among the top 75 resort courses in the country and among the top 10 in Arizona); an Elizabeth Arden spa (featuring 18 private treatment rooms and 2 outdoor settings, a eucalyptus sauna, European steam rooms, and a menu of spa therapies); two of Tucson's best restaurants (Janos and J BAR—see chapter 5); 5 swimming pools (one of which features one of Tucson's longest resort water slides); 10 championship tennis courts (voted among the country's top 50 by *TENNIS Magazine*); and accommodations that, among other features, include wood-burning fireplaces, private balconies, tiled floors, handmade maple furniture, and natural stone and glass bathrooms.

WESTWARD LOOK RESORT

520-297-1151, 1-800-722-2500
www.westwardlook.com
245 E. Ina Rd., Tucson, AZ 85704
Price: Expensive
Credit Cards: AE, CB, D, DC, MC, V
Handicapped Access: Yes
Pets: Yes

Located high in the Catalina foothills, the Westward Look Resort offers 241 guest rooms (204 of which are suites with separate living and sleeping areas) scattered around 80 acres of prime Sonoran Desert, at the center of which is an original homestead estate dating back to 1912, months before Tucson became a state. Rooms mix modern convenience with traditional Southwest motifs and feature 42-inch televisions and high-speed wireless Internet. Spa services like massage, mud treatments, and ancient desert rituals offer rest and rejuvenation from daylong horseback rides, high desert hiking or biking, tennis on one of eight courts, or golf at one of three nearby courses. Gold, the resort's fine-dining restaurant, features innovative contemporary American cuisine, while the Lookout Bar & Grill offers more casual fare and terrace views.

Westward Look Resort at sunset   Courtesy Westward Look Resort

Chapel at DeGrazia Gallery VDA © Metropolitan Tucson Convention & Visitors Bureau

4

Culture

Multicultural Convergence

At the intersection of the United States and Mexico, at the intersection of the Southwest and the West, at the intersection of different people from a myriad of backgrounds is Tucson, Arizona. Unlike other places that try to keep things neat and compartmentalized, Tucson embraces its diversity. Among those who live here—whether they are hippies or hipsters, snowbirds or firebirds, those of European, Asian, African, or Mexican descent— there is an understanding: This is a place they can all share.

People who live in the desert have to be hearty to survive the summer heat and to patiently understand the other creatures that make this landscape their home. Perhaps that's the reason there is such a sense of hospitality here. Don't be surprised if your waitress gives you tips about her favorite places as she sets your table, or if random strangers share bits of history with you when you meet them on a park bench. Something about the warm weather permeates people's attitudes. They are genuinely happy to have you here and to share the things they love about their home.

At this crossroads of geography and culture, there is much to explore, historically and culturally. From the Native American tribes who have lived here for thousands of years, such as the Tohono O'odham, to the Spanish missionaries who came in the 1700s, the ethnographic and anthropological roots of this area are fascinating to discover, and there are countless opportunities to do so in the various museums and historical sites and tours in town.

Artists and musicians of all types find inspiration in the natural beauty of the desert in the form of the creatures, the plant life, and the purple and pink mountain ranges that provide the backdrop for the buildings and seem to be constantly peering down upon the city.

This chapter will give you a sense of the arts and entertainment the city has to offer, from music and museums to cinema and sites of historic significance. In admiring the artistic endeavors of those who make Tucson home, you will also encounter the many reasons natives love this desert city.

ARCHITECTURE AND HISTORIC SITES

If your perfect day involves strolling down streets to take in the craftsmanship of archways and columns, and discovering the myths and legends behind historic buildings, you will not be disappointed by what Tucson has to offer. From historic adobe buildings to modern architectural designs, the city's most striking buildings only further the natural beauty of

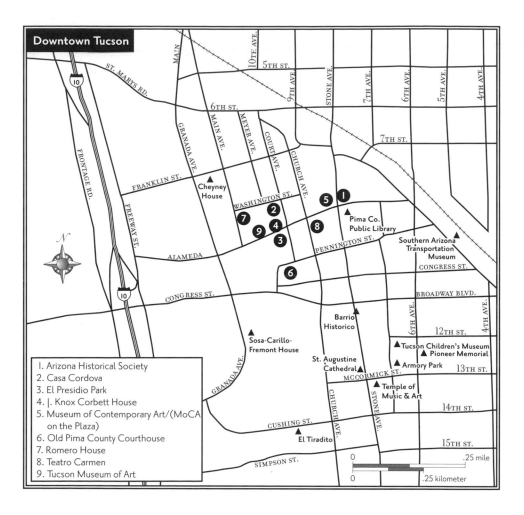

Downtown Tucson

1. Arizona Historical Society
2. Casa Cordova
3. El Presidio Park
4. J. Knox Corbett House
5. Museum of Contemporary Art/(MoCA on the Plaza)
6. Old Pima County Courthouse
7. Romero House
8. Teatro Carmen
9. Tucson Museum of Art

the desert. Where downtown Tucson now stands used to be the entire area of the city before the turn of the 20th century. Tucson's origins were in *el presidio del Tucson,* established by Spanish colonials in 1775, and remnants of this walled city still exist, deep under modern government and office buildings. The Arizona Historical Society (520-622-0956; 949 E. Second St.) offers walking tours of downtown Tucson—and you can always explore the city's streets on your own. The self-guided **Presidio Trail Historic Walking Tour** takes the pilgrim back to the time when the city was merely a small fort surrounded by an adobe wall. Begin at the northeast corner of the historic presidio at the intersection of Church and Washington streets. The complete walk, which has markers of sites of significance along the way, is 2.5 miles and typically takes one and a half to two hours.

Then you can stop by the places that have been religious homes to Tucsonans for more than a century. Just beyond the economic center of Tucson is **St. Augustine Cathedral** (520-623-6251; www.staugustinecathedral.com; 192 S. Stone Ave.). The current cathedral, begun in 1866, was constructed in the Romanesque Revival style. Deemed inappropriate for its "French style," the towers and facade were rebuilt using sandstone and plaster in the 1920s to give the building a Spanish Colonial Revival appearance that was more suited to its location. The crisp white of the towers contrasts nicely with the carved beige sandstone facade. Outside the church and beside the bronze statue of St. Augustine are carvings of desert scenes featuring saguaros, yucca, prickly pear cacti, and even a horned toad. The inside of the church features a 17-foot-tall, 2-ton *Risen Christ* statue originally carved in Spain. Because of its size and weight, the statue had to be rolled down the main aisle and raised by a cable that was lifted by a crane through a drilled hole in the ceiling. Below this statue is the "cathedra," or Bishops Chair, without which a church cannot rightly be called a cathedral. Every Sunday, the cathedral has a mariachi mass, which is open to the public. Guided cathedral tours are available by calling 520-770-1245.

Just down the street from the cathedral is the first Jewish house of worship in the territory of Arizona. The **Historic Stone Avenue Temple** (564 S. Stone Ave.), originally built in 1910 and restored in 2000, is now used as a cultural center and features Greek, Moorish, and Roman decor.

A different kind of shrine can be found in the Barrio Historico (Historic District) at **El Tiradito** (356 S. Main Ave., between Cushing and Simpson streets). Known locally as "the wishing shrine," El Tiradito is the grave of a young sheepherder named Juan who was murdered as the result of a fateful love triangle back in the 1870s. Meaning "the castaway," El Tiradito is said to be the only shrine in the country that is dedicated not to a saint or religious leader but to, as the plaque reads, A SINNER BURIED IN UNCONSECRATED GROUND. Tucsonans and visitors come here to say prayers, light candles, and leave a *milagro* (a small religious charm). The legend is that if your candle is still burning come morning, whatever you prayed for will come to be. Years ago, this little wishing shrine saved the Barrio Historico, as its status as on the National Register of Historic Places prevented a highway from being built to cut through the historic district.

The **Barrio Historico** is also sometimes known as Barrio Viejo (Old District) or Barrio Libre (Free District), the latter because its Mexican inhabitants were free to create and follow their own laws long ago. While the area is no longer home to just Mexican Americans, the cultural heritage of the place is still present in the adobe houses with flat roofs made of ribs of saguaro cacti and dirt floors. The homes here are still private residences, but you can admire them while taking a stroll down the streets.

Also in the Barrio are the offices of *El Fronterizo* (475 S. Stone Ave.), a still-operative Spanish-language newspaper founded by Carlos Y Velasco in 1878, and **Teatro Carmen** (380 Meyer Ave.), a landmark built in 1915 that was one of the first theaters in Tucson developed exclusively to present plays in Spanish. The theater, named after its founder, Carmen Soto Vasques, was featured in the film *Boys on the Side,* starring Whoopi Goldberg.

In the spirit of its nearby neighbor Tombstone, Tucson was a pioneer town, a rough-and-tumble, no-holds-barred kind of town. This spirit, however, could not be fully maintained with the entrance of the railroad to the city in 1880. The railroad brought not only material things but also a link to the ideas of civilization in the rest of the country. The history of this transformation can be witnessed at the **Historic Depot** (400 E. Toole Ave.). Built in 1907 and restored a few years back, the depot is home to the Southern Arizona Transportation Museum and showcases an old freight-hauling locomotive that was featured in the film *Oklahoma.*

Built in 1913 when the Phelps Dodge Mining Company extended its El Paso and Southwestern Railroad to Tucson, the **El Paso & SW Depot** (419 W. Congress St.) was abandoned just over 10 years later when Southern Pacific purchased the railroad. The building now houses an office building and a restaurant.

Entrance to the Corbett House David Jewell © Metropolitan Tucson Convention & Visitors Bureau

No visit to downtown Tucson is complete without seeing the **Old Pima County Court-house** (115 N. Church Ave.), one of Tucson's architectural treasures. The Spanish Colonial Revival building, with its ornate carved facade, is capped off by a green, yellow, blue, and red mosaic dome. Built in 1929 but still relevant today, the building is used for court and county offices, and the courtyard inside is frequently a site for special events.

West of the Old Pima County Courthouse is **El Presidio Park** (55 W. Alameda St.). Established in 1775 by Col. Hugo O'Connor, the park is the site of the Plaza de las Armas, the southern part of the Spaniards' frontier presidio. Tucson's Vietnam Veterans Memorial is also located here. The park is often used as a gathering place for community festivals and events.

The nearby **James A. Walsh Federal Courthouse** (38 S. Scott Ave.) was originally built in 1929 to serve as Tucson's post office. The Neoclassical building is now home to the U.S. Bankruptcy Court.

In addition to government buildings and cultural centers, Tucson has many restored homes dating back to the 1800s. The **Tucson Museum of Art & Historic Block** (140 N. Main Ave.) is notable not only for the art inside its walls but the architecture of them. The complex contains several 19th-century adobe houses, including **La Casa Cordova**, which is believed to be the oldest existing structure downtown, and the 1908 Mission Revival–style **J. Knox Corbett House**. The **Romero House**, built in 1868, is believed to contain portions of the original wall of El Presidio de Tucson. The Tucson Museum of Art offers tours of the houses.

The site of Tucson's first maternity ward, dating back to 1922, the appropriately named **Stork's Nest** (223 N. Court Ave.) is a Sonoran home in El Presidio Historic District, and it still gets visits from people who were born there.

With a blend of Mexican and Victorian design, the **Charles O. Brown House** (40 W. Broadway Blvd.) dates to the mid-1800s. Its owner and namesake was the administrator of the Congress Hall Saloon, where notable legislators from the territory came to meet. Among those currently residing in the house is El Centro Cultural de las Americas, a non-profit that organizes and hosts multicultural events.

In the downtown district formerly known as Snob Hollow are some of the most striking mansions in town. The **Cheyney House** (252 N. Main Ave.) was slated to be demolished because of costly but necessary repairs, but it was saved when two El Presidio neighbors purchased the home to buy some time, and then two out-of-town experts in architectural preservation stepped in and offered to restore the house at their own cost. The inside of the Mission Revival house is not accessible to the public, though you can view the restored face of the mansion.

Just a block from the Cheyney house is the **Steinfeld Mansion** (300 N. Main Ave.). Originally built in 1900, the building was purchased by Albert Steinfeld, a prominent Tucsonan and proprietor of a Tucson department store. Some features of the house include an arched portico and tiled roof, reminiscent of Southwestern style and Spanish influence. Private offices occupy the inside, but you can sit in the courtyard and enjoy the view.

The **Stevens House** (520-624-2333; 150 N. Main Ave.) has a history right out of a scary movie. The home is the site of an attempted murder and a successful suicide. In fact, the house is said to be haunted by the ghost of the suicidal Hiram Stevens. A businessman and politician, Stevens built the first Stevens House in 1866, but he added onto it and renovated it, with the current home having been completed by 1870. Stevens died in 1893, shooting himself after he failed to kill his wife. The legend is that her life was spared by a Spanish comb that deflected the bullets. The tragic events that took place in the house led to its abandonment by the Stevens family, and the house has changed hands a number of times since then. After a stint as a home to another family, the Stevens House has been repurposed as a teahouse, an artist's colony, and an upscale restaurant.

The **Armory Park** neighborhood began its resurgence after the railroad moved to town. The historic neighborhood offers homes in many different architectural styles, including Spanish, Victorian, Queen Anne, mission, Spanish Colonial Revival, and California Bungalow.

One of the landmarks in this neighborhood is the Spanish Colonial Revival–style **Temple of Music and Art** (330 S. Scott Ave.), which was built in 1926 and used to be home to Tucson's Saturday Morning Music Club. In addition to its large auditorium, the building features a café, gallery, gift shop, and courtyard with a Mexican tile floor. The building is now used for theatrical productions and musical events, most notably by the resident company, the Arizona Theatre Company.

Created by San Francisco architect Bernard Maybeck and artist Benjamino Bufano in 1920, the **Pioneer Memorial** (200 Sixth Ave.) is the oldest public art piece in Tucson. Because it was designed and sculpted by California artists, the neoclassical memorial was transported to Tucson by train. The monument to Tucson's persistent pioneers now rests in front of the Tucson Children's Museum, the former Carnegie Library.

Away from downtown but at the heart of what makes Tucson tick is the **University of Arizona** (520-621-5130; www.arizona.edu; UA Visitor Center, 811 N. Euclid Ave.). Opened in 1891 with a freshman class of six, the University of Arizona is now home to nearly 37,000 students. Known for its beauty, the U of A's uniform red brick and landscaping of cacti and olive and palm trees is a perfect setting for a morning or afternoon stroll.

A prominent Tucson architect designed many of the early buildings, including the **Arizona State Museum** (the oldest anthropology museum in the Southwest) and **Centennial Hall** (home to the UA Presents Series), and the use of red brick has continued in the construction of the rest of the buildings, even if it is just an ornamental accent so the campus has an architecturally cohesive feel.

Past the historic main gate and at the center of the university campus is **Old Main**, the oldest building on campus, which had its groundbreaking in 1887. The **Memorial Fountain**, in front of Old Main, was built in 1919 to honor UA students who lost their lives during World War I.

In addition to the historical architecture, you can take in some of the more modern, innovative architecture, including the **Stevie Eller Dance Theatre**, which was designed to replicate motion itself with its modern, twisting rust metal facade. Other modern buildings of note are the corrugated copper-skinned **Chemical Sciences Building** and the six-story glass-covered **Meinel Building**, housing the College of Optical Sciences on the mall.

The university has made a commitment to use the campus's landscape as an arboretum. Botanist and professor James W. Toumey began the university's first cactus garden, located in front of Old Main, in 1896. Now the entire campus is covered in plants from around the world, which are labeled for walkers, and the Krutch Cactus Garden features the tallest boojum tree in the state.

Start at the visitors center, where you can pick up a map and get directions to the places you want to visit. While you are on campus, consider a visit to the **University Museum of Art** or the **Center for Creative Photography** (where Ansel Adams's work is archived), or one of the other great museums the university is host to.

Resting in the foothills of the majestic purple Catalina Mountains is one of the largest Episcopal churches in the country. **St. Philip's in the Hills** (520-299-6421; 4440 N. Campbell Ave.) is known as much for its beautiful views as for the architecture of the building. Take in the surrounding desert from its 12-foot arched window. Designed by Josias Joesler in the 1930s, the mission-style building also features a gallery with the work of local artists. The church hosts free musical events throughout the year.

Historic Sites Outside of Tucson

Fifty miles south of Tucson near the Santa Cruz River is the quirky artist town of **Tubac** (520-398-0007; Tubac–Santa Cruz Visitors Center, 4 Plaza Rd., Ste. E, Tubac). Stop by the visitors center to pick up maps and brochures about local attractions. The main town area is a charming place to stroll, where you can take in the various boutiques, galleries, and shops with handmade work and crafts created by local Native American tribes. One of the highlights of the area is the scenic Tubac Presidio State Historic Park, whose history dates to 1752. The park features historical and archaeological exhibits and also walking trails. The Anza Trail between the park and Tumacácori National Historic Park crosses the Santa Cruz River. Get your feet wet while you take in the local flora and fauna.

Tumacácori National Historical Park (520-398-2341; www.nps.gov/tuma; 1891 E. Frontage Rd., Tumacácori) has its origins as a Native American village. It was later a mission established by Father Kino, the same priest and missionary who is responsible for San Xavier del Bac. After repeated hostile attacks by the Apache, the mission was abandoned, but you can visit the mission's ruins and the preserved adobe church there. The visitors center houses artifacts in its small museum.

There are even more historic sites to see when venturing a bit outside the city. Take, for

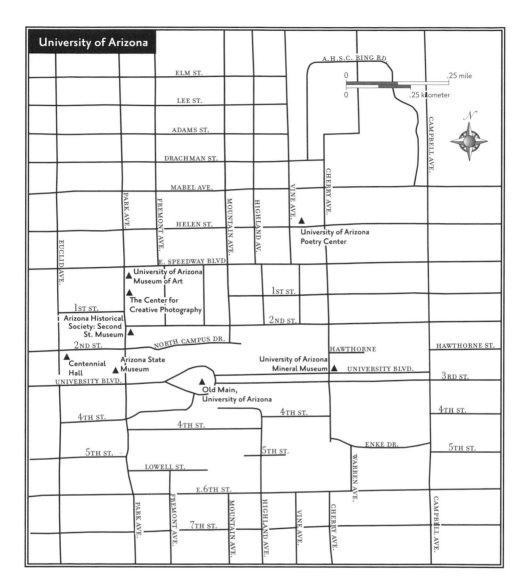

instance, **Sentinel Peak,** more commonly known as "A" Mountain for the *A* that University of Arizona students paint annually on the mountainside. Located just a few miles from the university, the peak can be reached by climbing Sentinel Peak Road, a 1.5-mile-long paved road that rises and loops, coming to a rest just below the *A*. It is a popular lookout spot to view Tucson.

In the Santa Cruz valley south of Tucson on the Tohono O'odham settlement is the famous "White Dove of the Desert": **Mission San Xavier del Bac** (520-294-2624; www.sanxaviermission.org; 1950 W. San Xavier Rd., San Xavier District, Tucson) was founded by Jesuit missionary and explorer Father Eusabio Francisco Kino in 1700, with the original church built about 2 miles from the current one. The mission's name comes from Kino's patron, St. Francis Xavier, and the longstanding name of the area. The settlement

Mission San Xavier del Bac Kathryn Alvarado

has always been known to natives as Bac, "the place where water appears," because of the Santa Cruz River, which was underground, and invisible, for a distance before reappearing nearby. Built between 1783 and 1797 by the Franciscan fathers Juan Bautista and Juan Bautista Llorenz, the building is a fine example of mission architecture, a blend of Moorish, Byzantine, and late Mexican Renaissance architecture. The restored white walls of the church's parapets, dome, and body stand like paper cutouts against the bright blue of the sky and the burnt sienna of the ground. You might be struck, as most visitors are, at the asymmetrical towers, one unfinished. Some say this was done intentionally to avoid paying taxes on the building since it was never technically "finished." The altar, decorated in crimson, dark green, and navy, has been restored using techniques of the Vatican in Rome. Various artifacts are housed inside the church. After exploring the church and small museum, you can stop and feast on the many kinds of fry breads offered by members of the Tohono O'odham outside the mission. San Xavier serves as the parish church for the tribe but is open to all. If you are visiting during the second weekend in March, you can witness the Tohono O'odham's annual powwow at the mission, where ritual dances and drumming circles are performed in addition to the showcase of traditional arts and crafts.

ART CLASSES

If, after visiting some of Tucson's galleries, you feel inspired to create art yourself, consider taking a course at one of the many studios and art centers Tucson has to offer.

BICAS ART

520-628-7950
www.bicas.org
E-mail: bicasunderground@yahoo.com
44 W. Sixth St., Tucson, AZ 85705

Tucson's famous bicycle cooperative, BICAS, or the Bicycle Inter-Community Action and Salvage, not only offers classes where guests can build their own bikes or receive help on their bikes from trained professionals, but also offers open workshop hours to make art out of discarded bicycle parts. It's recycling at its most interesting. You will probably see some of the BICAS garbage cans while walking down Fourth Avenue. Come view the bicycle-part creations already made, or make your own inner tube wallets, tire belts, mobiles, or whatever other creation comes to mind.

THE DRAWING STUDIO

520-620-0947
www.thedrawingstudio.org
33 S. Sixth Ave., Tucson, AZ 85701

This artist cooperative offers artists of all ages and skill levels the opportunity to learn and grow in their art. In addition to scheduled classes in design, drawing, painting, printmaking, and multimedia arts, the Drawing Studio holds open figure-drawing studios each week for $7; no reservations are required.

The interior of Mission San Xavier del Bac   Rick Machle © Metropolitan Tucson Convention & Visitors Bureau

EXPRESSIONS ART GLASS

520-806-7720
www.expressionsartglass.com
8002 E. Broadway Blvd., Tucson, AZ 85710

This family-owned shop offers classes in stained glass, ranging from beginner level to highly skilled. Make your own stained-glass hangings, pendants, or Tiffany lamp shades.

THE SONORAN GLASS ART ACADEMY

520-884-7814
www.sonoranglass.org
E-mail: info@sonoranglass.org
633 W. 18th St., Tucson, AZ 85701

If you've always been curious about those lovely glass bowls and how they get their shape and luminous color, you can learn by doing at the Sonoran Glass Art Academy. Named for the desert where it is located, the school of skilled artisans teaches furnace glassblowing, lampworking, fusing and slumping, and kiln casting in their state-of-the-art facility, which includes a hot shop for furnace glassblowing, a cold shop for cold-working the glass, and classrooms for lampworking and beadmaking. Intimate class size allows for students to get quality one-on-one attention as they learn.

TUCSON CLAY CO-OP

520-792-6263
www.tucsonclayco-op.com
E-mail: tucsonclaycoop@yahoo.com
340 N. Fourth Ave., Tucson, AZ 85705 (in the El Ojito Springs Center for Creativity)

For an affordable, fun place to throw, sculpt, glaze, and bake, visit Tucson Clay Co-Op. The community-based pottery center offers classes for adults and children in the making of clay art. All of their classes include free practice time, and courses range from beginner to advanced levels.

TUCSON STAINED GLASS

520-745-8844
www.tucsonstainedglass.com
E-mail: tucstainedglass@aol.com
4444 E. Grant Rd. #107, Tucson, AZ 85712

This studio offers classes in everything from beadmaking and mosaics to fusing, slumping, and creating kaleidoscopes. Classes range from beginner to advanced.

Arts Councils

THE ARIZONA MEDIA ARTS CENTER

520-882-0204
www.azmac.org
E-mail: reelfrontier@yahoo.com
P.O. Box 431, Tucson, AZ 85702

The organization behind Tucson's renowned International Film Festival, the Arizona Media Arts Centers holds events year-round to promote the appreciation and production of and discourse about media arts. In addition to supporting emerging and established artists, the arts center provides resources so that the community can witness innovation in media. This includes working with educators and students, and producing multicultural, multimedia exhibitions.

CENTRAL TUCSON GALLERY ASSOCIATION

520-629-9759
www.ctgatucson.org

Comprised of 10 of the most reputable and eclectic art galleries in town, the Central Tucson Gallery Association fosters community support of and engagement in the visual arts. They organize several events including three first-Saturday Art Walks in downtown Tucson, an Art Safari every February, the Summer Art Cruise in June, and the Big Picture in October.

TUCSON PIMA ARTS COUNCIL (TPAC)

520-624-0595
www.tucsonpimaartscouncil.org
E-mail: info@tucsonpimaartscouncil.org
10 E. Broadway Blvd. #106, Tucson, AZ 85701

TPAC aspires to support art and cultural awareness and enrichment in the city of Tucson and Pima County. Since 1971, TPAC has done this through their economic and institutional support of local artists, their educational and public arts programming, and their promotion of the Tucson area's rich and diverse cultural heritage. It was a group of dedicated citizens that formed TPAC, and this grassroots community investment still resonates with the organization today. TPAC provides grant opportunities, free workshops and education programs throughout the city, and coordinates a central calendar of arts activities throughout the county.

CINEMA

Besides providing the backdrop for such films as *Tombstone* and *Lonesome Cowboys*, Tucson also supplies the foundation for a diverse and eclectic film community. While this community is small, you can still find many worthwhile events at theaters like the Loft and at the various film festivals held in the city annually.

Theaters

CROSSROADS FESTIVAL CINEMAS 6

520-327-7067
4811 E. Grant Rd., Tucson, AZ 85712

Just because it's cheap doesn't mean it's not high quality. Crossroads Festival has long been making film accessible to everyone in the Tucson community by showing current films at discount prices. With markdowns not only on tickets, but also on snacks, you'll get the movie-theater experience for about as much as your microwave popcorn and video rental at home. Crossroads is also the main 35 mm site for the Arizona International Film Festival.

THE FOX THEATRE

520-624-1515
www.foxtucsontheatre.org
E-mail: info@foxtucsontheatre.org
17 W. Congress Ave., Tucson, AZ 85701

Enjoy movies like they used to in the glory days of Hollywood film at the Fox Theatre, Tucson's only movie palace. Although also home to musical and theatrical events nowadays, the Fox Theatre still stays true to its original mission: movies, movies, movies. Meander under the grand marquee to see old classics, new documentaries, and everything in between. As you sit in the proscenium theater, you'll have the chance to admire more than the stars on the silver screen as you enjoy the picturesque setting, replete with art deco ceilings and walls, and light fixtures with a Southwestern flair.

THE LOFT

520-795-7777 (showtimes), 520-795-0844 (box office)
www.loftcinema.com
3233 E. Speedway Blvd., Tucson, AZ 85716

One of Tucson's cultural treasures, the Loft offers independent and artistic films in a relaxed, low-key setting. In addition to the traditional popcorn and soda fare, you can enjoy a slice of pizza with a tall beer or a glass of wine as you take in the show. In 2007, the Loft instituted a free movie night called Essential Cinema where Tucsonans and visitors alike are treated to a must-see classic film followed by a question-and-answer period with one of the film's directors or actors. The Loft also holds a Tucson International Children's Film Festival in July, and each summer it screens classic films outdoors at a plaza in downtown Tucson. In addition to independent, foreign, documentary, and alternative and classic narrative films, the Loft features late-night cult classics.

THE SCREENING ROOM

520-882-0204
www.azmac.org/scroom
127 E. Congress St., Tucson, AZ 85701

A cross between a trendy art gallery and a minimalist movie theater, the Screening Room offers a modern, unique twist on your trip to the movies. Local artists showcase their work on the walls of the theater, and the foyer offers an intimate place for filmmakers to discuss their work with attendees after screenings. The Screening Room works in opposition to the priorities of many theaters, showing rarely screened films from around the globe instead of the latest blockbuster. Just steps away from Hotel Congress, the Rialto Theatre, and other downtown institutions, the Screening Room has established itself as a vital part of the film scene in Tucson and is also the home base for the annual Arizona International Film Festival.

Other Movie Theaters

AMC Loews Foothills 15 (520-742-6174; 7401 N. La Cholla Blvd. # 144)
Century 20 El Con (520-202-3343; 3601 E. Broadway Blvd.)
Century 20 Park Place (520-742-7200; 5870 E. Broadway Blvd.)
De Anza Drive-In Theatres (520-745-2240; 1401 S. Alvernon Way)

Ceiling design of the historic Fox Theatre David Jewell © Metropolitan Tucson Convention & Visitors Bureau

Grand Cinemas (520-327-7067; 4811 E. Grant Rd.)
Oracle View (520-292-2430; 4690 N. Oracle Rd.)

Film Festivals

ARIZONA INTERNATIONAL FILM FESTIVAL

520-882-0204
www.filmfestivalarizona.com
E-mail: reelfrontier@yahoo.com
Films screened at various venues; see Web site

Each spring, the Arizona Media Arts Center presents the Arizona International Film Festival, Arizona's longest running and largest festival. In addition to local filmmakers, the 80-plus films shown are representatives of the handiwork of artists who hail from more than a dozen countries around the globe. The festival also aims to engage the community beyond what's on the screen, sponsoring panels and workshops on various topics from language extinction to memory loss. Awards for excellence in independent media and in films done by youth are given to winning participants.

TUCSON FILM AND MUSIC FESTIVAL
www.tucsonfilmandmusicfestival.com
E-mail: filmfest@upstairsfilm.com
Rialto Theatre
318 E. Congress St., Tucson, AZ 85701

Originating in 2005 as a way to combine two longstanding artistic traditions of Tucson, the Tucson Film and Music Festival integrates the work of filmmakers and musicians who use the Southwest as their subject matter or muse. Run by indie film collective Upstairs Film and the legendary Hotel Congress, the August festival is a weekend-long, multiscreen, multistage production with dozens of local bands and scrupulously selected films. The films shown—feature, short, documentary, and music videos—have been gleaned by film-makers who are either connected to the state or emphasize music in their work.

TUCSONFILM.COM SHORT FEST
www.tucsonfilm.com
Crossroads Festival Cinemas
4811 E. Grant Rd., Tucson, AZ 85712

Brief but beautiful. Short but sassy. These are the thoughts behind the films showcased as part of the annual TucsonFilm.com Short Fest, whose motto is "short films, big ideas." A grassroots event run by local filmmakers, the festival features independent shorts from around the globe and awards cash prizes to winners. They also archive the films online for Web-surfing film lovers to view.

Video Stores

CASA VIDEO
520-326-6314
www.casavideo.com
2905 E. Speedway Blvd., Tucson, AZ 85716

More than your typical video store, Casa is held in high regard by many Tucsonans. They have your basic sections you will see in most any store—drama, comedy, foreign film—but that is supplemented by new ones you might be surprised by, such as "cult classics" and Criterion Collection flicks. Pick up a bag of free movie theater popcorn to munch on as you peruse and pick a film.

DANCE

From traditional ballet to folk dance and capoeira, Tucson is host to companies who express the beauty of movement in many different ways. Whether you like to watch dancers in their element or enjoy dancing yourself, you can find the spaces that inspire dance here.

BALLET FOLKLÓRICO TAPATÍO
520-622-0231

www.dancingtapatio.com
2100 S. Fourth Ave., Tucson, AZ 85713

Ballet Folklórico Tapatío is a school and performing troupe that is rooted in the rich cultural history of Mexican regional dances. The troupe not only continues the tradition of Mexican folk art, but seeks to tell the stories of the people of Mexico through their elaborate choreography and colorful costumes so that future generations will know them.

CAPOEIRA MALANDRAGEM

520-603-8043
www.capoeiramalandragem.com
E-mail: besouro@capoeiramalandragem.com
55 N. Sixth Ave., Tucson, AZ 85701

Beginning in the 16th century, slaves were shipped from Portugal to South America, with Brazil being the most popular destination. It was in Brazil that the ritual martial art capoeira was ingrained as an important part of the slaves' culture. There are disagreements about capoeira's exact origins: Some say it already existed in Africa as a courtship dance, but others claim it was created in Brazil by African slaves. A martial art, capoeira was disguised by slaves on coffee and sugarcane plantations as a dance so as to not anger their masters. Since 1997, Tucson's Capoeira Malandragrem has followed in the tradition of the form, encouraging its students in building physical strength, flexibility, and endurance in addition to expanding their mental capacity for reflectivity and growth. The most famous act of capoeira is a physical game called jogo, during which two skilled dancers engage in a series of offensive and defensive movements in a ritualized combat. Capoeira Malandragem is committed to reaching disadvantaged youth and empowering them through learning this physical and mental art form. All classes—which cover basic techniques, rhythms, instruments, and Portuguese songs—are open to beginners. Capoeira Malandragem also performs at local events and festivals.

FLAM CHEN PYROTECHNIC THEATRE COMPANY

www.flam-chen.com

A mix between circus act, performance art, mime, and modern dance, Flam Chen has been surprising Tucson audiences with its spectacular displays since 1994. You can find them pretty easily—look for the ones who are clothed in flowing ram costumes and towering above you on stilts, coming down from the wide blue Tucson sky on enormous red balloons, or encircling themselves in rings of fire.

NEW ARTICULATIONS DANCE THEATRE

520-250-4664
www.newarticulations.org
620 E. 19th St., Tucson, AZ 85719

Edgy. Experimental. Quirky. Clever. All of these words can be used to describe Tucson's New ARTiculations Dance Theatre. Founded in 1997, the professional dance company does not shy away from traditional modern and postmodern style but adds its own flair. Incorporating storylines into their pieces, they strive to not only empower emerging dancers and choreographers, but to collaborate with guest artists. The group sponsors a Youth Dance

Ensemble as part of its community outreach and offers master classes to local high schools. New ARTiculations also runs the DanceLoft studio, which offers ongoing adult dance classes—including modern, hip-hop, ballet, salsa, jazz/theater, and belly dancing—as well as classes that appeal to dancers and nondancers alike, such as Pilates.

SCHOOL OF DANCE AT THE UNIVERSITY OF ARIZONA

520-621-4698
http://web.cfa.arizona.edu/dance
E-mail: dance@cfa.arizona.edu
The University of Arizona
1713 E. University Blvd., Ina Gittings Building, Room 121, Tucson, AZ 85721

The University of Arizona's dance program is among the top in the country. The school offers specializations in modern, jazz, and ballet and frequently features performances from both undergraduate and graduate students, rising stars in the dance world. Even if you do not attend a performance, consider checking out the Steve Eller Dance Theatre on the main university mall. The modern building's architects designed the building not only so the inside would be suited to dance but so that the outside, a blend of rust-colored metal mesh and glass, would replicate the movement of dance. In fact, the design is based on a dance notation system.

SHALL WE DANCE

520-327-7895
www.shallwedanceaz.com
101 E. Grant Rd., Tucson, AZ 85705

Whether you want to shake your hips with a little salsa or partner up for an elegant fox trot, you can learn how to do it at Shall We Dance. Begun by competitive dancers Bob Blake and Deborah Frechette in 1997, the studio is dedicated to making ballroom dancing accessible to all who want to learn. Private lessons are offered by appointment for both singles and couples.

TUCSON CREATIVE DANCE CENTER

520-327-7453
www.dancecreative.org
E-mail: mabdance@aol.com
3131 N. Cherry Ave., Tucson, AZ 85719

Based on the principles of individual and group dance improvisation of Barbara Mettler, the Tucson Creative Dance Center is a place where you can let your inner dancer, however coordinated or not, roam free. The center has studio rooms but also holds dance classes outdoors. Classes are typically held on Wednesday mornings.

TUCSON REGIONAL BALLET

520-886-1222
www.tucsonregionalballet.org
E-mail: lwalker@tucsonregionalballet.org
See Web site for venue information

The scenery surrounding Tucson is often dramatic. L.S. Warhol

Encouraging promising talent in traditional ballet, the Tucson Regional Ballet produces several full-scale productions each year. They are known locally for their annual production of *A Southwest Nutcracker,* a Tucson take on the traditional ballet, which features coyotes, cavalry, and rattlesnakes in addition to the large growing Christmas tree. Performances are usually held at the Leo Rich Theatre in the Tucson Convention Center.

ZUZI! DANCE COMPANY

520-629-0237
www.zuzimoveit.org
E-mail: zuzi@zuzimoveit.org
738 N. Fifth Ave., Tucson, AZ 85705

From modern and jazz to aerial dance, ZUZI! Dance Company is on the forefront of innovation in dance. The professional performance company doesn't limit its influences—it borrows from modern dance, classical ballet, as well as Skinner Releasing and Dance Therapy. ZUZI! also features the unique youth aerial company Many Limbs, with 11 youngsters aged 9 to 15.

GALLERIES

The unique beauty of the Southwest has inspired many artists. From Georgia O'Keeffe to Ted DeGrazia, artists have recognized that the burnt umber wide-open spaces make the colors of the ocotillo, wildflowers, hummingbirds, and other desert creatures pop out. In Tucson, you can exhaust yourself visiting the dozens of art galleries that feature the sculpture, paintings, and pottery of Arizona artisans.

ANTIGUA DE MEXICO, INC.

520-742-7114
www.antiguademexico.us
E-mail: info@antiguademexico.us
3235 W. Orange Grove Rd., Tucson, AZ 85741
Open: Mon. through Sat. 10–5

If you aren't going to Mexico but want to take back something with that flavor, stop at Antigua de Mexico. The 10,000-square-foot showroom features such items as Colonial furniture, custom-made wrought-iron work, glassware, folk art, jewelry, and ceramics.

DAVIS DOMINGUEZ GALLERY

520-629-9759, 1-866-629-9759
www.davisdominguez.com
E-mail: info@davisdominguez.com
154 E. Sixth St., Tucson, AZ 85705
Open: Tues. through Fri. 10–5; Sat. 10–4

The building where the Davis Dominguez Gallery rests was once a very different kind of studio space. Built to house a Packard car dealership in the late 1930s, the building was remodeled in 1998 to suit the Davis Dominguez Gallery, which holds Tucson's largest exhibit of contemporary art. While the outside appears true to its industrial roots, the stark white walls and exposed beam ceilings of the 5,400-square-foot warehouse space allows both the viewers and the art being showcased room to breathe. The gallery accommodates new exhibits every six weeks and features the art of James Cook, Bruce McGraw, and Mark Rossi, among others.

DEGRAZIA GALLERY IN THE SUN

520-299-9191
www.degrazia.org
4300 Swan Rd., Tucson, AZ 85718
Open: Daily 10–4 except New Year's Day, Easter, Thanksgiving, and Christmas
Special Features: Gallery gift shop with DeGrazia reproductions and consignment originals

Nestled in the scenic foothills of the Santa Catalina Mountains is a gallery celebrating the life and art of Ettore "Ted" DeGrazia. Famous for his pastel images of Native American children of the Southwest, the late artist designed and began building his Gallery in the Sun complex from the ground up in the 1950s. His Native American friends crafted traditional adobe bricks on-site for the buildings: the Mission in the Sun as well as the artist's home, studio, and gallery. The gallery rotates some of DeGrazia's 15,000 oils, watercolors, sketches, serigraphs, lithographs, sculptures, and ceramics. Visitors will also appreciate the Mission in the Sun building, which the artist built in honor of Padre Kino and our Lady of Guadalupe, and which features DeGrazia murals leading up to a view of the Tucson sky.

DESERT ARTISANS' GALLERY

520-722-4412
www.desertartisansgallery.com
E-mail: info@DesertArtisansGallery.com
6536 E. Tanque Verde Rd., Tucson, AZ 85715 (located in La Plaza Shoppes Center)
Open: Mon. through Sat. 10–5; Sun. 10–1:30

Founded more than two decades ago by a local artist who wanted a place to sell creative work, Desert Artisans' Gallery is the oldest cooperative gallery in Tucson and is committed to showcasing and selling the work of Tucson artists. Beyond its former role as an arts and crafts space, the gallery now features the contemporary painting, sculpture, photography, jewelry, and ceramic and glass work of more than 30 Tucson artisans. You can also purchase this original work directly from the artists showcased.

DINNERWARE ARTSPACE

520-792-4503
www.dinnerwarearts.com
E-mail: dinnerware@dinnerwarearts.com
264 E. Congress St., Tucson, AZ 85701
Open: Tues. through Sat. noon–5

Rumor has it that the idea for Dinnerware Artspace, formerly the Dinnerware Gallery, was conceived over a couple of beers. Tucson artists would gather for casual meetings, drinking a few beers and discussing their current work at the Fourth Avenue haunt the Shanty. One of them mentioned that there was a space opening up for rent on Congress Street, near the current site of the gallery. The building for rent had been a dinnerware store selling ceramic cups and plates, hence the gallery's name. Since its beginnings in 1979, Dinnerware has refused to honor the traditional boundaries of artistic work, introducing not only visual art exhibits but also performance art and poetry readings into its spaces. Dinnerware Artspace continues in this custom, hosting 7 UP Open Performance Nights showcasing local performance artists in addition to their exhibitions of contemporary Tucson artists, which rotate every 30 days. The Dinnerware Artspace also sponsors three other galleries: the Shane House Gallery in central Tucson, the Arts Incubator Gallery in downtown Tucson, and the Brick Gallery, which houses Dinnerware's permanent collection. The nonprofit gallery, which has education and community building as part of its mission, is supported in part by the Tucson/Pima Arts Council and the Arizona Commission on the Arts.

ERIC FIRESTONE GALLERY

520-577-7711
www.ericfirestonegallery.com
4425 N. Campbell Ave., Tucson, AZ 85718
Open: Tues. through Sat. 11–5 and by appointment

Housed in two historic Josias Joesler adobe houses from the 1930s, the Eric Firestone Gallery designs its exhibitions to cater to the talent and interests of the local art community. The intimate gallery frequently changes exhibits and ranges from American modernist and regional artworks to American arts and crafts and decorative items.

ETHERTON GALLERY

www.ethertongallery.com
E-mail: info@ethertongallery.com
Main Gallery: Downtown
520-624-7370
135 S. Sixth Ave., Tucson, AZ 85701
Open: Tues. through Sat. 11–5; Thurs. 11–7
Temple Gallery
520-624-7370
330 S. Scott Ave., Tucson, AZ 85701 (located upstairs at the Temple of Music and Art, home of the Arizona Theatre Company)
Open: Mon. through Fri. 10–6; weekends call 520-622-2823

Voted Best Gallery in Tucson by natives every year since 1997, Etherton Gallery's two sites offer viewers a look into vintage and contemporary photography, paintings, prints, sculptures, and mixed media works. Since 1981, the gallery exhibited local and regional art, including photography by such illustrious artists as Ansel Adams, Danny Lyon, Paul Caponigro, Harry Callahan, Aaron Siskind, Mark Klett, Kate Breakey, Graciela Iturbide, and Joel-Peter Witkin. The main gallery, in downtown Tucson, is housed in the historic Oddfellows Hall, built in 1914, while the Temple Gallery, opened in 1990, features six exhibits a year that showcase the work of Tucson artists working in diverse mediums.

GROGAN GALLERY OF FINE ART

520-577-8787
www.ggrogangallery.com
E-mail: contact@ggrogangallery.com

2890 E. Skyline Dr., Tucson, AZ 85718
Open: Mon. through Sat. 10–6

Grogan Gallery is a meeting of man and nature. Set off by the drama of the Catalinas, the gallery features contemporary art in a stark, industrial setting. The gallery focuses on the work of midcareer artists who have already experimented and who have found their style and ways of expression in form. These experienced artists' work, in various mediums, coincides with the gallery's vision to support progression and innovation in art.

JOSEPH GROSS GALLERY & LIONEL ROMBACH GALLERY

520-626-4215
http://web.cfa.arizona.edu/galleries
School of Art, the University of Arizona
Corner of Speedway Blvd. and Park Ave., Tucson
Open: Mon. through Fri. 9–4

Located on the University of Arizona campus and run by the School of Art, both of these galleries are dedicated to supporting the artistic work of those at the university. The Joseph Gross Gallery includes professional artists, both emerging and established, in addition to their exhibition of student and faculty work. The Lionel Rombach Gallery provides exhibition space with the vision of both allowing students to showcase their work and to learn about gallery management at the same time.

MEDICINE MAN GALLERY

1-800-422-9382
www.medicinemangallery.com
E-mail: art@medicinemangallery.com
7000 E. Tanque Verde Rd., Ste. 16, Tucson, AZ 85715
Open: Mon. through Sat. 10–5 Sept. through Apr.; Sun. 1–4 Dec. through Apr.; Tues. through Sat. 10–5 May through Aug.

If seeing art and craftwork that has its origins and traditions in the Southwest is your desire, consider a visit to the Medicine Man Gallery. The gallery features a large selection of Southwest Native American craftwork, including baskets, beadwork, jewelry, and pottery. Also on display are fine-art pieces from early Western artists and contemporary painters and sculptors, as well as antique furniture pieces.

OLD TOWN ARTISANS

520-623-6024, 1-800-782-8072
www.oldtownartisans.com
E-mail: info@oldtownartisans.com
201 N. Court Ave., Tucson, AZ 85701
Open: Mon. through Sat. 9:30–5:30 Sept. through May; Sun. 11–5 and Mon. through Sat. 10–4 June through Aug.

Built in 1755, El Presidio San Augustin del Tucson was a fort where Spanish settlers lived while trying to claim the area. Now Old Town Artisans occupies the land where the fort's horse stables originally stood. The adobe buildings, built in the 1850s, house a variety of shops and galleries that offer art visitors can take home with them, including fine-art pieces, jewelry, pottery and glassworks, and Native American crafts. Former tenants of the

Cottonwood trees often grow along streams and riverbanks.   L.S. Warhol

buildings included a grocery store, private residences, and a distillery. The original ceilings of the shops are made of the ribs of saguaro cacti, and old packing crates and whiskey barrels are stored there.

PHILABAUM GLASS GALLERY

520-884-7404
www.philabaumglass.com
E-mail: philabaumgallery@qwestoffice.net
711 S. Sixth Ave., Tucson, AZ 85701
Open: Tues. through Sat. 10–5

Gallery founder and glass artisan Tom Philabaum originally opened the gallery in 1982 with a small retail space. A few years later, the gallery moved to the site of what was an old fast-food restaurant in downtown Tucson and added a glassblowing facility. In addition to viewing the showcase of glass artisans from across the country, visitors can also watch glass being blown in the studio or purchase some of the contemporary glass pieces.

SETTLERS WEST GALLERIES

520-299-2607
www.settlerswest.com
6420 N. Campbell Ave., Tucson, AZ 85718
Open: Mon. through Sat. 10–5

For more than 30 years, Settlers West Galleries has been committed to revealing the history and culture of the West through exhibiting western and wildlife art. Their Tucson gallery has been home to work by such artists as Howard Terpning, Bob Kuhn, Kenneth Riley, Pino, Francois Koch, and William Acheff. Their Contemporary Fine Arts and Graphics Gallery in Tucson makes this artwork available to collectors in the form of limited-edition prints, serigraphs, giclée canvas prints, and original artwork.

LIBRARIES AND LITERARY ARTS

There's something about the sparseness of the desert that heightens its beauty. Beauty is typically viewed as being lush, vibrant, and rich in color, but here, the sameness of the miles of beige dirt serves as a stark contrast to the yellow blooms of the saguaro. The wide-open robin's egg sky offers inspiration to those who view it. The desert landscape's artistic powers have been evidenced in the many thinkers, artists, and writers who have decided to make their home in the Tucson area. Home to writers' retreats, various libraries, and one of the largest poetry archives in the country, Tucson's literary community continues in the tradition of its landscape; it is both modest and blooming, both the same and innovative.

ANTIGONE BOOKS

520-792-3715
www.antigonebooks.com
E-mail: antigonebooks@qwest.net
411 N. Fourth Ave., Tucson, AZ 85705
Open: Mon. through Thurs. 10–7; Fri. and Sat. 10–9; Sun. noon–5

There are places where you can buy books, and then there are bookstores that are the living rooms and dens of the community, where patrons come not only to purchase books but to discuss ideas. Antigone Books is one of the latter. The bookstore's namesake is Greek heroine Antigone, the daughter of Oedipus who took her father's exile as her own and attempted to reunite her brothers. Antigone, the store, offers a feminist perspective on the literary—showcased not only in the book offerings but in the cards, bumper stickers, T-shirts, and other paraphernalia for sale. Dedicated to fostering appreciation in literary arts, Antigone Books regularly holds readings for both local and national poets and prose writers.

CASA LIBRE EN LA SOLANA

520-325-9145
www.casalibre.org
E-mail: casakeepers@casalibre.org
228 N. Fourth Ave. #2, Tucson, AZ 85705
Open: See Web site for upcoming events
Admission: Varies

Just steps away from one of Tucson's most bustling streets is an oasis for writers and literati alike. Open the rustic red door and walk into Casa Libre, a writers' retreat where the primary belief is that the creation of a comfortable, inspiring ambience is essential to producing and appreciating literary art. The name comes from the Spanish, and roughly translated it means "Free House in the Sun." With a solarium and patio filled with trees and native plants, a library for reading and discussion, and vibrant Southwestern decor, Casa Libre is truly a place to concern oneself not with work but with creation, not with errands but ideas. The nonprofit resource center and inn gathers the community for free readings as well as workshops, meetings, and literacy programs. Casa Libre also provides a supportive community for writers and opportunities for those within the Tucson writing community to form connections. Combining the hum of Fourth Avenue and the homey feel of Casa Libre, writers are both reminded of their arts connection to the world and given the privacy they need to create it.

NUESTRAS RAÍCES LITERARY ARTS FESTIVAL

www.library.pima.gov/spotlight/nuestras

One of the largest cultural markers of Tucson stems from its close proximity to Mexico, and the meeting of these two worlds is celebrated each March through the Nuestras Raíces Literary Arts Festival. This multiday, multimedium festival honors the work of Mexican American authors as well as the Mexican American culture at large. Authors, artists, and craftspeople present their work, and local musicians perform as part of the event, which is sponsored in part by the Pima County Public Library.

PIMA COUNTY PUBLIC LIBRARY

Joel D. Valdez Main Library
520-594-5500
www.library.pima.gov
101 N. Stone Ave., Tucson, AZ 85701
Open: Mon. through Wed. 9–8; Thurs. 9–6; Fri. 9–5; Sat. 10–5; Sun. 1–5

The Pima County Public Library offers the Tucson community free access to learning tools, including books and periodicals, as well as free Wi-Fi and Internet access at their many branches. Readings, workshops, and events are also held in support of the library's commitment to lifelong learning.

TUCSON POETRY FESTIVAL
www.tucsonpoetryfestival.org
E-mail: info@tucsonpoetryfestival.org

Since 1982, the Tucson Poetry Festival has celebrated the style and craft of the poem. The festival focuses on a different aspect of the poetic experience with varying themes each year, such as "Poetry's Connection to Voice." A literary festival created both by and for the Tucson community, the event celebrates the written and spoken words of renowned local and national poets. Over the four-day event, readings are given, discussion groups and panels are held, and a poetry slam invites viewers to witness the power of poetry. The Tucson Poetry Festival also presents awards to the winners of statewide contests, on both professional and high school levels.

THE UNIVERSITY OF ARIZONA POETRY CENTER
520-626-3765
www.poetrycenter.arizona.edu
E-mail: poetry@email.arizona.edu
508 E. Helen St., at Vine Ave., Tucson, AZ 85705
Open: Hours vary by season; please see Web site

For years, one of the largest poetry archives in the country was packed up in storage and gathering dust, with only a rotating selection of books available for viewing in the University of Arizona's small center. Those days are over. With the opening of its new building in October 2007, the University of Arizona Poetry Center is now not only a container for works of art but a work of art itself. The contemporary, asymmetrical building in shades of silver and charcoal is a fitting casing for a place dedicated to preserving and promoting modern poetry. The center, started in 1960 with the mission to allow people "to encounter poetry without intermediaries," has a collection that comprises more than 60,000 items, including books, anthologies, literary journals, chapbooks, photographs, and critical works by poets. In addition to the printed archives, the center has audio archives of poets such as Gary Snyder, Robert Hass, Mona Van Duyn, and W. S. Merwin reading their work. The poetry center participates in promoting poetic literacy in the community, holding free literary readings, lectures, and workshops and doing educational outreach in Tucson. The center also has a residence for visiting poets and writers.

MUSEUMS

With a history as rich and complicated as Arizona's, it shouldn't be surprising that Tucson is host to a multitude of museums focusing on the art, culture, and livelihood of the Southwest. One benefit of being a large university town is the ability to support museums and artistic centers, and Tucson—with its University of Arizona—is certainly no exception. Whether photography, ethnography, or astrology is your passion, you can find it in the museums of Tucson.

The University of Arizona Poetry Center

ARIZONA HISTORICAL SOCIETY DOWNTOWN MUSEUM

520-770-1473
www.arizonahistoricalsociety.org
140 N. Stone Ave., Tucson, AZ 85701
Open: Tues. through Fri. 10–4
Admission: $3 adults, $2 seniors and students 12–18, free for children under 12; free first
Fri. of each month

To learn about the history of Tucson in the heart of the city, visit the Arizona Historical
Society Downtown Museum. The museum features an exhibit entitled "History in the Heart
of Tucson" that traces the history of the community—from police and military history to its
education and economic systems—from its era as a Spanish presidio in the late 1700s to
today.

ARIZONA HISTORY MUSEUM

520-628-5774
www.arizonahistoricalsociety.org
949 E. Second St., Tucson, AZ 85719
Open: Mon. through Sat. 10–4; library open Mon. through Fri. 10–3, Sat. 10–1
Admission: $5 adults, $4 seniors and students 12–18, free for children under 12; free
admission the first Sat. of each month

The largest of the Arizona Historical Society's museums in Tucson, the Arizona History Museum tells the story of the people who have made Arizona home over the past two centuries. Exhibits, both interactive and traditional, offer opportunities to learn about Tucson's past, including an underground copper mine, exhibit of both ranch and town life in the late 1800s, period rooms from the Victorian era, and a historical stagecoach. Visitors are also invited to view the museum's extensive library, archive, and artifact collections.

ARIZONA STATE MUSEUM

520-621-6302
www.statemuseum.arizona.edu
1013 E. University Blvd., P.O. Box 210026, Tucson, AZ 85721 (University of Arizona campus)
Open: Mon. through Sat. 10–5; Sun. noon–5
Admission: Free

Discover the history of the people who have made Arizona the cultural mecca it is today. Established in 1893, the Arizona State Museum is the oldest and largest anthropology museum in the Southwest. Affiliated with the Smithsonian Institute and located on the University of Arizona campus, the museum features the artifacts and history of indigenous peoples of the American Southwest and of northern Mexico. The museum holds the largest whole-vessel collection of Southwest Native American pottery and is home to an extensive Navajo textile collection comprised or more than 150,000 archaeological and ethnographic artifacts.

THE CENTER FOR CREATIVE PHOTOGRAPHY

520-621-7968
www.creativephotography.org
1030 N. Olive Rd., Tucson, AZ 85719 (University of Arizona campus)
Open: Mon through Fri. 9–5; Sat. and Sun. noon–5
Admission: Free

Take in the beautifully rendered landscapes of photographer Ansel Adams at the Center for Creative Photography (CCP). Cofounded by the legendary artist in 1975, the CCP holds more archives and individual works by 20th-century North American photographers than any other museum in the nation. Rotating exhibitions are displayed year-round, but the public is also invited to request viewings from the extensive archives of more than 50 photographers, including Richard Avedon, Lola Alvarez Bravo, Edward Weston, and Louise Dahl-Wolfe. (For more information, see sidebar on page 104.)

FORT LOWELL MUSEUM

520-885-3832
www.oflna.org/fort_lowell_museum/ftlowell
Old Fort Lowell Park, 2900 N. Craycroft Rd., Tucson, AZ 85712
Open: Wed. through Sat. 10–4
Admission: $3 adults, $2 seniors and students 12–18, free for children under 12; free first Sat. of each month

Run by the Arizona Historical Society, the Fort Lowell Museum harkens back to military life on the Arizona frontier in the late 1800s.The museum is housed in the reconstructed and renovated commanding officer's quarters of Fort Lowell, which were constructed out of

Exhibit at the Arizona Historical Society Downtown Museum Courtesy Metropolitan Tucson Convention & Visitors Bureau

adobe, pine logs, and saguaro ribs. Those stationed at Fort Lowell, founded in 1866 and abandoned in 1891, were commissioned with the duties of protecting settlers, patrolling the border, guarding supplies, and instigating engagement with the Apache. Take in the exhibit on your own, or attend a walking tour, lecture, or one of the museum's living-history events.

MUSEUM OF CONTEMPORARY ART (MOCA ON THE PLAZA)

520-624-5019
www.moca-tucson.org
E-mail: info@moca-tucson.org
149 N. Stone Ave., Tucson, AZ 85701 (next to the main library)
Open: Mon. and Thurs. through Sat. noon–5
Admission: Free to members, $5 nonmembers; free admission every third Thurs. and Apr. 26

Nestled in the heart of downtown Tucson, the Museum of Contemporary Art's mission is "to provide a forum for the development and exchange of ideas about the art of our time," and it does so by inviting the community to view its collection and by hosting programs, lectures, and special events where people can engage in and discuss visual art. Featuring artists from the 1970s to the present day, the museum plans exhibits so as to expose people to the diverse work in the international contemporary arts scene. Six to eight temporary exhibitions are mounted each year, and the museum is currently in the process of building its permanent collection.

PIMA AIR & SPACE MUSEUM

520-574-0462
www.pimaair.org
6000 E. Valencia Rd., Tucson, AZ 85756
Open: Daily 9–5, except for Thanksgiving and Christmas; last admittance at 4
Admission: June through Oct.: $11.75 adults, $9.75 seniors, $8 children 7–12, free for children under 7; Nov. through May: $13.50 adults, $10.75 seniors, $9 children 7–12, free for children under 7

While staying in Tucson, you might suddenly find your ears filled with a cacophony of zooming noises. Look up to see the jets from the Davis-Monthan Air Force Base flying above you. The endless skies of Tucson have long been residence to planes of all kinds. You can find out more about this aviation history at the Pima Air & Space Museum, one of the largest air and space museums in the world. The museum, second only in size and diversity to the Smithsonian's International Air and Space Museum, is host to more than 275 aircraft and spacecraft, from the United States and beyond, and more than 125,000 artifacts. Many of these are among the most significant and technically advanced crafts ever made. Experience a guided walking tour or explore the 177,000 square feet of exhibition space in the hangars on your own. Among the crafts are President John F. Kennedy's *Air Force One* and the presidential aircraft used by presidents Nixon and Johnson, a B-29 Superfortress, a SR-71 Blackbird, and a rare World War II German V-1 "buzz bomb." The museum grounds include the Arizona Aviation Hall of Fame and the 390th Bombardment Group Memorial Museum, where you can learn about the World War II bombing cadre. The museum also operates free tours of the Aerospace Maintenance and Regeneration Group, more popularly known as the Boneyard—a plane graveyard where planes no longer operable or relevant meet their final rest. It's located across the street from the museum at Davis-Monthan Air Force Base.

THE POSTAL HISTORY FOUNDATION
520-623-6652
www.postalhistoryfoundation.org
E-mail: phf3@mindspring.com
920 N. First Ave., Tucson, AZ 85719
Open: Mon. through Fri. 8–3
Admission: Free

Sure, you might know where your mail comes from now, but to find out about the history of the postal service in times before automobiles, planes, and the Internet, pay a visit to Tucson's Postal History Foundation. The foundation's library has more than 25,000 U.S. Post Office and U.S. Postal Service publications, specializing in Civil War literature and memorabilia. Postal history exhibits change periodically inside the turn-of-the-20th-century building. The foundation is also a fully operative post office that has all of the current stamps, so if you collect stamps or just want to send your postcards back home, this should be a stop on your itinerary.

SOSA-CARRILLO-FREMONT HOUSE
520-622-0956
www.arizonahistoricalsociety.org
151 S. Granada Ave., Tucson, AZ 85701
Open: Wed. through Sat. 10–4
Admission: $3 adults, $2 seniors and students 12–18, free for children under 12; free the first Sat. of each month

To step into the life of a 19th-century Hispanic pioneer, stroll through the period rooms of the historic Sosa-Carillo-Fremont House. Built in the 1870s, the adobe house gets its name from the families who took up residence there. You can also sign up for a walking tour of historic downtown Tucson at the museum or see if any special events are scheduled for while you are in town.

SOUTHERN ARIZONA TRANSPORTATION MUSEUM
520-623-2223
www.tucsonhistoricdepot.org
414 N. Toole Ave., Tucson, AZ 85701
Open: Tues. through Thurs. 11–3; Fri. and Sat. 10–4; Sun. 11–3
Admission: Free

Celebrating a time when everyone rode the rails, the Southern Arizona Transportation Museum takes visitors back in time through exhibits, oral history, and archival collections. The museum itself is an artifact, as it resides within the restored main depot building in downtown Tucson. Highlights include a historic steam locomotive and the restored depot lobby, which was restored to look as it did in 1942.

TUCSON CHILDREN'S MUSEUM

520-792-9985
www.tucsonchildrensmuseum.org
200 S. Sixth Ave., Tucson, AZ 85701 (in the historic Carnegie Library Building)
Open: Tues. through Sat. 10–5; Sun. noon–5; closed Thanksgiving and Christmas Day
Admission: $7 adults, $5 seniors, $5 children ages 2–18, free for children under 2; free
admission day once a month

If traveling with little ones, the Tucson Children's Museum is a must-stop. With exhibits
and interactive, hands-on learning activities meant to inspire creativity and a spirit of discovery, the museum is a treat for kids of any age. The 11,000-square-foot museum features
12 permanent exhibits in addition to special events and traveling exhibits. Feeding off the
cultural influences of Tucson, the museum has a social powwow program as well as a Dia de
los Muertos exhibit, which coincides with the city's celebration of the Day of the Dead.

TUCSON MUSEUM OF ART AND HISTORIC BLOCK

520-624-2333
www.tucsonmuseumofart.org
140 N. Main Ave., Tucson, AZ 85701
Open: Tues. through Sat. 10–4; Sun. noon–4
Admission: $8 general admission, $6 seniors, $3 students, free for members and children
12 and under; free to all the first Sun. of each month

To get a feel for Tucsonans who walked this ground years ago, long before the city was
known as Tucson, visit the Tucson Museum of Art and Historic Block. The museum, nestled
inside five houses built between the mid-1850s and 1907, holds more than seven thousand
pieces, specializing in art of the American West and the Americas, and folk art from the
Spanish Colonial and post-Colonial periods. In addition to its modern collection, the
museum holds historically significant works, such as the central Mexican piece *Stela,* which
dates back to between 100 B.C. and 250 B.C. Its permanent collection is supplemented by
four private collections featuring pre-Columbian, 20th-century modern, and American
West art.

TUCSON RODEO PARADE MUSEUM

520-294-1280, 520-741-2233
www.tucsonrodeo.com
4823 S. Sixth Ave., Tucson, AZ 85714
Open: Seasonal; see Web site
Admission: Minimum donation $5 adults; free for children under 16

February in Tucson is rodeo time. If you are visiting during that time and want to know a
little history behind the cowboys and cowgirls who have spent the last century roping
steeds and riding broncos, visit the Tucson Rodeo Parade Museum. Located on the grounds
of the Tucson Rodeo, the seasonal museum, which is housed in what was Tucson's first air-
plane hangar, was founded in 1962 to show Tucsonans and visitors alike the history behind
the rodeo parade. A museum still in progress, it currently features more than 150 buggies
and wagons from pioneer days to the present day, in addition to other Old West artifacts.
Among the vehicles are those that were once ridden in films by Maureen O'Hara, Ava Gard-

Cowboy statue outside the Tucson Museum of Art   David Jewell © Metropolitan Tucson Convention & Visitors Bureau

ner, and the cowboy's cowboy, John Wayne. Stroll down a street re-created to represent what Tucson would have looked like back in the time when the Wild West was a reality.

THE UNIVERSITY OF ARIZONA MINERAL MUSEUM

520-621-4227
www.uamineralmuseum.org
1610 E. University Blvd., Tucson, AZ 85719 (University of Arizona campus)
Open: Thurs. 9–3; Fri. 9–3 and 6–9; Sat. noon–9; Sun. noon–5
Admission: $7.50 adults, $5 children ages 4–10, free for children under 4

Some of the mineral collection at the University of Arizona Mineral Museum is almost as old as the university itself, dating back to 1892. The museum is open to the public, and visitors can view more than 2,000 minerals on display. The collection also features meteorites collected from around the world and a micromount exhibit where visitors can view minerals not visible to the naked eye.

THE UNIVERSITY OF ARIZONA MUSEUM OF ART AND ARCHIVE OF VISUAL ARTS

520-621-7567
www.artmuseum.arizona.edu
1031 N. Olive Rd., Tucson, AZ 85721 (University of Arizona campus)

Open: Tues. through Fri. 9–5; Sun. noon–4
Admission: $5 adults, free for students and faculty with ID, children, and museum members

Located on the University of Arizona campus, the museum houses collections of more than 5,000 paintings, sculptures, prints, and drawings in addition to its rotating exhibitions. The focus is on European and American fine art from the Renaissance to today.

Museums Outside of Tucson

THE AMERIND FOUNDATION: A MUSEUM OF
NATIVE AMERICAN ARCHAEOLOGY, ART, HISTORY, AND CULTURE
520-586-3666
www.amerind.org
E-mail: amerind@amerind.org
100 N. Amerind Rd., Dragoon, AZ 85609
Open: Tues. through Sun. 10–4; closed Mon. and major holidays
Admission: $5 adults, $4 seniors, $3 students and youth 12–18, free for children under 12

Set among the picturesque tan granite rocks of Texas Canyon with a backdrop of the purple Little Dragoon Mountains are several Spanish Colonial–style buildings that house the Amerind Foundation, an anthropological and archaeological museum and research center that houses Native American art and artifacts. William Fulton, a Connecticut native, became infatuated with the history and culture of the Southwest after several trips to Arizona. His endeavors into archaeology and anthropological research that began as a hobby soon turned into scholarly work, and he created the foundation in 1937 to further research the ancient peoples and landscape of the Southwest. Not limited to Native Americans of the Southwest, the museum's exhibitions explore the history of America's first inhabitants from the tip of Alaska to South America and from the last ice age to today. The museum hosts Native Arts weekends, where visitors can view Native American artists demonstrating their skills and creating their artistic work in the main gallery. While in Texas Canyon, take in the natural surroundings, and bring your guidebooks to decipher the wide range of flora and fauna that call this area home.

CASA GRANDE VALLEY HISTORICAL SOCIETY & MUSEUM
520-836-2223
www.cgvhs.org
E-mail: info@cgvhs.org
110 W. Florence Blvd., Casa Grande, AZ 85222
Open: Mon. through Sat. 1–5 Sept. through May, except major holidays
Admission: $3 adults

Halfway between Phoenix and Tucson is the city of Casa Grande, the place where the road used to end—the railroad, that is. The city's roots trace back to 1879, when the city was founded, taking its name from the Hohokam Indian ruins nearby. The Casa Grande Valley Historical Society & Museum explores the history of this southern Arizona region, including its history in mining and agriculture. Take a tour, attend a lecture, or just explore the exhibit on your own. You can visit the historic one-room barn that was once an African American grammar school and the historic stone Heritage Hall church.

While in Casa Grande, you can also visit the historic railroad station and other buildings of significance or stop by the Casa Grande Art Museum. If you're there in February, you can partake in the annual O'Odham Tash celebration, a gathering of Native American tribes replete with ceremonial dances, rodeos, powwows, and parades.

Music

Whether you want a mariachi band to accompany your munching on chips and guacamole, a singer-songwriter to serenade you in a mellow bar, or a symphony to reveal its mastery in a performance of Bach, Tucson is the place for you. Because of its placement in the Southwest and its proximity to the Mexican border, Tucson's streets are alive with music from a multitude of persuasions. Although it isn't typically the stop-off point for the big headliners, Tucson's position between Austin and Los Angeles means that local venues are able to book many artists passing through on their tours. In addition to local artists, Tucson venues feature many up-and-coming artists, as well as those who have a strong fan base but sometimes fall below the mainstream radar. If you are more traditional in your musical tastes, Tucson can assist you, as the city also has a symphony, opera company, and jazz society.

Venues

CLUB CONGRESS
520-622-8848, 1-800-722-8848
www.hotelcongress.com/club
311 E. Congress St., Tucson, AZ 85701

Located in the historic Hotel Congress, Club Congress is a hot spot for Tucson nightlife, showcasing musical acts and dance DJs in a trendy, vintage environment. Club Congress began in 1985 as a once-weekly showcase for Tucson artists and now has grown to a club featuring live music or DJs nightly. The adjoining taproom features cowboy art, a Wurlitzer jukebox, and a decent selection of brews. Built in 1919, the same year as its neighbor, the Rialto Theatre, Hotel Congress is the longest continually operating hotel in Arizona. It's most famous moment came on January 22, 1934, when a fire started in the basement of the hotel and led to the historic arrest of notorious criminal John Dillinger, who had been hiding out on the third floor with his buddies under assumed names. Allegedly, upon being captured, Dillinger appeared stunned and uttered just four words: "Well, I'll be damned!"

FOX THEATRE
520-624-1515
www.foxtucsontheatre.org
E-mail: info@foxtucsontheatre.org
17 W. Congress St., Tucson, AZ 85701

The Fox Theatre movie palace was the place to be during the heyday of Hollywood film. However, when the glamor and prestige of that era was fading, the Fox Theatre was rendered obsolete and then abandoned. The venue reopened in the spring of 2000 after an extensive face-lift, and the stately historic theater, now returned to its previous glory, is now home not only to motion pictures but to live music and performances of all kinds.

THE HISTORIC RIALTO THEATRE

520-740-1000
www.rialtotheatre.com
318 E. Congress St., Tucson, AZ 85701

If you are looking for some history to go along with your musical outing, consider seeing a show at the Historic Rialto Theatre. Situated in downtown Tucson, the Rialto takes its name from the famous medieval covered bridge in Venice, Italy, which is surrounded by novelty shops. When the Rialto first opened in 1920, Hollywood motion pictures, including the premiere of Tucson's first talkie film, were shown on its silver screen. Later, vaudevillians and touring groups found their way to the Rialto's stage, with the theater scoring such illustrious acts as Ginger Rogers, prima ballerina Anna Pavlova, and the Sistine Choir, the official chorus of the Pope. Despite the celebrities who have graced its stage, the theater has not been unmarred by history. In the 1940s, a piano player seated in the orchestra pit fell back against a concrete slab and was crushed by his piano, dying from his injuries. Some claim his ghost still haunts the theater. Then, in the 1970s, the Rialto, then operated under a different name, had a short run as a porn theater. One Tucsonan was so appalled by the showing of the movie *Deep Throat* that after being forcibly removed from the theater on multiple occasions, she poured gasoline down the balcony stairs and lit a match. Although this incident caused minimal damage, the theater would not be so lucky when its boiler exploded in 1984. Only one person suffered minor injuries, but damage to the theater was extensive. It wouldn't be repaired until 1995, when new owners renovated the place, renamed it the Rialto, and opened it as a concert venue. Today, the Rialto hosts national and local acts, including folk and country bands, rock bands, jam bands, comedians, and hiphop and jazz musicians. In a tip of the hat to its previous life, the venue also occasionally screens films.

PLUSH

520-798-1298
www.plushtucson.com
340 E. Sixth St., Tucson, AZ 85705

Situated on the bustling corner of Fourth Avenue and Sixth Street, this bar and club combines plush furniture and quirky decor for a charming setting to grab a cocktail or listen to bands perform. With both small and large stages, Plush presents local and national musical acts almost daily. Sit out on the patio and enjoy the Tucson weather while you wait for the show, or hang out on the sofas inside, partaking in the comfort that gives the club its name.

SOLAR CULTURE

www.solarculture.org
E-mail: info@solarculture.org
Stone Ave. and Toole Ave., Tucson, AZ 85701

Representing the laid-back, New Age attitude of certain parts of Tucson is the nonprofit performing-arts venue Solar Culture. In addition to offering gallery and studio space for visual artists, Solar Culture showcases local and national performers. Solar Culture's mission is to "foster an exchange of ideas and information with the artists we present that is mutually inspirational." Most events start at 9 PM, and tickets are sold at the door. Although refreshments aren't served, patrons are welcome to bring their own food and beverages.

Groups and Associations

ARIZONA FRIENDS OF CHAMBER MUSIC

www.arizonachambermusic.org
E-mail: office@arizonachambermusic.org
Leo Rich Theater, 260 S. Church Ave., Tucson, AZ 85701

For more than 60 years, Arizona Friends of Chamber Music has brought renowned chamber ensembles to the city of Tucson. Six times a year, the Evening Concert Series is host to diverse chamber music ensembles. The concert series Piano and Friends is dedicated to aficionados of the black-and-white keys, performing solo or paired with another instrument. Finally, the end of the year is topped off with the weeklong Tucson Winter Chamber Music Festival, which not only features concerts but a gala dinner, open dress rehearsals, and master classes with the festival performers. Arizona Friends of Chamber Music is also active in keeping the genre of chamber music alive, commissioning new works for their concerts.

ARIZONA OPERA

520-293-4336
www.azopera.com
E-mail: info@azopera.com
Tucson Music Hall, 260 S. Church Ave., Tucson, AZ 85701

If, during your stint in Tucson, you would like to spend some time with a mysterious mezzo soprano or a boisterous baritone, look no further than the Arizona Opera. Begun in 1971 by a group of Tucson opera devotees, Arizona Opera has grown from a fledgling company drawing on a mix of local and regional talent for two performances to a professional company with talent from all over the globe producing five operas. Arizona Opera also takes its place as one of only three U.S. opera companies that perform in two cities, Tucson and neighboring Phoenix. For the 2007–2008 season, Arizona Opera established the Marion Roose Pullin Arizona Opera Studio program in order to provide training—in the form of master classes, vocal coaching, acting, movement, and conducting—to emerging opera singers and conductors.

TUCSON JAZZ SOCIETY

520-903-1265
www.tucsonjazz.org
E-mail: office@tucsonjazz.org
Various venues

The Tucson Jazz Society, one of the country's largest jazz societies, has one goal at its core: to promote and preserve jazz, America's music. Started in 1977, the nonprofit organization works to expose the Tucson community to jazz music and also to encourage musicianship in local youth. Some of the artists presented by the Tucson Jazz Society include Tito Puente, Marian McPartland, Clark Terry, Buddy DeFranco, and Brian Bromberg. The society sponsors regular events like its Blues, Brews and BBQ brunch each Sunday, as well as annual seasonal events like the Summer Series and the Primavera Women in Jazz Concert.

Plush is a popular nightlife venue.

TUCSON SYMPHONY ORCHESTRA

520-882-8585 (box office), 520-792-9155 (administrative office)
www.tucsonsymphony.org
Tucson Symphony Center, 2175 N. Sixth Ave., Tucson, AZ 85705

The first performance of the Tucson Symphony Orchestra in 1929 took place in a high school auditorium with volunteer musicians. That's quite a modest beginning for a musical ensemble that has the longevity and has received the accolades of this one. More than 75 years later, the professional musicians that make up the Tucson Symphony Orchestra continue to perform, both as a large group and in smaller performances, delighting the Tucson community with their interpretations of classical music. The Tucson Symphony Orchestra often plays with its own chorus, which made its debut in 2003 with Handel's *Messiah*. The Tucson Symphony Orchestra is also involved in educational outreach, which often culminates in concert performances.

THE UNIVERSITY OF ARIZONA SCHOOL OF MUSIC

520-621-1655
http://web.cfa.arizona.edu/music
E-mail: musicweb@cfa.arizona.edu
1017 N. Olive Rd., Tucson, AZ 85721 (Music Building, University of Arizona)

Since the 1800s, the University of Arizona has offered promising musicians an opportunity to hone their skills. Today, the university continues in that tradition, training instrumentalists, vocalists, and conductors for their future in the music field. A team of nationally and internationally renowned faculty leads the school's 485 music majors. The school regularly showcases music—from the UA Philharmonic or UA Chorus to solo performances by student vocalists and instrumentalists.

NIGHTLIFE

While Tucson is home to a large university, there is a plentiful nightlife scene for those no longer in their teens and twenties. In addition to the bars and clubs that feature live music on a regular basis, there are plenty of things to do in the Old Pueblo once the sun goes down.

If stargazing and being out in nature at night is what you desire, there are many options. In summer months, the **Arizona-Sonora Desert Museum** (520-883-1380; www.desertmuseum.org; 2021 N. Kinney Rd.) offers night programs where you can watch animals like mountain lions, beavers, and bats in their natural environs. Museum docents run special talks and lectures where they explain the habits of desert animals and the wonders of the night sky, among other topics. You can also dine at the on-site restaurant, the acclaimed **Ocotillo Café Restaurant.**

For a better view of the night sky, you can make a reservation through the **Kitt Peak Night Visitor Program** (520-318-8726; www.noao.edu/outreach/nop). Although the visitors center typically closes at 4, you can arrange to be there after hours, when you can utilize their high-tech telescopes to get a majestic view of the sky. Kitt Peak is about an hour-and-a-half drive from Tucson.

To witness your favorite classic movies out in the open, take a picnic to **Cinema La Placita** (www.cinemalaplacita.com; La Placita Village, 110 S. Church Ave., southwest corner of Broadway and Church avenues in downtown Tucson). Free movies are shown every Thursday evening from May to October.

If you want to kick up your heels 1950s-style, bop on over to **Fenderskirts** (520-722-1214; 140 S. Kolb Rd.) to dance to the music and be part of the old-style flavor. If you'd rather dance the night away with Latin flair, spend your Friday night visiting the acclaimed salsa night at **El Parador Resaurant** (520-881-2808; www.elparadortucson.com; 2744 E. Broadway). Tropical plants and decor set the mood for a night of mambo and cha-cha to live Latin dance music. The $7 cover also takes care of the dance lessons that start around 10 PM The restaurant also has salsa dancing every third Saturday.

Tucson's countryside can be seen at local bars that offer good ol' Western fun. **Cactus Moon Café** (520-748-0049; www.cactusmooncafe.com; 5470 E. Broadway), the official hot spot for the Tucson Rodeo, has a large dance floor used for two-step and country swing dancing. Wet your whistle and pop in for swing lessons when the music begins.

Maverick (520-298-0430; 6622 E. Tanque Verde Rd.) is another popular honky-tonk where cowboys and cowgirls show up to take a spin around the floor. Western dress is not required, but you won't be out of place if you wear your cowboy boots and Western shirts here.

So your skill is not in the legs but in the vocal cords. Karaoke has spread like wildfire in Tucson over the past decade. Make sure to call to ensure days and times haven't changed, and check the *Tucson Weekly* for the dozens of places that offer karaoke nights. Wednesday nights are for the singers at **French Quarter of Tucson** (520-318-4767; 3146 E. Grant Rd.), Tucson's own Cajun Kitchen and Bayou Bar. They have live local music on Friday and Saturday, and their menus feature Cajun and Creole dishes from Louisiana. Sunday-night karaoke is at **Club Congress** (520-622-8848; 311 E. Congress St.), where the cool kids go to sing.

To try your luck in the desert, visit one of Tucson's casinos. **Casino Del Sol** (1-800-344-9435; www.casinodelsol.com; 5655 W. Valencia Rd.) not only has hundreds of slot machines, blackjack, poker, and bingo, but it also holds concerts by touring musicians in its outdoor amphitheater. **Desert Diamond Casino** (520-294-7777; www.desertdiamondcasino.com; 7350 S. Nogales Hwy.) is a concert venue as well, and it's also become somewhat of a destination for live boxing.

Tucson's only comedy club, **Laffs Comedy Club and Café** (520-323-8669; www.laffscomedyclub.com; 2900 E. Broadway Blvd. #154), offers both local and national comedians in a cozy cabaret-style setting. In additional to traditional stand-up performers, Laffs hosts specialty acts like ventriloquists, hypnotists and magicians. Laffs also has an extensive menu including steaks, burgers, salads and sandwiches.

Want to catch some sports while you are in town? If you don't mind bumping arms with some undergrads, you can try **O'Malley's on Fourth** (520-623-8600; 247 N. Fourth Ave.) or **Maloney's** (520-388-9355; 213 N. Fourth Ave.). **Jeff's Pub** (520-886-4299; 112 S. Camino Seco Ave.), Tucson's home of off-track betting, is a lively atmosphere to watch

Arizona-Sonora Desert Museum Gill Kenny © Metropolitan Tucson Convention & Visitors Bureau

sporting events. Take in a game near the university at **Bob Dobbs'** (520-325-3767; 2501 E. Sixth St.), where you can also admire the creative words of patrons lining the walls. Bring a permanent marker and join in the conversation. Some other places to catch the big game are **Sports Page Lounge** (520-887-3096; 915 W. Prince Rd.), **Trident Grill & Bar** (520-795-5755; 2330 E. Speedway Blvd.), or **Trophies Bar and Grill** (520-323-6262; Sheraton Hotel & Suites, 5151 E. Grant Rd.).

If you are more in the mood to play games, stop by **Click Billiards** (520-887-7312; 3325 N. First Ave.) It has 14 professional pool tables, foosball tables, pinball games, and electronic dartboards, so you can encourage your competitive spirit.

For a more upscale evening, stop for a cocktail at **The Arizona Inn** (520-325-1541; www.arizonainn.com; 2200 E. Elm St.). Listen to the nightly music in the piano bar or browse through the books and periodicals in the library, with its comfortable armchairs and high wooden-beamed ceilings. You can also take a stroll through the upscale hotel's manicured garden.

Just steps away from downtown in the Barrio Historico is the classy but cozy **Cushing Street Bar and Restaurant** (520-622-7984; www.cushingstreet.com; 198 W. Cushing St.). Cushing Street, housed in an 1860 historic adobe building, has a stylish main dining room or a lovely garden patio for when Tucson weather is at its best. On the drink menus are specialty drinks, like their to-die-for mojito. The patio is also the place for live music on the weekends.

For a trip back to the 1960s, take in the kitschy but classy scene of **The Shelter** (520-326-1345; 4155 E. Grant Rd.). A former fallout shelter, the odd-shaped building houses a retro bar with strong drinks and fun and quirky decor, including velvet paintings of the Kennedys, red-light-bulbed chandeliers, and leopard prints.

The Shanty of Tucson (520-623-2664; 401 E. Ninth St.) is anything but shabby. The Fourth Avenue bar has one of the best selections of beers in Arizona, with brews hailing from all over the world. Play a game of pool and feast on the complimentary snacks inside, or enjoy the fountain and junglelike garden on the patio. Jazz guitarist Joe McNeil is featured on Sunday nights.

Listen to jazz while overlooking the city of Tucson at the **Cascade Bar** (520-299-2020; 7000 N. Resort Dr.). The piano bar has music Thursday through Sunday nights.

Located in the historic El Presidio District and run by the same family as the adjacent famous El Charro Café, **Toma!** (520-622-1922; 311 N. Court Ave.) is the most festive place to have a margarita in the city. Have a traditional one or sample one of their delightful variations—including mango, melon, and peach.

Tucsonans love their beer, and to taste their favorites, visit one of the many breweries in town. **Nimbus Brewing and Tap Room** (520-745-9175; www.nimbusbeer.com; 3850 E. 44th St.) allows you to hang out with the locals as you sample one of Tucson's most famous microbrews. In the heart of the city's warehouse district, the taproom is the foyer of the brewery itself, and they often have live music playing.

On University Boulevard, just blocks from the main gate of campus, is **Gentle Ben's** (520-624-4177; 865 E. University Blvd.), a favorite among the university community that has been around since the 1970s. The restaurant and microbrewery's name was chosen through a communitywide contest. A university professor thought the establishment's manager looked like Dan Haggerty from the TV show *Grizzly Adams,* and Haggerty's cohort was a bear with the moniker Gentle Ben. The brewery began in 1991 with three different beers, but now there are eight different kinds to sample, in addition to seasonal brews.

Thunder Canyon Brewery (520-797-2652; 7401 N. La Cholla Blvd.) is an offshoot of the Prescott Brewing Company located north of Phoenix. In addition to their IPA and other beers, the brewery has a full-menu restaurant.

Known for its selection of brews and huge menu, **BJ's Restaurant and Brewhouse** (520-690-1900; 4270 N. Oracle Rd.) is part of a small West Coast–based chain. Some popular brews include the hoppy Piranha Pale Ale and the brown Nutty Brunette.

Although both are full restaurants, **Kingfisher** (520-323-7739; 2564 E. Grant Rd.) seafood restaurant and **McMahon's Prime Steak House** (520-327-2333; 2959 N. Swan Rd.) have extensive wine lists. McMahon's also has a cigar and martini lounge.

THEATER

While not a theater mecca like New York or Los Angeles, Tucson does offer a strong theater community, committed not only to producing quality theater but also to making it accessible to the community at large. From more traditional theaters dedicated to classics to activist ones that produce plays to instigate and challenge the status quo, the stages of Tucson have something for everyone.

ARIZONA ONSTAGE PRODUCTIONS

520-270-3332, 520-882-6574
www.arizonaonstage.org
E-mail: azonstage@yahoo.com
Venues vary

With a goal to create theater that is not only entertaining but also complicated and challenging for the viewer, Arizona Onstage Productions presents dynamic and engaging musical theater. To perform their shows, Arizona Onstage employs not only professionals but draws on the talents of the community found at the University of Arizona, ZUZI! Dance Lab, and middle and high school Basis Tucson. The company performs musicals—new and old, funny and dark—for the city community.

ARIZONA REPERTORY THEATRE

520-621-1162
http://web.cfa.arizona.edu/theatre/art
Peter Marroney Theatre and Laboratory Theatre, University of Arizona

To see emerging actors, directors, stage designers, and playwrights in the act of forming their art, attend a production of the Arizona Repertory Theatre. The professional training company of the University of Arizona School of Theatre Arts, Arizona Repertory Theatre features rising young artists in six plays each year. The plays range in style from classical dramas to comedies, musical theater, and contemporary plays.

ARIZONA ROSE THEATER COMPANY

520-888-0509
www.arizonarose.cc
E-mail: roseinfo@arizonarose.cc
The Berger Performing Arts Center, 1200 W. Speedway Blvd., Tucson, AZ 85745 (venue varies from season to season)

Center for Creative Photography

If the museums and galleries around the city haven't satisfied your thirst for art, be sure to stop by the University of Arizona's Center for Creative Photography (CCP). This research center and museum first gained prominence when it obtained the collections of a few well-known photographers— among them that master of the American landscape, Ansel Adams. The museum now houses eighty thousand photographs from more than two thousand artists, making it the largest archive of 20th-century North American photography in the nation. Exhibitions have included the works of old pioneers like Edward Weston and Eugene Smith, as well as the efforts of more recent innovators, such as Richard Avedon, Philip di Corcia, and Sally Mann. But artists are not just represented by their works; world-famous artists and art historians have taken the time to visit this center's auditorium in person, as well. For example, performance artist and musician Laurie Anderson spoke about her experience as NASA's artist in residence in 2007, and Belgian art collector Stephane Janssen introduced the opening of his personal photography collection at the CCP in 2008. Because of the center's strong focus on education, you may see classes from the university analyzing the exhibitions, as well as curators leading educational tours and archive tutorials. This is also an excellent location to visit if you like to shop, as the store in the CCP's lobby has a variety of unique photography books, and monographs, posters, postcards, and other materials available for purchase. Visit the museum's Web site (www.creativephotography.org) for information, or make an appointment to arrange a tour by calling 520-621-7968.

The desert is an unlikely place to find a rose, but one exists in the form of the Arizona Rose Theater Company. Two theater, film, TV, and recording industry veterans, Cynthia and Terry Howell, founded the community-based theater company in 1986. Their mission was bifold: to produce quality theater without funding from public sources and to only put on shows that had positive messages and resolutions. They tapped into their own experience and the talent pool of the Tucson community, and the result is 30 years' worth of all-original musicals. The Arizona Rose, called the Rose by Tucsonans, produces four main stage productions each year.

ARIZONA THEATRE COMPANY

520-622-2823
www.aztheatreco.org
Temple of Music and Art, 330 S. Scott Ave., Tucson, AZ 85701

Founded in 1967 as the Arizona Civic Theatre, the Arizona Theatre Company serves both Tucson and Phoenix. They seek diversity with their productions by seeking out classic and new musicals and plays. From the *Pajama Game* to *Dr. Jekyll and Mr. Hyde* and from Shakespeare to Stoppard, the Arizona Theatre Company aims to both honor the history of theater and be on the forefront of the theater of today. Committed to making theater accessible to people of all income levels, the Arizona Theatre Company keeps ticket prices down and recoups the production cost through community contributions and grants.

BEOWULF ALLEY THEATRE COMPANY

520-882-0555
www.beowulfalley.org

E-mail: theatre@beowulfalley.org

11 S. Sixth Ave., Tucson, AZ 85701

Beowulf Alley's mission and theatrical priorities can be explained by its moniker: The first part of its name was inspired by the epic poem *Beowulf,* recognized as the oldest literary work, and this reflects the theater's commitment to traditional and classical theater, while the second part of its name, *Alley,* suggests modern, cutting-edge, and urban theater. Located in historic downtown Tucson, Beowulf Alley's physical theater space is humble, and while it lacks the charm of some of Tucson's older theaters, it offers a private space in which to view performances. Over the past several years, Beowulf Alley has premiered several productions on both a state and national scale.

BORDERLANDS THEATER

520-882-7406

www.borderlandstheater.org

Administrative office at El Centro Cultural de las Americanas, 40 W. Broadway Blvd., Tucson, AZ 85701 (plays held at various venues)

The belief that theater is a political vehicle and is a means to subvert the mainstream is at the root of Borderlands Theater. As the name evokes, the theater company's productions and educational programs focus on issues and voices coming out of the Southwest border region of the United States. The company is concerned with both physical and social borders, and their plays primarily work to project the voice of Latino/Chicano people. Founded in 1986, Borderlands Theater grew out of Teatro Libertad, a community-based "activist" company that was interested in exploring Chicano culture during the time of the civil rights movement. Borderlands produces six plays a year and supports the work of emerging playwrights and artists through the Border Playwrights Project, which has commissioned and developed more than 50 plays.

BROADWAY IN TUCSON

520-903-2929

www.broadwayintucson.com

E-mail: info@broadwayintucson.com

260 S. Church Ave., Tucson, AZ 85701 (most performances at Tucson Music Hall)

Part of the national Nederlander Producing Company of America, Broadway in Tucson offers high-quality Broadway musicals. Broadway in Tucson began in 2003 when the city commissioned Nederlander to present a series of musicals and musical events downtown, recognizing the value of experiencing such musical events as a way of building community. Debuting with *Movin' Out,* the musical based on the music of Billy Joel, Broadway in Tucson has continued to create a gathering place downtown to see such shows as *Chicago, Thoroughly Modern Millie,* and *Evita.* Broadway in Tucson has also presented musical guests and comedians like B. B. King and Jerry Seinfeld. Tucsonans seem to enjoy it: attendance of more than 83,000 for a six-week run of *The Lion King* broke Tucson box-office records and made *The Lion King* the best-attended and longest-running production in Tucson theater history.

CATALINA PLAYERS' THEATRE

520-409-8407

Academy Hall, 6653 E. Carondelet Dr., Tucson, AZ 85710

Begun in 1983 by a group of local actors in search of a way to produce plays and continue to learn their art, Catalina Players is a supportive, professional theater company working to share their love of drama with the Tucson community. Over the years, the company's beginnings as a small ensemble of church-based performers has evolved into a nonprofit open to public participation, both as players and audience, relying on the talent of its community for its plays and musical revues. The theater group works to encourage diversity both in the pieces it produces and the cast that performs them, and it often partners with groups like the National Association of Women Business Owners and the Tucson Hispanic Chamber of Commerce to attract new and diverse participants.

THE GASLIGHT THEATRE
520-886-9428
www.thegaslighttheatre.com
7010 E. Broadway Blvd., Tucson, AZ 85710

Unapologetically melodramatic and over the top, the Gaslight Theatre offers wacky, off-the-wall live musicals while you dine. Begun by University of Arizona drama students in 1977, the Gaslight Theatre offers an interactive experience: cheer for the heroes, boo at the villains, and stomp your feet as the honky-tonk piano plays and the ensemble performs their original dialogue and songs.

THE INVISIBLE THEATRE
520-884-0672
www.invisibletheatre.com
1400 N. First Ave., Tucson, AZ 85719

A nonprofit theater named after the intangible connection formed between performer and audience during a play, the Invisible Theatre has been a fixture in the Tucson community since 1971. The theater originated as a showcase for Tucson playwrights but has now expanded to include adaptations of classics and current off-Broadway plays and musicals, as well as locally produced plays and readings. The theater typically produces six plays a season in addition to special events. One of their events, Project Pastime, is an educational program for the mentally challenged, which introduces theatrical ideas and encourages discussion and dialogue. The small physical space, comprised of 80 seats and converted from an old Laundromat, forges an intimate connection between viewer and actor.

LIVE THEATRE WORKSHOP
520-327-4242
www.livetheatreworkshop.org
E-mail: livethworkshop@qwest.net
5317 E. Speedway Blvd., Tucson, AZ 85712

Live Theatre Workshop is a community-based theater designed to make theater accessible to people of all ages, backgrounds, and income levels. Their programs and theatrical productions focus on developing emerging theatrical talents in addition to providing entertaining plays. Founded in 1994 with its first main stage season of productions such as Synge's *The Playboy of the Western World,* the Live Theatre Workshop now produces a full season of plays in addition to their family theater series, school productions, and free Readers'

Series productions. They have also added a theatrical event called ETCETERA, LTW Late Nights to spice up the late-night theater scene in Tucson. From tragedy to comedy, from classics to modern pieces, from Shakespeare to Shaw and Vogel to Durang, you can find them all at the Live Theatre Workshop.

THE OLD PUEBLO PLAYWRIGHTS

520-743-0940
www.oldpuebloplaywrights.org
Venues vary

The Old Pueblo Playwrights is made up of Arizona playwrights who gather to read and workshop each other's work, put on new plays several times a year, and host the annual Festival of New Plays. They also host the annual Play in a Day Festival, where a half dozen plays are written, cast, rehearsed, and performed in less than 24 hours.

THE ROGUE THEATRE

520-551-2053
www.theroguetheatre.org
Various venues

Named out of a desire to "poke and prod and kick over a few sand castles" with their work, the Rogue Theatre strives to not only produce quality theater, but theater that provocatively pushes the bounds of social, political, and personal issues. Whether that is done through the work of Anton Chekhov or Edward Albee, the Rogue will not only entertain you for a few hours, but it will get you thinking for the rest of the night—or for the rest of your stay in Tucson.

SEASONAL EVENTS

Tucson is an enjoyable place to visit any time of year. Visitors love the hospitality and friendly nature of the locals, and it's hard not to fall in love with the rose- and purple-toned mountains that embrace the city. However, there are certain times of year when Tucson is spectacular. Whether you're a baseball fan, a treasure hunter, an anthropology whiz, or a cowboy or cowgirl at heart, it would serve you well to consider visiting Tucson during one of these seasonal events.

All Souls Procession (www.allsoulsprocession.org) Each year, Tucson's streets flood with people dressed head to toe in black, their faces painted to resemble skulls. It's not Halloween. On a day close to November 2, Tucsonans come out in full force at the All Souls Procession for Dia de los Muertos (the Day of the Dead) to celebrate the legacy and spirit of their ancestors. The celebration, infused with Latin traditions, began in 1990 with a performance piece created by local artist Susan Johnson to honor the death of her father. Now, in its modern incarnation, elaborate decorative floats and puppets move down the street alongside stilt walkers and ten thousand participants during the 2-mile walk. Enjoy the procession as a spectator, or dress up and join in the walk from Fourth Avenue all the way to downtown Tucson. The march concludes with a communal celebration near the railroad tracks, where a large urn—containing the written hopes, offerings, and wishes for those who have passed—is set afire.

Annual Waila Festival (520-628-5774; www.arizonahistoricalsociety.org) Sponsored by the Arizona Historical Society, the Waila Festival celebrates the culture of the Tohono O'odham, or Desert People. Located to the west of Tucson, the Tohono O'odham Nation is the second-largest Native American reservation in the United States and is roughly the size of Connecticut. The free festival provides an opportunity to experience the Tohono O'odham culture by sampling food like fry bread, tepary beans, squash, and cholla buds, and participating in social dancing to waila music. *Waila* comes from the Spanish word for "dance" and is the fiddle-driven music of the O'odham that evolved from their adaptations of European and Mexican tunes. The fiddle was initially introduced to the tribe by missionaries who wanted them to play for church services, but today a waila group typically includes multiple fiddles, as well as accordions, saxophones, electric and bass guitars, and drums. The principal purpose of the music is to inspire dancing, whether that be the chote (a modified two-step) or the waila (a polka-style dance). Workshops are held for youth musicians. Some of the musicians have been featured in the Smithsonian's Folk Masters Series. The festival's goal is to counteract prominent stereotypes of who American Indians are and to celebrate the rich culture of this tribe of Native Americans.

Cinco de Mayo (520-292-9326; Kennedy Park, 3700 S. Mission Rd.) Each May, Tucson celebrates Mexico's victory against France in 1862 with a four-day-long Cinco de Mayo festival. The free festival culminates on May 5, and it features live music, dancing, crafts, and tasty food. There are also opportunities to learn about Mexican history and culture. Also held around May 5 each year is the annual Cinco de Mayo 10K (www.azroadrunners.org/events/cinco) race, which winds through Star Pass in the foothills of the Tucson Mountains. As a reward for completing the race, participants are given free burritos and treated to mariachi music.

El Nacimiento (www.tucsonarts.com; La Casa Cordova, Tucson Museum of Art Historic Block, 140 N. Main Ave.) Tucson rings in the holiday season each year in its own unique way. The historic adobe La Casa Cordova (part of the Tucson Museum of Art Historic Block) houses a traditional Mexican nativity scene display that features three hundred earthen figurines. This annual event coincides with Fiesta Navidad, a Mexican mariachi Christmas celebration.

El Tour de Tucson (520-745-2033; throughout Tucson) Tucson's streets are filled with two-wheeled vehicles instead of the four-wheeled kind when El Tour de Tucson comes to town each year. Since the race's inception in 1983, cyclists from all over the world have visited the city to ride in the 109-mile race, the largest perimeter cycling event in the United States. Open to both amateurs and professionals, the event always takes place on the Saturday before Thanksgiving, and such notable cyclists as Greg LeMond, Jeannie Longo, Lance Armstrong, and Floyd Landis have participated.

Family Arts Festival (520-624-0595; downtown Tucson) Run by the Pima County Arts Council, the annual Family Arts Festival sprawls across downtown Tucson and offers kids of all ages the opportunity to explore their creative side. Held in January, the festival celebrates the art and cultural heritage of the Tucson area with live musical and theatrical performances, dance, and folklorico, and showcases of the work of visual artists. There are also opportunities for children and adults to engage in hands-on activities and demonstrations, such as alabaster stone carving and watercolor painting. A past festival featured a Carnivale parade showcasing the antics and acrobatics of renowned Tucson-based performance troupe Flam Chen.

GLBT Tucson

One evening in November 2008, almost one thousand students, teachers, doctors, waitresses, and families marched to the Tucson City Hall in order to protest against a ban on gay marriage. Earlier that June, thousands turned out for activities related to the gay, lesbian, bisexual, and transgender (GLBT) **Tucson Pride Week** (www.tucsonpride.org), which included a week of events at parks, coffeehouses, and the local art-house film theater. While the city is small, its GLBT community is reasonably strong. This could be thanks to a number of well-orchestrated organizations, like the twenty-year-old nonprofit organization **Wingspan** (520-624-1779; www.wingspan.org), which offers outreach, counseling, and programming to the southern Arizona GLBT community. It could also be due to the many establishments that have made a special point of welcoming GLBT customers, like **Bentley's Coffee and Tea** (520-795-0338; www.bentleyscoffeehouse.com), located near the University of Arizona campus. If you are looking to socialize, **The Biz** (520-318-4838; www.thebiztuc.com) and **IBT's** (520-882-3053) cater primarily to Tucson's GLBT community. **Antigone's Bookstore** (520-792-3715; www.antigonebooks.com) carries an array of titles that will be of interest to readers of all stripes, but the owners are expressly oriented toward issues that relate to feminism, and they carry a wide selection of GLBT-related literature and media. If you are looking for a GLBT-friendly place to worship, the **Water of Life Metropolitan Community Church** (520-292-9151) has expressed interest in reaching out to the GLBT community and its allies. Looking for a place to stay? Consider the **Royal Elizabeth Bed and Breakfast** (520-670-9022), which is not only GLBT-friendly but gay owned. Visit www.gaytucson.com for more details on eateries, retailers, hotels, events, and news of interest to the GLBT community in Tucson.

Fiesta de San Augustin (St. Augustine Cathedral, 192 S. Stone Ave.) Each August, Tucson celebrates its relationship to its patron saint with the Fiesta de San Augustin, which includes a special mass, exhibits, speakers, stalls, dances, and live music. Held at the downtown St. Augustine Cathedral, the festival honors the history of Tucson and its affiliation with the saint, which begun with the Spanish missionaries in the 1700s.

Folk Festival (520-792-6481; El Presidio Park, downtown Tucson) Legendary trumpeter Louis Armstrong once said, "All music is folk music. I ain't never heard a horse sing a song." You can enjoy all kinds of folk music at Tucson's annual Folk Festival the first weekend in May. The free two-day event, held during one of the most beautiful times of year, celebrates acoustic music and other folk arts, and showcases not only nationally known headline acts but also musical groups from Tucson and other parts of Arizona. In addition to featuring about one hundred musical groups, the festival holds workshops for attendees where you can learn how to yodel or play blues guitar.

Fourth Avenue Street Fair (520-624-5004; Fourth Ave.) Throughout the year, Fourth Avenue is a bustling, entertaining street, catering to locals and tourists alike with it's quirky cafés, trendy and vintage boutiques, and diverse restaurants. But twice a year, in March and December, artists, merchants, and musicians bring their special flair to the street for the Fourth Avenue Street Fair. Buy wares crafted by more than 100 artisans or just walk around and admire their handiwork while sampling more than 40 kinds of food and listening to music by Tucson bands.

Pro Baseball Spring Training (520-434-1000; Kino Sports Complex, 500 E. Ajo Way) Although Arizona's pro baseball team, the Diamondbacks, belongs to the city of

Phoenix, the months of February and March mean that Tucson is home to the spring training sessions for the team. Sit back, relax, and take in the backdrop of the majestic Santa Catalina Mountains while watching pro baseball players gear up for the coming season. The smaller, intimate setting of Tucson Electric Park, nicknamed "the jewel of the desert," lets baseball fans take in the action up close. You might even see your hometown team take on the Diamondbacks. Or check out the Colorado Rockies, who train at Hi Corbett Field (1-800-388-7625; 3400 E. Camino Campestre).

Tucson Gem & Mineral Show (520-322-5773; Tucson Convention Center, 260 S. Church Ave.) Everyone from gem experts and jewelry designers to those who just appreciate colorful, gleaming things gathers in Tucson each February for the Tucson Gem, Mineral & Fossil Showcase. The showcase is made up of more than 40 gem, jewelry, bead, mineral, and fossil shows spread throughout the city of Tucson, and it finishes off with the main event, the Tucson Gem & Mineral Show, which takes place downtown during the final weekend. Treasure hunters can find everything from glass beads, gold, and rubies to granite tabletops and ancient dinosaur fossils. Most shows are open to the public, while some are only open to wholesale buyers (and require credentials for entry).

Tucson International Mariachi Conference (520-838-3913; www.tucsonmariachi.org; 502 W. 29th St.) They're not just performing at your tableside in restaurants—mariachi is a longstanding musical tradition in Mexico. Each April, the La Frontera Tucson International Mariachi Conference is held in Tucson, treating participants to a weeklong series of events showcasing established and emerging talents of mariachi and baile folklorico. Originally, Mariachi were Mexican street performers or buskers, but now many mariachi groups make their living performing. Usually a mariachi group consists of three violins, two trumpets, one Mexican guitar, one vihuala (a high-pitched, five-string guitar), and a small acoustic bass. In addition to promoting awareness of this musical tradition, the conference works to foster awareness of and generate funding for La Frontera Center, a nonprofit behavioral health agency serving Tucson children, families, and adults.

Tucson Meet Yourself (520-792-4806; downtown Tucson) Tucson Meet Yourself, in early October, provides both locals and visitors the chance to celebrate the diverse people that make up the Tucson community. Since 1974, festivalgoers have been given the opportunity to experience the food and folk art of the many cultures that live here.

World Famous Tucson Rodeo (520-741-2233 or 1-800-965-5662; Tucson Rodeo Grounds, 4823 S. Sixth Ave.) In some parts of the country, real-life cowgirls and cowboys still exist. They're out there roping steers, riding horses, and grazing cattle. See them in action at the annual La Fiesta de Los Vaqueros (Celebration of the Cowboys) in February. Begun in 1925 as a small festival and competition, the rodeo now touts nine days of celebration and rodeo events including bull riding, bareback and saddle bronc riding, and steer wrestling. The air is filled with the nostalgia of the Old West as the announcers interact with cowboys and the crowd responds with laughter and rows of nodding cowboy hats. If you are in the mood for shopping, there's no shortage of cowboy hats, brass belt buckles, and rhinestone-studded Western gear. You can also take in the Tucson Rodeo Parade, featuring Western-themed floats and buggies, historic horse-drawn couches, folk dancers, and marching bands and dance teams from local schools.

Yaqui Deer Dances (520-791-4609; 785 W. Sahuaro St.) Each year, from Lent to Easter, the Yaqui Native Americans participate in ritualized dances that celebrate their culture and traditions. The sacred dances, songs, and prayers are a mix of ancient Yaqui beliefs and the Catholic traditions introduced by early-18th-century Spanish missionaries. From a young age, children are trained in the practices and assigned roles to perform in the ceremonies, which depict the Passion of the Christ. All those that participate do so under a manta—a promise or vow—as a result of receiving aid from Jesus or Mary. The most honored role is that of the Deer Dancer, who dons the head of a deer and carries a gourd rattle in each hand. The dance involves the Pascals, or old men of the fiesta, attempting to persuade the deer to sacrifice himself to the hunters for the welfare of the people. The sacrifice depicted in this ritual has obvious parallels to the story of Jesus Christ. Although visitors are invited to attend, photographs are prohibited as this is a sacred spiritual ceremony.

Janos Wilder of Janos Restaurant and J BAR Courtesy Westin La Paloma

5

RESTAURANTS & FOOD PURVEYORS

¡Salud!

In the last decade, Tucson has come into its own as a food destination. It has long been known for its Sonoran (and other regional) Mexican food, and this is truer than ever, as more and more locals head to South Tucson in search of real home cooking. The invisible Tucson–South Tucson border that once kept residents in their respective quarters no longer exists.

"American" food in Tucson is heavily influenced by its neighbor California, always a culinary pioneer. And now there are also respectable Italian, French, Thai, and even Malaysian options. Because of the large university subculture, there are lots of cafés that take their coffee—and their café atmosphere—seriously.

The newest trends are toward small-plate menus, wine bars, and casual bistro ambience. There is still some fusion cooking going on (Asian fusion being the most popular), but the cutting-edge restaurateurs prefer simple tradition over wild invention. Local and sustainable food is gaining in popularity as diners become more conscious about where their food comes from.

This chapter categorizes restaurants geographically, by cuisine, and then alphabetically. The price codes reflect the cost of one meal, including an appetizer, main course, and dessert—but not cocktails, wine, or beer. Food purveyors (at the end of the chapter) are categorized by type, then alphabetically. There are two restaurant indexes in the back of the book, one grouped by cuisine and one by price. Every restaurant appears in the general index as well.

Dining Price Codes

Inexpensive	Up to $15
Moderate	$15–30
Expensive	$30–65
Very Expensive	$65 or more

The following abbreviations are used for credit card information:

AE: American Express
CB: Carte Blanche
D: Discover Card
DC: Diner's Club
MC: MasterCard
V: Visa

Restaurants in Tucson Proper

American
ACACIA

520-232-0101
www.acaciatucson.com
4340 N. Campbell Ave., Tucson, AZ 85718
Price: Moderate
Credit Cards: AE, D, DC, MC, V
Hours: Sun. through Thurs. 11–10; Fri. and
Sat. 11–11 (hours may vary seasonally)
Reservations: Recommended
Handicapped Access: Yes
Special Features: Patio dining, live music,
Sun. brunch

Acacia promises nothing if not elegance.
The centerpiece of the main dining room
(there are two, as well as a bar area and a
patio) is a beautiful wall of colored tiles over
which flows a sheet of water, a sight
matched only by the waitstaff, which is
impeccable and fleet. And then there's the
artfulness of the food. Lunch at Acacia is a
curious mixture of simple comfort foods
(grilled cheese with a cup of tomato soup;
tuna melts) and more refined fare, such as a
wok-charred salmon salad or a broiled
paupiette of Pacific sole filled with lobster,
crab, shrimp, and wild mushrooms. For
dinner, both the sweet corn and green chile
custard and the pan-seared diver scallops
(with pancetta crisps and sambal mashed
Yukon potatoes) shine with Southwestern
flavors. Chef-owner Albert Hall also offers a
three-course tasting menu that changes
weekly and comes with or without recommended wine pairings. Jazz brunch draws
crowds on Sunday.

ANTHONY'S IN THE CATALINAS

520-299-1771
www.anthonyscatalinas.com
6440 N. Campbell Ave., Tucson, AZ 85718
Price: Expensive
Credit Cards: AE, D, DC, MC, V
Hours: Daily 5:30–10 PM
Reservations: Highly recommended
Handicapped Access: Yes
Special Features: Patio dining, views,
extensive wine list, valet parking

That a restaurant can keep limited hours
and serve only dinner generally indicates
that it is destination dining for a devoted
clientele. Such is the story of Anthony's,
which continues to attract loyal, button-
down foothills crowds, as it has for decades.
Winner of *Wine Spectator*'s Grand Award and
AAA's Four Diamond Award, Anthony's
serves traditional Continental cuisine in a
lofty foothills setting. The atmosphere here
is decidedly rarified with tuxedoed waiters,
elegant dining rooms (there are several),
and a dinner menu featuring classics like
beef Wellington, châteaubriand, and veal
Piccata. Wine isn't just an afterthought at
Anthony's. Running more than one hundred pages and featuring 1,700 bottles from
around the world, the wine list is big, deep,
and filled with impressive and expensive
wines.

ARIZONA INN

520-325-1541
www.arizonainn.com
2200 E. Elm St., Tucson, AZ 85719
Price: Expensive
Credit Cards: AE, CB, DC, MC, V
Hours: Breakfast daily 7:30–10; lunch Mon.
through Sat. 11:30–2; dinner daily 6–10;
Sun. brunch 11:30–2
Reservations: Recommended for dinner in
the main dining room; not accepted for bar
or patio dining
Handicapped Access: Yes
Special Features: Patio dining, live music on
nights and weekends, weekend brunch,
tasting menu

Located in a sleepy midtown neighborhood
on 14 splendid acres of manicured gardens,
pristine courtyards, and flowing stone
fountains, and nationally recognized as one
of the best luxury resorts in the country,
Tucson's Arizona Inn exudes class. Cathedral ceilings, Spanish Colonial furniture,

and a corner fireplace lend a Southwestern charm to a main dining room that, on milder days, extends onto a garden patio. Lunch and dinner menus balance regionally accented dishes (like a seared red chile glazed salmon) with more international fare (like braised beef under pearl onions, mushrooms, and Burgundy sauce). Chef Odell Baskerville also offers a four-course tasting menu that changes weekly and comes with or without wine pairings. Those looking for a little history with their cocktails would do well to visit the Audubon bar, where live piano and an extensive wine and spirits lists conjure 1930s elegance. Breakfast is served daily, but it's the lavish poolside brunch buffet on weekends that is really worth the splurge.

BARRIO GRILL

520-629-0191
135 S. Sixth Ave., Tucson, AZ 85701
Price: Moderate
Credit Cards: AE, DC, MC, V
Hours: Lunch Mon. through Fri. 11–5 and Sat. noon–5; dinner Tues. through Thurs. 5–10, Fri. and Sat. 5–midnight, Sun. 5–9
Reservations: Recommended for dinner
Handicapped Access: Limited access to parts of the dining room
Special Features: Patio dining

Tucson's downtown Barrio Grill serves regionally accented American cuisine in a casual bistro setting replete with comfortable booths, muted lighting, and a lively bar serving everything from draught beer to wine flights. Chef Jeffrey Glomski's lunch menu includes a sumptuous steak sandwich (grilled New York strip on a kaiser roll with sautéed poblano chiles, caramelized shallots, oyster mushrooms, and Havarti cheese) and a delectable ensalada de pescado (mixed greens, sunflower sprouts, and pineapple relish tossed with a papaya-cilantro vinaigrette and topped with pan-blackened fresh fish of the day). Dinners at Barrio feature fish tacos (usually grilled

cabrilla or salmon with black beans and guacamole, served with a habanero tomatillo salsa and grilled pineapple salsa) and the papaya and mango pasta (grilled chicken reduced in a chipotle chardonnay cream tossed with linguine and finished with basil chiffonade). Barrio's proximity to downtown galleries, theaters, and concert halls makes it the perfect place to grab pre- or post-show dinner and drinks.

B LINE

520-882-7575
www.blinerestaurant.com
621 N. Fourth Ave., Tucson, AZ 85705
Price: Inexpensive
Credit Cards: MC, V
Hours: Mon. through Thurs. 7:30 AM–9 PM; Fri. and Sat. 7:30 AM–10 PM; Sun. 7:30 AM–8 PM
Reservations: Not accepted
Handicapped Access: Stairs limit access to the cash register and ordering
Special Features: Wi-Fi access

Lacquered wood counter tops, cold-rolled-steel accents, a wire cable that zips handwritten orders from the front register to the back kitchen—all of it lends a cool, industrial vibe that belies the appealing simplicity of B Line's Southwestern-inspired menu. Breakfast highlights include crêpe cakes (served with a ramekin of whipped honey butter, pecans, and maple syrup), made-from-scratch buttermilk biscuits, and burritos (stuffed with one variation or another of scrambled egg, beans, jack cheese, chorizo, and potatoes), while the combined lunch and dinner menu features unpretentious fare like tortilla soup, a blackened mahimahi burro (pan seared spicy mahimahi, coleslaw, achiote rice), and an incredible steak salad (seared flank steak on a bed of fresh greens under a mild avocado dressing). Most items on the menu pair nicely with B Line's selection of 11 draught microbrews and its small but smart selection of imported and California wines.

B Line also features fresh fruit pies, cakes, and tarts made on the premises by its own in-house pastry chef.

BLUEFIN

520-531-8500
www.bluefintucson.com
7053 N. Oracle Rd., Tucson, AZ 85704
Price: Moderate
Credit Cards: AE, D, DC, MC, V
Hours: Sun. through Thurs. 11–9; Fri. and Sat. 11 AM–midnight
Reservations: Recommended for dinner
Handicapped Access: Yes
Special Features: Oyster bar, late-night menu, Sun. brunch

Bluefin has fast distinguished itself as a hipper (if pricier) version of its sister restaurant, Kingfisher, due in no small part to its chic foothills digs. While many of the offerings here overlap with those found at Kingfisher (oyster varieties are sourced from the same area of the Pacific Northwest; starters like the Old Bay gulf shrimp and scallop seviche are given only subtle twists; fish is fresh and given the same gentle treatment), it's the increased size and variety of the dinner menu that distinguishes Bluefin. Whereas Kingfisher features six or seven appetizers and seafood entrées, Bluefin's menu boasts nearly double that number and also includes steamed Maine lobster and Alaskan king crab legs. Of the two, Bluefin is also the only one to offer Sunday brunch, though the only alcohol served here anytime is wine.

CUSHING STREET

520-622-7984
www.cushingstreet.com
198 W. Cushing St., Tucson, AZ 85701
Price: Moderate
Credit Cards: MC, V
Hours: Tues. through Sat. 4–10
Reservations: Accepted
Handicapped Access: Limited in places by a few stairs
Special Features: Garden patio dining, live music on nights and weekends

Tucked away in Barrio Viejo, Cushing Street has long been a mainstay of the downtown restaurant scene, serving up a well-prepared mix of contemporary American fare. With high ceilings, an antique cut-glass chandelier hung above a wood and brass bar, and a centennial Steinway piano that still gets some use on weekends, the atmosphere at Cushing Street is classy. The selection of main courses is more modest than most downtown restaurants, but at least two superb selections stand out: a sweet and spicy ancho-maple glazed meat loaf, and bacon-wrapped pork tenderloin with tomato couscous and braised apples. Those looking for conversation over drinks should try Cushing Street's mojito, a refreshing brace of white rum, lime, mint, sugar, and soda water. While this house specialty takes a little longer getting to the table because of how the lime and mint are hand crushed with mortar and pestle, it's the perfect drink for an evening with friends on Cushing's Street's fabulous garden patio.

THE DISH

520-326-1714
www.dishbistro.com
3131 E. First St., Tucson, AZ 85716
Price: Moderate
Credit Cards: AE, MC, V
Hours: Tues. through Sat. 5–midnight
Reservations: Highly recommended
Handicapped Access: Yes
Special Features: Adjoins a wine shop; wine tastings

With around 30 seats in the whole place, the Dish is tiny. With its burnt orange walls, blond wood accents, and closely spaced tables, it's also as intimate a bistro as you're likely to find in Tucson. Among the many areas of the menu worth lingering over are the "deep dishes," in particular the steamed mussels, which are transcendent and come

The fruits of the Prickly pear cactus are bright pink on the inside; they're also delicious.

steeped in warm saffron broth with diced tomato, garlic, and fresh oregano. "Bigger" dishes like the herb rubbed lamb rack (with baked semolina custard, sautéed spinach, and trumpet mushrooms) or the New York strip (under a brandied demiglaze with crispy shallots, mashed potatoes, and grilled asparagus) are each a carnivore's dream. Like everything on the menu, they pair well with an outstanding international wine list that draws from the vast reserves of the adjoining Rumrunner wine shop (see *Food Purveyors* later in this chapter).

FEAST

520-326-9363
www.eatatfeast.com
4122 E. Speedway Blvd., Tucson, AZ 85712
Price: Moderate

Credit Cards: AE, D, MC, V
Hours: Tues. through Sun. 11–9
Reservations: Not accepted
Handicapped Access: Yes
Special Features: Take-out

With an insistence on pristine, seasonal ingredients, an inventive *nouvelle* American menu that changes monthly, and a casual atmosphere that's one part bistro, one part wine bar, Feast has quickly risen to the level of Tucson phenomenon. On any given month, Feast features three to four appetizers, three to four salads, several sides à la carte, and a half dozen entrées, such as pan-roasted monkfish with asparagus risotto, Swiss chard–wrapped spoon bread and sunchoke hash, or saddle of rabbit stuffed with chicken livers, pancetta, artichoke hearts, and leeks. The wine selection (available by the bottle, half bottle, and glass) is an appealing, imaginative, well-thought-out list featuring more than five hundred bottles, from sparkling whites to fruit-driven reds. Like the food, any bottle in the house is available to go.

FLEMING'S PRIME STEAKHOUSE

520-529-5017
www.flemingssteakhouse.com
6360 N. Campbell Ave., Tucson, AZ 85718
Price: Expensive
Credit Cards: AE, D, MC, V
Hours: Sun. through Thurs. 5–10; Fri. and Sat. 5–10:30
Reservations: Recommended
Handicapped Access: Yes
Special Features: Private dining rooms, live music on nights and weekends, take-out

Casual, clamorous, and classic, Fleming's, a chain with 30 or so franchises scattered around the country, is one of the truly upscale steakhouses in Tucson. Dark lacquered woods, framed prints of wine bottles, and an inconspicuous little wine room lend a touch of minimalism to the decor, a minimalism that also carries over to the menu—which, not surprisingly, features mostly meat. Steaks range from petite filet mignons to bone-in New York strips, and all come with peppercorn, béarnaise, and Madeira sauces upon request. Fleming's also offers chops (of veal, lamb, and pork) and a standard seafood selection including seared scallops, lobster tail, and Alaskan king crab legs. Sides like baked potatoes and vegetables are ordered à la carte. Compared to other upscale restaurants around town, the wine selection here is modest, with about one hundred wines available by glass or flight and a small, mostly California, reserve list.

THE GRILL AT HACIENDA DEL SOL

520-529-3500
www.haciendadelsol.com
5601 N. Hacienda del Sol Rd., Tucson, AZ 85718
Price: Expensive
Credit Cards: AE, D, DC, MC, V
Hours: Mon. through Sat. 5:30–10; Sun. 10–2 and 5:30–10
Reservations: Recommended
Handicapped Access: Yes
Special Features: Garden patio dining, Sun. brunch, tasting menu

Few dining experiences in Tucson offer as much in the way of history and character as the Grill at Hacienda del Sol. Tucked away in the rolling foothills of the Catalinas, on the grounds of a former dude ranch and in a 1920s hacienda-style building surrounded by lush, flowering gardens, the Grill's menu is always an ode to the seasons, culling, as it does, many of its ingredients (fruits, herbs, vegetables) from Hacienda del Sol's kitchen gardens. Think salads with spinach, truffle vinaigrette, house-cured duck prosciutto, and marinated organic heirloom tomatoes, or, as an entrée, the *loup de mer,* a seasonal herb risotto with lobster beurre blanc and lemon arugula pesto. The sprawling international wine list, 12-time winner of *Wine Spectator*'s Award of Excellence, features more than two thousand bottles. For those looking for a more casual (and slightly less expensive) experience, the adjoining Terraza del Sol features an exhibition grill, a full-service bar, an all-season patio, and live music on weekends. Sunday brunch, while pricier than others around town, is unrivaled in taste and includes everything from ricotta cottage cheese blintzes (with blueberry vanilla coulis) to salads like roasted new potato, bacon, and caramelized onion in a cilantro lime vinaigrette.

JANOS

520-615-6100
www.janos.com
3770 E. Sunrise Dr., Tucson, AZ 85718
Price: Expensive
Credit Cards: AE, DC, MC, V

Hours: Mon. through Thurs. 5:30–9; Fri. and Sat. 5:30–9:30
Reservations: Highly recommended
Handicapped Access: Yes
Special Features: Outdoor dining, views, tasting menu, valet parking

Named by the prestigious James Beard Foundation as the top chef in the Southwest for 2000, Janos Wilder is something of a living legend, having adapted classic French techniques to seasonal, sustainable, locally grown ingredients and almost single-handedly putting the *nouvelle* in nouvelle Southwestern cuisine. It's the kind of cooking that's been on full display for 25 years at Janos, where plush, French-influenced interiors and lofty mountain views harmonize with a menu that changes both daily and with the seasons. In winter, Janos might offer a lobster and mascarpone relleno (fennel and Pernod-flamed Maine lobster fried in light, crispy batter and served with fennel flan and smoked paprika oil) or a California halibut and seafood tomalito (halibut glazed with orange and fennel served with griddled seafood tomalito in lobster broth with grilled fennel and kumquat salad). Whatever the season, always expect to find regional chiles, corn, and herbs on Janos's five-course tasting and prix-fixe menus. J BAR, Janos's convivial companion bar and grill, is a great place for late-night drinks and stunning city views (see below). The wine list at Janos features more than five hundred bottles and is one of the choicest in the city.

JAX KITCHEN

520-219-1235
www.jaxkitchen.com
7286 N. Oracle Rd., Tucson, AZ 85704
Price: Moderate
Credit Cards: AE, MC, V
Hours: Lunch Tues. through Sat. 11:30–2:30; dinner Sun. through Thurs. 5–9, Fri. and Sat. 5–10
Reservations: Accepted
Handicapped Access: Yes
Special Features: Sharing menu

Nowhere else in town will you find cookies (sugar, peanut butter, chocolate chunk) and bourbon-spiked milk on the dessert menu, to say nothing of Jax's lunches and dinners that do well as reinterpretations of modern American comfort foods. For lunch, the grilled cheese (whipped Brie and Gruyère on brioche) is a minor miracle of contrasting textures and pairs well with a bowl of the potato leek soup, here topped with crispy prosciutto and chives. It's hard to find a more alluring dish on the dinner menu than the duck leg confit with green bean and potato hash, truffle butter, and dried raz cherries, though the hanger steak with olive oil smashed red potato certainly doesn't disappoint either. Jax also offers an innovative "For 2" menu, and while it includes only two options (a whole salt-crusted roasted chicken or a dry aged 24-ounce rib eye steak), the spirit of sharing each invokes complements the lively, upbeat atmosphere of Jax's spacious dining room.

J BAR

520-615-6100
www.janos.com
3770 E. Sunrise Dr., Tucson, AZ 85718
Price: Moderate
Credit Cards: AE, MC, V
Hours: Daily 5–9:30 PM (bar open until 1 AM Mon. through Sat.)
Reservations: Highly recommended
Handicapped Access: Yes
Special Features: Patio dining, views

One of the most beloved dining spots in Tucson, J Bar is also the more raucous counterpart to Chef Janos Wilder's adjacent fine-dining restaurant, the eponymously named Janos. The flavors at J Bar derive from Mexico, Latin America, and the Caribbean, as does the ambience, which combines Southwestern chic with panoramic views of the entire city. The centerpiece of the restaurant is the open kitchen, where Scottish salmon (served on creamy polenta with cranberry broth, green beans, and pistachio-orange relish) and bistro steak (with garlic-mint recado, basil chimichurri sauce, chipotle molasses sweet potatoes, and sauté of summer squash) are grilled to order over open flames and served family style. As evenings progress, much of the energy is redirected around the bar, where drinks such as watermelon margaritas and Guadalajara Coolers (Mexican quince liquor, cranberry, and soda water) flow until well past midnight on J Bar's covered patio. Big or small, no meal is complete without an order of the chocolate jalapeño ice cream, one of the more delicious desserts to be found anywhere in the city.

JONATHAN'S CORK

520-296-1631
www.jonathanscork.com
6320 E. Tanque Verde Rd., Tucson, AZ 85715
Price: Moderate
Credit Cards: AE, MC, V
Hours: Sun. through Thurs. 5–10; Fri. and Sat. 5–11 (bar open until 1 AM)
Reservations: Accepted
Handicapped Access: Yes
Special Features: Late-night dining, outdoor patio

If you're in the mood for dependable, meat-and-potatoes dining, the kind that shirks aesthetics for simple charbroiled or blackened fare, Jonathan's is your place. Exposed wood-beam ceilings, painted adobe walls, Moorish-style archways, and beehive fireplaces do little to distract from the menu, which offers both traditional meats (prime rib, chicken, pork, lamb, and fish) as well as more unusual options, like ostrich and bison steaks. Chef Jonathan Landeen's wine list features mainly West Coast vineyards that pair surprisingly well with just about everything on the menu. There is late-night dining at the bar or on Jonathan's brick patio.

KINGFISHER

520-323-7739
www.kingfishertucson.com
2564 E. Grant Rd., Tucson, AZ 85716
Price: Moderate
Credit Cards: AE, D, DC, MC, V
Hours: Mon. through Fri. 11 AM–midnight; Sat. and Sun. 5–midnight (bar open later)
Reservations: Recommended for dinner
Handicapped Access: Yes
Special Features: Oyster bar, late-night menu, extensive cocktail list

Awarded *Wine Spectator*'s Award of Excellence for more than a decade and designated Best Seafood for almost that long by readers of *Tucson Weekly,* Kingfisher is the place to go for fish and shellfish. Most impressive is Kingfisher's oyster bar, which, in addition to a savory bay scallop ceviche and house-smoked trout with red onion jam, offers a variety of seasonal oysters by the half dozen and dozen, as well as more than 15 varieties of specialty oysters sourced from the Pacific Northwest. All the fish on the menu is fresh and simply prepared, some with a touch of imagination, such as the macadamia-nut-crusted Hawaiian fish (which changes seasonally) that comes in a creamy lemongrass butter sauce with steamed rice and fried sweet potatoes. For those out for cocktails and a nosh, Kingfisher also offers an abbreviated late-night menu that cherry-picks from its lunch and dinner menus some of the restaurant's simpler offerings: steamed mussels, littleneck clams, pan-fried shrimp cakes, baked oysters Rockefeller, and grilled fish sandwiches. There isn't a thing on the menu here that doesn't pair well with Kingfisher's extensive wine and spirits lists, highlights of which include Kingfisher's specialty martinis, its selection of 30 Scotch whiskies, and its two dozen artisanal tequilas.

MCCLINTOCK'S

520-579-2100
www.mcclintocks-restaurant.com
3755 W. Conrads Way, Tucson, AZ 85742
Price: Expensive
Credit Cards: AE, D, DC, MC, V
Hours: Sun. through Thurs. 5–10; Fri. and
Sat. 5–11
Reservations: Required
Handicapped Access: Yes
Special Features: Rooftop dining, outdoor
fireplace

On the grounds of Saguaro Ranch, a 1,035-acre luxury residential retreat set amid the sprawling Sonoran Desert, McClintock's specializes in hearty organic American cuisine. The dining room itself is rustic, modern, and attractively understated, while the covered rooftop porch features a roaring fireplace and dusky mountain views that lend a touch of Western romance to any evening's meal. Chef Virginia Wooters's menu is robust fare served in generous portions, revolving around simply prepared game, meats, and organic vegetables. Highlights include the beef tartar (finely sliced beef, red onions, whole grain mustard, capers, and black truffle), the braised buffalo barley soup to start, and the lemon gnocchi sautéed with asparagus, sunchokes, basil, and parsley. The international wine list features more than three hundred bottles (with specific attention paid to the regions of Italy, California, and France), as well as a fine selection of imported and domestic after-dinner cigars.

MCMAHON'S

520-327-2333
www.metrorestaurants.com
2959 N. Swan Rd., Tucson, AZ 85712
Price: Expensive
Credit Cards: AE, D, DC, MC, V
Hours: Mon. through Fri. 11:30–10; Sat.
5–10:30; Sun. 4–9
Reservations: Recommended
Handicapped Access: Yes

Special Features: Patio dining, live music

Meat headlines the menu at this locally owned steakhouse that also features fresh seafood and fine-dining appetizers like escargot bourguignon (snails in garlic, butter, and red wine) and baby beef Wellingtons (tenderloin wrapped in puff pastry and served over Madeira demiglaze). The best of the beef is the Baseball Cut. Aged more than 28 days and "as thick as a baseball," this steak arrives under one of three toppings: portobello mushrooms, garlic, and aged Romano cheese; tequila, lime, and green chile salsa; or a mushroom, shallot, garlic, and port wine demiglaze. Sides like creamed spinach, mashed potatoes, and fresh corn on the cob are available à la carte. At 2,600 bottles (450 of which are offered by the half bottle), the wine list is wide ranging.

MONTANA AVENUE

520-298-2020
www.foxrc.com
6390 E. Grant Rd., Tucson, AZ 85715
Price: Moderate
Credit Cards: AE, D, DC, MC, V
Hours: Mon. through Thurs. 11–9:30; Fri.
and Sat. 11–10:30; Sun. 9:30–9:30
Reservations: Recommended for dinner
Handicapped Access: Yes
Special Features: Patio dining, outdoor fireplace

Like North, Wildflower, and Blanco, Montana Avenue projects a decidedly trendy vibe, due in part to a design that marries the voyeurism of an exhibition kitchen to a dining room richly appointed with sleek wood beams, exposed duct work, and etched glass partitions. The concept here is contemporary American eatery, so expect classic comfort foods to be given a twist. Generous portions of buttermilk chicken or barbecue pork tenderloin arrive with simple sides like mac and cheese, creamed corn, or green beans. Even the wine selection keeps it simple with a workmanlike list of a dozen or so each of reds and whites, with the emphasis almost all on California. Those looking to take their meal (or one of Montana's signature cocktails, like the green and red mojito) on one of Montana Avenue's two patios will admire the enormous walk-through fireplace that, on cooler nights, makes outdoor dining here truly memorable.

PASTICHE

520-325-3333
www.pasticheme.com
3025 N. Campbell Ave., Tucson, AZ 85719
Price: Moderate
Credit Cards: AE, MC, V
Hours: Mon. through Fri. 11:30 AM–midnight; Sat. and Sun. 4:30–midnight
Reservations: Recommended for dinner on weekends
Handicapped Access: Yes
Special Features: Adjoins a wine shop; wine tastings

Pastiche means "blend," "mixture," and "collage." It also describes the fusion menu here, which is eclectic, adventurous, and combines American and world influences in a setting that is cheerful, welcoming, and quirky. For those looking to graze lightly, two of the menu's more praiseworthy features are the sizeable starter menu (there are 15 appetizers offered during both lunch and dinner) and Pastiche's bistro portions, which are smaller portions of the original and allow diners to sample Pastiche's ambitious menu, including such standouts as the thyme sea bass (in a smoked tomato-caper beurre blanc, Champagne cream sauce with mashed root vegetables) and the steak frites salad (seared beef, fresh greens, blue cheese, Roma tomato, and mustard vinaigrette with julienned pommes frites). For the eclecticism of its wine list (much of which is pulled from the adjacent gourmet food and wine shop), *Wine Spectator* has awarded Pastiche its Award of Excellence.

TOHONO CHUL PARK TEA ROOM

520-797-1222
www.tohonochulpark.org
7366 N. Paseo Del Norte, Tucson, AZ 85704
Price: Inexpensive
Credit Cards: AE, MC, V
Hours: Daily 8–5
Reservations: Accepted for groups of six or more
Handicapped Access: Yes
Special Features: Garden patio dining

In the West House, a territorial-style Spanish Colonial home set amid Tohono Chul Park, is the Tohono Chul Park Tea Room, one of the more tranquil dining spots in Tucson, serving breakfast, lunch, and, yes, tea both indoors and alfresco on its hummingbird garden patio. For breakfast, try the huevos enchiladas (scrambled eggs in corn tortillas, baked with red Hatch chile sauce, cheddar, and pepper jack), or if it's lunchtime, opt for the raspberry-chipotle chicken, a bowl of steamy tortilla soup, or a crispy quesadilla. Those with less of an appetite can enjoy an afternoon tea service that includes fresh-baked scones, finger sandwiches, and an assortment of pastries.

THE VENTANA ROOM

520-299-2020
www.ventanaroom.com
7000 N. Resort Dr., Tucson, AZ 85750
Price: Very Expensive
Credit Cards: AE, D, DC, MC, V
Hours: Tues. through Thurs. 6–9; Fri. and Sat. 6–10 (closed mid-Aug. to mid-Sept.)
Reservations: Required
Handicapped Access: Yes
Special Features: Strict dress code, prix-fixe and tasting menus, private dining room

In a city with no shortage of fine dining, the Ventana Room at the Loews Ventana Canyon Resort (one of only two AAA Five Diamond restaurants in Arizona, and one of only 50 nationally) easily wins top honors. In fact, for those unaccustomed to such opulence,

After dining at the Tohono Chul Park Tea Room, you can shop for a cactus at the greenhouse.
David Jewell © Metropolitan Tucson Convention & Visitors Bureau

the Ventana Room is as much a classic four-star restaurant as it is an opportunity to live, if only for a few hours, a certain lifestyle. Velvet wing chairs and an enormous, central stone hearth lend unpretentious formality to the main dining room, while the wine room, an intimate dining space lined in fine woods and even finer wines, offers the most exclusive atmosphere for private parties of two to four. Waiters at the Ventana Room have a preternatural ability to anticipate your every whim, and their knowledge of the menu impresses, particularly given how often it changes. If you're sparing no expense, Chef Marc Ehrler's six-course tasting menu with sommelier-guided wine pairings represents the most rarified (and priciest) dining option, though those of more modest means will luxuriate in anything on the menu, including the Arizona Jojoba beef tenderloin, which comes with Tohono O'odham white tepary beans and a pomegranate port reduction, or the broiled piquillo pepper, filled with confit of zucchini and rice Riviera, toasted pine nuts, ricotta salata, and ratatouille jus.

VIN TABLA

520-577-6210
www.vintabla.com
2890 E. Skyline Dr., Ste. 100, Tucson, AZ 85718
Price: Moderate
Credit Cards: AE, D, DC, MC, V
Hours: Sun. through Thurs. 4–9; Fri. and Sat. 4–10

The Ventana Room Courtesy Loews Ventana Canyon Resort

Reservations: Recommended
Handicapped Access: Yes
Special Features: Adjoins a wine shop; wine tasting

Wine store, raw seafood bar, artisanal cheese shop, salumeria, patisserie, an inside-outside bar—Vin Tabla is one of Tucson's most versatile eateries. While there are a few traditional entrées here (the goat-cheese-crusted lamb T-bone is particularly good), the concept here is more decidedly à la carte. Much of the menu is divided among small plates or is otherwise priced by the inch (like the dried, cured Spanish chorizo) or the ounce (like the Purple Haze, a northern California goat cheese blended with lavender and fennel pollen). Such a menu (which also features nuts, olives, and wood-fired pizzetta) provides particularly fine grazing for an award-winning wine selec-tion that hiply divides itself into categories like "juicy and lush" for reds and "creamy and soft" for whites. On Monday nights, Vin Tabla offers special sommelier-hosted dinners. Co-owner Laura Williamson is one of 130 Master Sommeliers in the world.

WILDFLOWER GRILL

520-219-4230
www.foxrc.com
7037 N. Oracle Rd., Tucson, AZ 85704
Price: Moderate
Credit Cards: AE, D, DC, MC, V
Hours: Mon. through Thurs. 11–9; Fri. and Sat. 11–10; Sun. 5–9
Reservations: Recommended for dinner
Handicapped Access: Yes
Special Features: Patio dining

The *new* in New American is often overused in culinary speak, though when applied to

Wildflower the descriptor is more than apt; the creative menu showcases contemporary American cuisine made from fresh, seasonal ingredients. Whether you take your meal on the all-seasons patio or inside, where Wildflower's exhibition kitchen overlooks an elegant dining room that mingles booths, half booths, and tables, expect food that is light, bright, and artfully rendered. While appetizers and salads, like the crispy calamari (with mizuna greens, yuzu vinaigrette, and toasted sesame seeds) and the warm Maine lobster salad (with grilled asparagus under a drizzle of white truffle vinaigrette), make up a sizable portion of the lunch and dinner menus, the subtle textures in entrées, like the lemongrass scallops with "forbidden" rice, sugar snap peas, and soy butter, more than hold their own. Winner of *Wine Spectator*'s Award of Excellence each year since 2005 for its more than 80 wines by the bottle and 25 by the glass, Wildflower promises one of the more pleasant fine-dining experiences in Tucson.

ZINBURGER

520-299-7799
www.foxrc.com
1865 E. River Rd. #101, Tucson, AZ 85718
Price: Inexpensive
Credit Cards: AE, D, DC, MC, V
Hours: Sun. through Thurs. 11–10; Fri. and Sat. 11–11
Reservations: Not accepted
Handicapped Access: Yes
Special Features: Outdoor patio and fireplace

Occupying the same space that was once Bistro Zin (formerly one of Tucson's best fine-dining restaurants), Zinburger is its downscale reincarnation, offering what is essentially gourmet fast food. Burgers here come classed up with toppings such as manchego cheese, Zinfandel-braised onions, and maple bacon, while side dishes include fancier variations on the french fry: sweet potato chips with yogurt dressing or zucchini fries with Parmesan and ranch. Zinburger's wine bar and low-key atmosphere—holdovers from its previous incarnation—make this spot a welcome addition to Tucson's burger scene.

Cafés & Wine Bars
ARMITAGE WINE LOUNGE AND CAFÉ

520-682-9740
www.armitagewine.com
2905 N. Skyline Dr. #168, Tucson, AZ 85718
Price: Moderate
Credit Cards: AE, D, DC, MC, V
Hours: Daily 11 AM–11:30 PM
Reservations: Accepted for parties of six or more
Handicapped Access: Yes
Special Features: Patio dining, live music, wine tasting, Sun. brunch

One of six chain restaurants thriving at the La Encantada shopping plaza, Armitage is a popular destination for foothills wining and dining. That vino is the focus here goes without saying, thanks in part to the interior's wine-cellar chic (crates and barrels decorate the two dining rooms), but even more so for the 30 or so wines (Californian, New Zealand, and Australian) available by glass or flight, and a reserve list predominantly made up of California cabernet sauvignons and blends. As for the food, the bruschetta and the daily cheese board (seasonal fruit, bread, crackers, and a choice of three to five imported and domestic cheeses) are each a great way to kick things off, while the seared yellowtail with orange soy syrup and wasabi cream, or the rosemary lamb sirloin (seared lamb served over asparagus risotto with a port wine demiglaze), are standout dinner options. Armitage also offers a Sunday brunch service that includes build-your-own omelets, brioche French toast, and Belgian waffles.

BLUE WILLOW

520-327-7577
www.bluewillowtucson.com

2616 N. Campbell Ave., Tucson, AZ 85719
Price: Inexpensive
Credit Cards: AE, D, MC, V
Hours: Mon. through Thurs. 7 AM–9 PM; Fri. 7 AM–10 PM; Sat. 8 AM–10 PM; Sun. 8 AM–9 PM.
Reservations: Accepted (excludes weekend mornings)
Handicapped Access: Yes
Special Features: Garden patio dining

Simple, straightforward home-style cooking and a quaint all-seasons patio (complete with greenery and fountains) make Blue Willow a local favorite. While omelets are generally considered Blue Willow's specialty (there are 13 different combinations), the Blue Willow Special (eggs scrambled with chicken, green chiles, tomatoes, chopped corn tortillas, cheddar, salsa, and sour cream) and the huevos rancheros (corn tortillas and pinto beans topped with two eggs, salsa, and cheddar cheese) are also notable standouts. Most dishes come with fresh fruit and potatoes, including lunch and dinner options like sandwiches, pasta dishes, and quiche plates.

CAFÉ 54

520-622-1907
www.cafe54.org
54 E. Pennington St., Tucson, AZ 85701
Price: Inexpensive
Credit Cards: MC, V
Hours: Mon. through Fri. 11–2
Reservations: Accepted for groups of five or more
Handicapped Access: Yes
Special Features: Menu changes daily

While this downtown café serves bistro-style meals to hungry lunch crowds, it also serves the public as an award-winning training program committed to reintegrating individuals recovering from mental illness. As such, the menu here is eclectic and changes daily. On any given day, expect to find simple sandwiches like the New Eng-

A mural graces the wall on the way out of El Charro Café.   Rick Machle © Metropolitan Tucson Convention & Visitors Bureau

land lobster roll (Maine lobster salad on a buttered hoagie roll) or items like the goat cheese tart (goat cheese and caramelized onions in a butter pastry crust, served over mixed greens). Café 54 also operates a small eatery at the Tucson Botanical Gardens.

THE CUP CAFÉ

520-798-1618
www.hotelcongress.com
311 E. Congress St., Tucson, AZ 85701
Price: Moderate
Credit Cards: AE, D, MC, V
Hours: Sun. through Thurs. 7 AM–10 PM; Fri. and Sat. 7 AM–11 PM
Reservations: Recommended for dinner and weekend brunch
Handicapped Access: Limited in some places by stairs
Special Features: Patio dining, live music, weekend brunch, Bloody Mary bar

What was once a shabby, hole-in-the-wall café has, after years of reimagination and renovation (including the installation of an entire floor made completely from pennies), become one of downtown Tucson's trendiest spots. Located inside Tucson's historic Hotel Congress (which also houses four separate bars, a dance club, and one of the country's best venues for emerging rock acts), The Cup serves up eclectic American fare in an atmosphere that's hip without being pretentious. The menu includes Latin-inspired appetizers such as Yucatan seafood ceviche and rich, well-executed entrées like tournedos of beef (grilled medallions of beef and braised red cabbage, served with roasted rosemary new potatoes and a Gorgonzola cream sauce). The Cup is also one of the best places in the town for weekend brunch, where live jazz and a do-it-yourself Bloody Mary bar lend a touch of charm to a menu that includes signature creations like Eggs and Gunpowder (roasted red potatoes topped with two eggs, turkey chorizo, and jack cheese) and enormous made-to-order omelets.

DELECTABLES

520-884-9289
www.delectables.com
533 N. Fourth Ave., Tucson, AZ 85705
Price: Inexpensive
Credit Cards: AE, D, MC, V
Hours: Sun. through Thurs. 11–9; Fri. and Sat. 11–11
Reservations: Not required
Handicapped Access: Yes
Special Features: Patio dining, Wi-Fi access

Whether for lunch or dinner, few eateries on Fourth Avenue offer as fresh and light a menu as Delectables, which draws on the best of Mediterranean cuisine and California spa fare, featuring healthy dishes like hummus plates, gazpacho, romaine salads, pasta dishes, and simple sandwiches on fresh-baked bread. Those looking for a quick bite might consider Delectables's "speedy lunch," a variation on call-ahead seating that not only reserves a table, but ensures your food is ready and waiting when you sit down. While the "speedy" option isn't available for dinner, vegetarian options like asparagus crêpes are, and they round out a dinner menu that also includes bistro plates such as *mousse truffée pâté* and prosciutto with melon. Delectables's bar serves wine flights, liquors, and cordials, as well as a select line of New Belgium beers.

EPIC CAFÉ

520-624-6844
www.epic-cafe.com
745 N. Fourth Ave., Tucson, AZ 85705
Price: Inexpensive
Credit Cards: MC, V
Hours: Daily 6 AM–midnight
Reservations: Not accepted
Handicapped Access: Yes
Special Features: Outdoor seating, Wi-Fi access

This bohemian refuge at the top of Tucson's historic Fourth Avenue attracts an eclectic crowd that includes hipster musicians, goateed artists, college students, avenue shoppers, and the occasional out-of-town visitor for whom the air of an unpretentious neighborhood café has an enduring appeal. Mismatched tables and chairs, brightly painted walls hung with local art (some of it good, some of it not so good), and at least two enormous couches lend a funky vibe to the place. Food includes an enormous selection of baked goods, soups of the day, salads, quiche plates, and foccacia sandwiches, which come loaded with sprouts and tomato. The long list of coffee and espresso drinks packs enough kick to keep anyone going.

THE GRILL

520-623-7621
www.myspace.com/redroomatthegrill
100 E. Congress St., Tucson, AZ 85701
Price: Inexpensive
Credit Cards: AE, MC, V
Hours: 24/7
Reservations: Not accepted
Handicapped Access: Yes
Special Features: Adjoins the Red Room bar; open 24 hours

Few downtown spots have as much character (and as many characters in them) as the Grill, which does one of the best impressions of an East Coast greasy-spoon diner as you're likely to find in Tucson. Open 24 hours a day, seven days a week, the Grill's hip, retro vibe (red leather booths, twirling stools at the counter) attracts an eclectic clientele with a menu that includes everything from Captain Crunch and tater tots to chicken fried steak and slightly out-of-place pasta dishes. On most nights and weekends, the Red Room, the Grill's adjoining bar, is one of the better venues in town to catch performances by up-and-coming local musicians.

Chinese
GUILIN HEALTHY CHINESE RESTAURANT

520-320-7768
www.guilintucson.net
3250 E. Speedway Blvd., Tucson, AZ 85716
Price: Inexpensive
Credit Cards: MC, V
Hours: Mon. through Thurs. 11–9; Fri. 11–10; Sat. 11:30–9:30; Sun. 11:30–9
Reservations: Not accepted
Handicapped Access: Yes
Special Features: Extensive vegetarian menu

For a city with a reputation for less-than-stellar Chinese food, this spot across from the Loft Cinema on East Speedway Boulevard proves the naysayers wrong. Nearly two-thirds of Guilin's menu is either vegetarian or vegan, making it one of the best destinations in town for healthy, affordable Chinese food. Vegetable dumplings, seaweed finger rolls, tempura pumpkin—the vegetarian options here exceed the typical tofu and bean sprout stir-fry, though you'll find that here, too. House specials like shrimp with scrambled egg and classics like sesame chicken make Guilin a dependable choice for quality Chinese.

P.F. CHANG'S

520-615-8788
www.pfchangs.com
1805 E. River Rd., Tucson, AZ 85718
Price: Moderate
Credit Cards: AE, D, DC, MC, V
Hours: Sun. through Thurs. 11–11; Fri. and Sat. 11 AM–midnight
Reservations: Recommended for dinner
Handicapped Access: Yes
Special Features: Full-service bar, patio dining, gluten-free options

P.F. Chang's dubs itself a "China bistro," and the description is apt. The plain white linens, chipped plates, and paper place mats redolent of the family-run Chinese restaurant have here been replaced with a sensibility that combines Western chic with Eastern elegance. Panoramic murals of 12th-century China, life-sized terra-cotta Xi'an soldiers, oiled woods, and silky fabrics lend authenticity and history to a menu that emphasizes variety. All the classics are here (orange peel beef, mu shu pork, lo mein), but so are more Americanized creations like crab rangoon (cream cheese and flaked crabmeat in a fried wonton). With a separate grill menu, a sleek full-service bar, and gluten-free options, P.F. Chang's takes Chinese food to richer heights.

Cuban
EL CUBANITO
520-623-8020
1150 E. Sixth St., Tucson, AZ 85719
Price: Inexpensive
Credit Cards: MC, V
Hours: Mon. through Sat. 11–7
Reservations: Not accepted
Handicapped Access: Yes
Special Features: Authentic Cuban coffee and tropical drinks

Typical of the Cuban comfort foods you'll find at this little, nondescript restaurant just south of the University of Arizona is the *ropa vieja* ("old clothes"), braised shredded beef brightly spiced with onion, red bell pepper, and tomato; *moros y cristianos* (black beans and rice); fried sweet plantains with a green "Creole" aioli sauce; and sandwiches like the Midnight (ham, roasted pork, pickles, and cheese served pressed between grilled bread). El Cubanito's exotic drink selection includes mango, banana, or papaya shakes; pineapple soda; and *malta,* a traditional drink made from sugarcane.

Ethiopian
ZEMAM'S
520-323-9928
2731 E. Broadway Blvd., Tucson, AZ 85716
Price: Inexpensive
Credit Cards: AE, MC, V

Hours: Tues., Thurs., and Sun. 11:30–9; Fri. 11:30–9:30
Reservations: Accepted for dinner
Handicapped Access: Limited
Special Features: BYOB

Situated back from busy Broadway Boulevard and occupying what was once a bungalow-style home is Zemam's, Tucson's only Ethiopian restaurant. The atmosphere here is intimate, with the dining area comprised of several small, whitewashed rooms. Keeping with Ethiopian custom, there are no utensils at Zemam's; each of the nine items on the menu require patrons to eat with their hands, or with an accompanying side of *injera,* a flatbread native to Ethiopa used for scooping and sopping. Even on Zemam's abbreviated menu, vegetarian dishes like *shiro* (puréed chickpeas and berbere) make up over half the offerings, and they typically include spices and aromatics like chiles, cardamom, onion, holy basil, mint, fenugreek, and ginger. Meat eaters will enjoy the *yebeg wat* (a savory lamb and chile stew) and the *lega tibs* (cubed beef simmered with tomatoes).

French
GHINI'S FRENCH CAFÉ
520-326-9095
www.ghiniscafe.com
1803 E. Prince Rd., Tucson, AZ
Price: Inexpensive
Credit Cards: AE, D, MC, V
Hours: Tues. through Sat. 6:30–3; Sun. 8–2
Reservations: Not accepted
Handicapped Access: Yes
Special Features: Take-out

With walls painted a sunny yellow, wooden tables and chairs, and sunflowers blooming from wine bottle centerpieces, you might think you've walked out of Tucson and into a small Provençal café. Which is exactly what Coralie Satta-Williams, Ghini's owner, wants you to believe. It's the same spirit that infuses the menu. Of course, it helps that

Cacti come in all shapes and sizes.

Ghini's shares space with La Baguette, a sister bakery that provides fresh bread for its breakfasts of fresh strawberry French toast and *tartines* (toasted slices of French baguette served with sweet cream butter and an assortment of jams), or for a lunch items like the ciabatta roast beef (rare roast beef on open-faced ciabatta bread with warm Brie, sliced tomato, and shredded basil) and Ghini's savory French onion soup.

LE DELICE BAKERY & CAFÉ

520-290-9714
www.le-delice.com
7245 E. Tanque Verde Rd., Tucson, AZ 85750
Price: Moderate
Credit Cards: AE, DC, MC, V

Hours: Breakfast daily 7–10:30 AM; lunch Sun. and Mon. 11–2, Tues. through Sat. 11–4:30; dinner Tues. through Sat. 5–8
Reservations: Recommended for dinner
Handicapped Access: Yes
Special Features: Take-out

The glass display cases at this small northside patisserie overflow with one kind or another of pastries (éclairs, madeleines, fruit tarts, flaky napoleons, brioches, palmiers, and chocolate tortes), cheeses (Emmental, Raclette, Crottin, Morbier, and Brie), and specialty meats (fresh rabbit, pâté, sausage, and head cheese). In a casual café atmosphere, Le Delice also serves full meals: delectable crêpes and bread baskets for breakfast, vichyssoise and quiche plates for lunch, and a dinner menu featuring classic French dishes like braised lamb shank, steak frites, and coq au vin.

LE RENDEZ-VOUS

520-323-7373
www.lerendez-vous.com/tucson-restaurant.htm
3844 E. Fort Lowell Rd., Tucson, AZ 85716
Price: Moderate
Credit Cards: AE, D, DC, MC, V
Hours: Lunch Tues. through Fri. 11:30–2; dinner Tues. through Sun. 5–10
Reservations: Accepted
Handicapped Access: Yes
Special Features: Excellent wine list

It may seem odd that some of Tucson's best French cuisine should be served at a restaurant with adobe walls and a Spanish tile roof, but Jean Claude Berger's Le Rendez-Vous has been doing so for decades and winning awards all along the way. The menu here is classic in temperament and limited by design, featuring traditional French delicacies like sweetbreads of veal, duck à l'orange, Dover sole, and, yes, escargots. It's no surprise that the wine list here is decidedly French, featuring lots of big, bold reds. While the ambience of the two dining rooms (one of which is a garden-style sunroom) doesn't exactly conjure Paris (too many pinks and teals invoke American design palettes of the early 1990s), the intimate, communal feel at Le Rendez-Vous still makes it destination dining for French epicures.

Greek
ATHENS ON 4TH AVENUE

520-624-6886
www.athenson4th.com
400 N. Fourth Ave., Tucson, AZ 85705
Price: Moderate
Credit Cards: AE, D, MC, V
Hours: Mon. through Sat. 11–10
Reservations: Accepted
Handicapped Access: Yes
Special Features: Outdoor dining

This small downtown restaurant evokes summer nights in Athens's *plaka* (old historic neighborhood), where candlelit tables line cobblestone streets. This setting is almost as idyllic, with its bougainvillea-enclosed patio and low-lit interior. Most dishes feature tomatoes, cucumbers, wild mountain greens, feta, and oregano (all Greek staples), along with fresh fish (usually snapper or cabrilla) and baby lamb. The cooking here is simple. Meats are broiled or stewed, and fish and shellfish are sautéed or roasted with olive oil and lemon. The wine list includes a few California selections but encourages experimentation with its focus on high-quality Greek imports, which match up better with the menu. Dessert choices include homemade baklava and *galactaboureko* (milk pie).

Indian
GANDHI

520-292-1738
www.gandhicusineofindia.com
150 W. Fort Lowell Rd., Tucson, AZ 85705
Price: Inexpensive
Credit Cards: AE, D, DC, MC, V
Hours: Daily 11–3 and 5–10
Reservations: Accepted
Handicapped Access: Yes
Special Features: Daily lunch buffet

Vegetarians, delight! Gandhi's offers more than two dozen meatless options, including *biryani masala* (a jambalaya-like stew made with raisins, cashews, peanuts, and almonds) and *navrattan* (a curried mix of eight vegetables). For meat eaters who like their Indian food spicy, the *paneer* (a mild cottage cheese pressed to a firm texture and mild in taste) on naan makes for a delicious complement to any one of Gandhi's 12 curry dishes, including the vindaloo, which, appropriately enough, comes with its own special warning right on the menu. Whatever your inclination, the daily lunch buffet is an inexpensive way to sample the full range of Gandhi's delicacies.

INDIA OVEN

520-326-8635
2727 N. Campbell Ave., Tucson, AZ
Price: Inexpensive
Credit Cards: AE, D, MC, V
Hours: Daily 11–2:45 and 5–9:45
Reservations: Accepted
Handicapped Access: Yes
Special Features: Daily lunch buffet

There's little to redeem India Oven's bland strip-mall exterior and underwhelming interior decor except, of course, its food, which is consistently rated among Tucson's best. This is due in no small part to India Oven's menu, which is ambitious in both scope (it draws inspiration from all over India) and quantity (there are more than one hundred dishes to choose from). Harmesh Bhatti and his brother Lekh make some of the best Samosa in town, but entrées like the chicken *karahai* (chicken and onions smothered in a creamy curry sauce) with a side of *aloo saag* (a mixture of spinach, potatoes, and cream) are especially good. India Oven's lunch buffet, which rotates up to seven main dishes daily, is always reasonably priced and as good as any in the city.

SHER-E PUNJAB

520-624-9393
853 E. Grant Rd., Tucson, AZ 85719
Price: Inexpensive
Credit Cards: AE, DC, MC, V
Hours: Daily 11–2:30 and 5–10
Reservations: Accepted
Handicapped Access: Yes
Special Features: Daily lunch buffet

For more than 10 years, Sher-E has been a favorite among Tucsonans for its ridiculously affordable, all-you-can-eat lunch buffet that offers 10 different classic Indian dishes rotated daily, allowing newcomers and regulars alike to sample from a wide swath of the vast menu. Those with more modest appetites might take the opportu-

nity to taste how regional differences can influence traditional Indian cooking: order anything cooked in the tandoor oven and taste the smokiness; Sher-E Punjab uses local mesquite wood to cook its meats, kebobs, and flatbreads.

Italian
ENOTECA

520-623-0744
58 W. Congress St., Tucson, AZ 85701
Price: Moderate
Credit Cards: AE, D, MC, V
Hours: Tues. through Thurs. 5–9; Fri. and Sat. 5–10
Reservations: Accepted
Handicapped Access: Yes
Special Features: Patio dining, live music, Wi-Fi access

On the corner of Church Avenue and Congress Street, in Tucson's downtown business district, is this small gourmet pizzeria and wine bar. Vibrant interior colors, black wood-trimmed tables, and muted ceiling lamps lend a warm, modern vibe to the restaurant, a feeling that also extends to the menu, which mixes both traditional and contemporary Italian temperaments. Standout appetizers include the bruschetta (grilled rustic flatbreads, sliced aged provolone, and six mix-and-match toppings) and the *cozze santa magherita* (mussels steeped in Pinot Grigio, garlic, herbs, and lemon). While the dinner menu here includes the requisite meat and pasta dishes, pizzas like the Napoletana (mozzarella, mushrooms, and veal sausage) and a reasonably priced wine list are how Enoteca keeps them coming back for more.

NORTH

520-299-1600
2995 E. Skyline Dr., Tucson, AZ 85718
Price: Moderate
Credit Cards: D, DC, MC, V
Hours: Mon. through Thurs. 11–10; Fri. and Sat. 11–11; Sun. noon–9

Reservations: Recommended for dinner
Handicapped Access: Yes
Special Features: Patio dining

One of Tucson's trendier spots, North specializes in refined rustic Italian. The atmosphere here is one part hipster living room (exposed brick walls and duct work, low-backed modern furniture), one part urban trattoria (sleek, dark woods and warmly glowing floor lamps), and one part romantic overlook (nearly the entire dining room enjoys full panoramic views of the city). The food itself is simple but elegantly prepared, and most dishes feature vegetables, meat, or seafood that is either wood roasted or grilled. North's house specialties include its line of gourmet specialty pizzas, as well as plates of the day like grilled flank steak with thick-sliced tomato, red onion, and Gorgonzola crumble, and braised duck risotto with black kale and spiced apple. The full-service bar (which boasts its own outdoor patio scene) makes North a popular destination for both young professionals and drop-in shoppers famished from a day's browsing La Encantada's upscale boutiques.

TAVOLINO

520-531-1913
7090 N. Oracle Rd., Tucson, AZ 85704
Price: Moderate
Credit Cards: AE, D, DC, MC, V
Hours: Mon. through Sat. 11–10
Reservations: Recommended
Handicapped Access: Yes
Special Features: Outdoor dining, take-out

Tavolino's mission is emphatically stated ("Simple. Classic. Italian"), and it is one well met by chef-owner Massimo Tenino, who, in a venue reminiscent of a cozy, urban trattoria, serves up northern Italian cuisine that resists American influence. Lunches here consist mainly of wood-fired pizzas and panini sandwiches, while the smaller dinner menu features handmade pastas (in one variation or other of olive oil or cream

sauce), as well as several heavier meat dishes like *bistecca alla Fiorentina* (grilled Angus rib eye with white beans and sautéed spinach) and *costolette d'agnello scottadito* (rosemary grilled lamb chops with roasted potatoes and sautéed fennel). The mostly Italian wine list takes its cue from the menu: short but select.

VIVACE

520-795-7221
4310 N. Campbell Ave., Tucson, AZ 85718
Price: Moderate
Credit Cards: AE, D, DC, MC, V
Hours: Mon. through Thurs. 11:30–9; Fri. and Sat. 11:30–10
Reservations: Recommended
Handicapped Access: Yes
Special Features: Martini bar

Chef Daniel Scordato's restaurant is widely recognized as one of Tucson's best for the understated elegance of its atmosphere and its rustic, back-to-basics Italian cooking. In two dining rooms—the one larger, louder, and more spacious than its smaller, quieter, more intimate counterpart—Vivace offers both lunch and dinner highlighted by Neopolitan-style pizzas (thin, crispy crust with toppings like sliced eggplant, smoked sausage, and quartered fresh tomatoes), antipasto salads (sweet roasted red peppers, marinated artichoke hearts, creamy goat cheese, crispy asparagus, and sautéed spinach), and chef specialties like the succulent osso buco and a moist crab-stuffed chicken breast. Vivace is also home to a popular wine and martini bar.

Japanese
RA SUSHI

520-615-3970
2905 E. Skyline Dr., Tucson, AZ 85718
Price: Moderate
Credit Cards: AE, D, MC, V
Hours: Daily 11–11
Reservations: Recommended for dinner
Handicapped Access: Yes

Special Features: Patio dining, sushi bar

The cherry reds and lacquered blacks that dominate Ra's interior lend a warm, mellow energy to this trendy foothills bar and sushi spot. Though purists may bristle at the thought of franchised sushi (the Benihana-owned chain operates 26 restaurants around the country), the good news is that the menu (including nonsushi dishes) is innovative, with the sushi and sashimi maintaining a high level of quality whatever the day of the week. More unconventional rolls here include the decadent Scallop Dynamite roll (*kani kama* and cream cheese rolled in rice and seaweed, tempura battered, topped with scallop and finished with eel sauce, red beet, and spinach tempura flakes) and the beef *tataki* roll (artichoke, asparagus, roasted red peppers, and avocado rolled and topped with seared steak and soy chile sauce, served with a creamy wasabi sauce). Particularly popular are Ra's happy-hour specials on select hand rolls, edamame, *gyoza* (pork dumplings), Japanese beers, and warmed sake. Ra's hip indoor-outdoor bar is a scene unto itself.

SKY BLUE WASABI

520-747-0228
250 S. Craycroft Rd. #100, Tucson, AZ 85711
Price: Moderate
Credit Cards: MC, V
Hours: Mon. through Fri. 11—2 and 5—10;
Sat. 5—11; Sun. 5—9
Reservations: Recommended
Handicapped Access: Yes
Special Features: Teppanyaki tables

Any Japanese restaurant whose specialty rolls include the Ultimate Roll (lobster, cucumber, avocado, and shrimp topped with 24-karat gold flakes) is out to do more than serve up traditional sushi; it's also about conveying an attitude and a sense of style. Thankfully, style meets substance at Sky Blue Wasabi, one of the newest (and best) additions to Tucson's sushi scene.

Reflective metals, sky-blue lighting, and flat-screen TVs give Sky Blue a crisp, clean feel that's matched only by the freshness of its fish and the innovation of its menu. If the Ultimate Roll seems too decadent, opt for the Sky Blue Wasabi roll (eel, avocado, special sauce, and strawberries) or classics like the white toro or eel roll, each of which is sweet and tender. Those looking for something other than sushi might take a seat at one of Sky Blue's five teppanyaki tables, where even the grilled appetizer themselves make a meal.

TAKAMATSU

520-512-0800
5532 E. Speedway Blvd., Tucson, AZ 85712
Price: Moderate
Credit Cards: AE, D, MC, V
Hours: Daily 11—10
Reservations: Accepted
Handicapped Access: Yes
Special Features: Teppanyaki tables, sushi bar, sushi buffet

It would be hard to categorize Takamatsu as strictly Japanese. That's because in addition to the largest sushi bar in Tucson and a lively teppanyaki room where entertaining showman chefs perform over sizzling hibachi grills, Takamatsu features an authentic Korean barbecue room where patrons cook their own meats to taste on in-table grills. First-time visitors navigating Takamatsu's vast menu may suffer the burden of too many choices, but the *kimchee bokeum* (hot and spicy stir-fried vegetables and pork), the *duk mandoo gook* (beef dumplings and rice cakes in broth), and the *chik naeng myun* (arrowroot noodles in cold beef broth with spicy sauce, topped with sliced beef and vegetables) are particularly tasty and mix and match well with any one of Takamatsu's 36 specialty sushi rolls.

YOSHIMATSU

520-320-1574

2660 N. Campbell Ave., Tucson, AZ 85719
Price: Inexpensive
Credit Cards: MC, V
Hours: Mon. through Thurs. 11:30–2:45 and
5–9; Fri. 11:30–2:45 and 5–10; Sat. and Sun.
5–9
Reservations: Accepted
Handicapped Access: Yes
Special Features: Sushi bar

Yoshimatsu is actually two restaurants
under one roof, but that hasn't stopped *Tucson Weekly* readers from voting it the single
best Japanese restaurant each year since
2004. On the smaller side of the restaurant,
diners can expect to find a traditional sushi
bar in a warm, bistrolike atmosphere, while
those in the larger main dining room will
wonder at the refreshingly bizarre decor
(inspired by Japanese television and pop
culture) and the full range of Yoshimatsu's
offerings, including deliciously offbeat
items like the Japanese pizza. Whichever
half of the restaurant you choose, all dishes
at Yoshimatsu are prepared without MSG,
using only the freshest organic vegetables,
natural flavorings like ginger and garlic,
and a wide range of soy foods, including
tofu, *natto*, miso, and edamame.

YUKI SUSHI

520-326-7727
2962 N. Campbell Ave., Tucson, AZ 85719
Price: Moderate
Credit Cards: AE, DC, MC, V
Hours: Mon. through Fri. 11–10; Sat. and
Sun. 5–10
Reservations: Accepted
Handicapped Access: Yes
Special Features: Sushi bar

Umami, the fifth primary taste (after sweet,
salty, sour, and bitter) is found in abundance at Yuki Sushi. A starter like the
sunomono salad (crispy cucumber and tender octopus lightly tossed in rice vinegar) is
an excellent choice, while those looking to
move straight to sampling the freshness of

the fish would do well to order the *chirashi*
(hand-formed rice boats topped with pristine cuts of ahi tuna, octopus, salmon,
shrimp, yellowtail, and mackerel) or Jun's
Boat (16 pieces of *nigiri* sushi, in addition to
a tuna roll, a California roll, and a cucumber
roll). Few places in Tucson serve better
soba, ramen, or *udon* noodles.

Malaysian
NEO OF MELAKA

520-299-7815
1765 E. River Rd., Tucson, AZ 85718
Price: Moderate
Credit Cards: AE, D, DC, MC, V
Hours: Daily 11–10
Reservations: Recommended for dinner
Handicapped Access: Yes
Special Features: Take-out

While in terms of ambience, Neo Melaka is
more elegant and upscale than its sister
restaurant, Seri Melaka (520-747-7811;
6133 E. Broadway Blvd.), both are run by
the same family, and both offer meticulously prepared pan-Asian fusion cuisine
that, along with a healthy dash of classic
Malay heat, includes lots of simmered
broths, noodles, chicken, seafood, coconut
accents, sautéed vegetables, pungent curries, and aromatic spices. Try starting with
the *tom yam* (fresh lime juice, crushed
Asian chile pods, and kaffir leaves in a
lemongrass broth with an assortment of
vegetables), and then move to the *lemak* (a
stew of shrimp and squid, coconut cream,
lemongrass, vegetables, and chunks of
pineapple).

Mexican (Sonoran)
BK HOT DOGS

520-295-0105
5118 S. 12th Ave., Tucson, AZ 85714
Price: Inexpensive
Credit Cards: Not accepted
Hours: Sun. through Thurs. 9 AM–midnight;
Fri. and Sat. 9 AM–2 AM

A mural graces the wall on the way out of El Charro Café. Rick Machle © Metropolitan Tucson Convention & Visitors Bureau

Reservations: Not accepted
Handicapped Access: Yes
Special Features: Outdoor dining only

BK Hot Dogs is a dive of the best kind, and it serves much more than its famed Sonoran-style hot dogs, which come in homemade buns. "All the way" means with *crema* (Mexican mayo), tomatoes, tomatillo salsa, onions, beans, and roasted chiles. Despite all these ingredients, the hot dogs are never overloaded. Carne asada and *cabeza* (beef cheek) are good choices from the regular menu, and they come in taco, *torta,* and burrito form. The only seating is outdoors, and no credit or debit cards are accepted. The patio has misters for hot summer days.

BLANCO

520-232-1007
2905 E. Skyline Dr. #246, Tucson, AZ 85718
Price: Moderate
Credit Cards: AE, D, DC, MC, V
Hours: Sun. through Thurs. 11–10; Fri. and Sat. 11–11
Reservations: Accepted for parties of eight or more
Handicapped Access: Yes
Special Features: Patio dining

Among the several upscale restaurants located at Tucson's posh La Encantada shopping plaza is Blanco, a nouveau Mexican hot spot. The bar (which serves up more than 30 artisanal tequilas, red and white sangrias, and, yes, margaritas) is the focal point of the restaurant's clean, minimalist dining room, though an even better choice for whiling away a meal is the open-air patio that, night or day, features stunning panoramic views of the Tucson valley. The menu is updated Sonoran-style Mexican and includes standout dishes like braised short ribs enchilada style with a *queso blanco* and ancho chile sauce, and the ahi tuna with chayote squash, sweet corn, and fire-roasted red peppers.

EL CHARRO CAFÉ

520-622-1922
www.elcharrocafe.com
311 N. Court Ave., Tucson, AZ 85701
Price: Inexpensive
Credit Cards: AE, D, DC, MC, V
Hours: Daily 11–9
Reservations: Recommended for dinner
Handicapped Access: Yes
Special Features: Adjacent cantina, patio dining

While Tucson's oldest family-run Mexican restaurant has greatly expanded its operations since first opening its doors in 1922, the original El Charro can still be found in the same stone building in Tucson's El Presidio Historic District. One its more unusual aspects is the metal cage atop the roof used for sun drying meat, including the beef in El Charro's signature *carne seca* (shredded beef grilled with green chile and onions) and its chimichangas (tortilla stuffed with shredded beef and cheese, deep fried and topped with guacamole, sour cream, and *pico de gallo* salsa), which, legend has it, were first invented here. Though the music and rowdiness of the adjoining cantina, ¡Toma!, can encroach on the dining rooms, the real action, whatever your taste, is in the restaurant. There are numerous additional locations in Tucson, including 6310 East Broadway Boulevard (520-745-1922), 100 West Orange Grove Road (520-

615-1922), 4699 East Speedway Boulevard (520-325-1922), and 6910 East Sunrise (520-514-1922).

EL GUERO CANELO

520-295-9005
www.elguerocanelo.com
5201 S. 12th Ave., Tucson, AZ 85706
Price: Inexpensive
Credit Cards: Not accepted
Hours: Mon. through Sat. 7 AM–midnight; Sun. 7:30 AM–midnight
Reservations: Not accepted
Handicapped Access: Yes
Special Features: Outdoor seating

What was once the Contreras family's modest taco stand has, since 1993, grown into a thriving business of two restaurants (the second location is at 2480 North Oracle Road; 520-882-8977). Both feature back-to-basics Sonoran-style comfort food in an outdoor patio setting. While the menu includes fresh, simply prepared Mexican standards like carne asada, quesadillas, and *burros*, El Guero Canelo is best known for its Mexican-style hot dogs, which come loaded with grilled onions, pinto beans, tomatoes, and salsa. On Sunday, El Guero Canelo serves *menudo*, a traditional Mexican soup made with tripe, hominy, aromatics, and chile peppers.

EL MINUTO

520-882-4145
354 S. Main Ave., Tucson, AZ 85701
Price: Inexpensive
Credit Cards: AE, D, MC, V
Hours: Mon. through Thurs. 11–10; Fri. and Sat. 11–11
Reservations: Not accepted
Handicapped Access: Yes
Special Features: Patio seating, live music

Downtown, on the edge of the Barrio Historico and next to El Tiradito shrine, is El Minuto, which, like many of Tucson's family-owned Mexican restaurants, attracts both Anglos and Latinos alike with its affordable prices, unpretentious atmosphere, and Mexican food that is at once both simple and flavorful. Patrons can expect to find traditional dishes like crunchy tostados and chiles rellenos, though those looking to be a little more creative would do well to try a red chile and bean *burro* combination, enchilada style. With a small outdoor patio, amazingly fast service, and the occasional mariachi guitarist strumming Mexican ballads, El Minuto continues its 60-plus years as a low-key neighborhood favorite.

EL TORERO

520-622-9534
231 E. 26th St., Tucson, AZ 85713
Price: Inexpensive
Credit Cards: Not accepted
Hours: Daily 10–10
Reservations: Not accepted
Handicapped Access: Yes

Despite the fact that it's housed in a hard-to-find, bright pink adobe building set back from 26th Street, El Torero is one of Tucson's quirkier landmarks. Bullfighter paintings and an enormous stuffed swordfish adorn the walls, while a jukebox belts out tunes into a brightly lit, no-frills dining room. As for the menu, it's diverse, with everything from tacos to off-the-bone turkey mole to a *topopo* (volcano) salad that arrives as a great tapering mound of greens, vegetables, and cheeses studded with a choice of chicken, shrimp, chili, guacamole, or *carne seca*.

MI NIDITO CAFÉ

520-622-5081
1813 S. Fourth Ave., Tucson, AZ 8571
Price: Inexpensive
Credit Cards: AE, D, MC, V
Hours: Wed. though Sun. 11–10
Reservations: Not accepted
Handicapped Access: Limited
Special Features: Bar

Like so many of Tucson's family-run Mexican restaurants, Mi Nidito (which literally means "my little nest") has grown from a modest café to a thriving restaurant and cantina where on weekends the line waiting to get inside sometimes runs out the door. The mood here is high-spirited and the portions enormous, often requiring a kitchen cart for delivery. Classics like tostados, tamales, enchiladas, and Mi Nidito's Mexican pizza (an enormous baked flour tortilla loaded with cheese, chiles, guacamole, and carne asada) are popular dishes, but none more so than the President's Plate, a sampler (named in honor of President Clinton, who ate here in 1999) that includes a bean tostada, a *birria* taco, a chile relleno, a chicken enchilada, and a beef tamale.

ROSA'S

520-325-0362
1750 E. Fort Lowell Rd. #165, Tucson, AZ 85719
Price: Inexpensive
Credit Cards: AE, MC, V
Hours: Daily 11–10
Reservations: Accepted
Handicapped Access: Yes

Few restaurants can claim as loyal a clientele as Rosa's, whose celebrity endorsers have included the man in black, Johnny Cash, and fellow Highwayman Willie Nelson. And there's good reason. Run by the Ortega family since 1970, this nondescript mom-and-pop restaurant hidden away at the back of a Campbell Avenue shopping plaza serves up some of the best *carne seca* (rehydrated dried spiced beef in onions and chiles) in town. If you go in the evening, expect to be greeted by Rosa herself, who makes a point of working the two dining rooms. Rosa's has good, cheap Mexican food and the margaritas to go with it.

Mexican (Other)
CAFÉ POCA COSA
520-622-6400
110 E. Pennington St., Tucson, AZ 85701
Price: Moderate
Credit Cards: MC, V
Hours: Tues. through Thurs. 11–9; Fri. and Sat. 11–10
Reservations: Recommended for dinner
Handicapped Access: Yes
Special Features: Menu changes daily, bar

The best restaurant for nuevo Mexican in Tucson is also one of the most celebrated restaurants in the city. Chef-owner Suzana Davila's signature mole dishes (of which there are 26 variations that rotate twice daily on and off Poca Cosa's portable blackboard menu) make a natural starting point. Try the chocolate mole (lean, roasted bone-in chicken covered with a rich red chile, dark chocolate, and red wine sauce), or the *pollo en pipian* (boneless chicken with a sauce of chocolate, crushed red chiles, Spanish peanuts, pumpkin seeds, and cloves). Dishes like the grilled carne asada (served with smoky chipotle pepper, tomato, and onion sauce) exhibit a more rustic flair and arrive with roasted whole vegetables and great piles of leafy greens, making portions at Poca Cosa large enough for two to share. Those looking to sample the menu should opt for the *plato poca cosa,* a chef-selected trio of items from the day's menu. The style of food here originates from central Mexico, so don't expect to find much (if anything) that is deep fried or drenched in melted cheese.

GUADALAJARA GRILL
520-323-1022
1220 E. Prince Rd., Tucson, AZ 8571
Price: Inexpensive
Credit Cards: MC, V
Hours: Daily 10–10
Reservations: Accepted
Handicapped Access: Yes
Special Features. Outdoor dining

Guadalajara combines a dedication to freshness with a flair for minor theatrics. The salsa here is made to order tableside by a *salsera* with mortar and pestle, and *tortilleras* hand-press and hand-roll the day's tortillas at an exhibition grill. The breakfast menu includes everything you'd expect: burritos, huevos rancheros, *chilaquels,* and omelets. If you're going for lunch or dinner, try the *burro pescado,* fish cooked with garlic and folded into a flour tortilla with lettuce, cheese, *pico de gallo,* and a creamy *diablo blanco* sauce.

MARISCOS CHIHUAHUA
520-623-3563
1009 N. Grande Ave., Tucson, AZ 85745
Price: Moderate
Credit Cards: AE, D, MC, V
Hours: Daily 9–9
Reservations: Accepted
Handicapped Access: Yes
Special Features. Outdoor dining

Mariscos, as the name suggests, is the best place in town for all manner of seafood. Try the tall cocktails (oyster, shrimp, fish) or seviche dressed with lime and Tapatío. If you're in the mood for something cooked, don't miss the whole fried fish, served with rice and fries.

TAQUERIA PICO DE GALLO
520-623-8775
2618 S. Sixth Ave., Tucson, AZ 85713
Price: Inexpensive
Credit Cards: MC, V
Hours: Daily 9–9
Reservations: Not accepted
Handicapped Access: Yes

One of the best (and cheapest) Mexican restaurants is this humble taqueria. Orders here are placed at a counter and come on Styrofoam plates with plastic utensils—but

Taqueria Pico de Gallo

don't let the casualness of the presentation fool you: the real frills are reserved for the food, which is terrific. Try the *coctel de elote* (a stew of warm corn kernels, melted cheese, hot chile, and lime) or the beef fajitas (sizzling seared beef, onions, and peppers folded into soft, warm corn tortillas). No visit would be complete without an order of *pico de gallo* ("rooster's beak"), a plastic cup filled with chunks of watermelon, coconut, pineapple, mango, and jicama speared with toothpicks and covered under a layer of chili powder and fresh-squeezed lemon juice. There's nothing else like it in Tucson.

TERESA'S MOSAIC CAFÉ

520-624-4512
2455 N. Silverbell Rd., Tucson, AZ 85745

Price: Inexpensive
Credit Cards: D, MC, V
Hours: Mon. through Sat. 7:30 AM–9:00 PM; Sun. 7:30–2
Reservations: Accepted for dinner same day before 5 PM
Handicapped Access: Yes
Special Features: Patio dining

If you're looking for authentic Oaxaca-style food in sunny, airy surroundings that boast lofty views of the Catalina Mountains and the city, Mosaic Café, on the near west side of town, is one of the more scenic spots for Mexican. While mole and margaritas make for great lunch, it's Mosaic's breakfasts that are truly outstanding. Try the *huevos divorceados* ("divorced" eggs, which come separated by beans and topped with two sauces, a salsa *roja* and a salsa *verde*) or the *chilaqui-*

les (simmered tortilla *totopos* topped with spicy chorizo and scrambled eggs). If you're thirsting for something more than the usual coffee or juice, the *horchata,* a spiced rice milk, makes a delicious alternative.

Middle Eastern
ALI BABA

520-319-2559
2545 E. Speedway Blvd. #125, Tucson, AZ 85716
Price: Inexpensive
Credit Cards: D, MC, V
Hours: Mon. through Thurs. 11–9; Fri. and Sat. 11–9:30; Sun. 11–8
Reservations: Not accepted
Handicapped Access: Yes
Special Features: Houses a Middle Eastern market, take-out

While the trompe l'oeil mural of the Mediterranean does little to distract from the cafeteria-style setting, Ali Baba's is a friendly restaurant that specializes in simple Lebanese dishes like tangy salads, falafels, baba ghanoush, and gently spiced grilled kebobs and rotisserie meats. A dish of *tzatziki* (yogurt and cucumber blended with a dash of mint) or hummus pairs well with Ali Baba's warm rounds of fresh baked pita bread. The *shawarma* plate (shaved lamb, chicken, or beef) is pleasant and light, and comes with rice, pickled vegetables, and tahini, or as a sandwich to go in a hand-wrapped pita. Ali Baba's also features desserts like *baklawa,* and a market stocked with all kinds of Middle Eastern foods and products.

LUXOR CAFÉ

520-325-3771
3699 N. Campbell Ave., Tucson, AZ 85719
Price: Inexpensive
Credit Cards: D, MC, V
Hours: Sun. through Thurs. 11 AM–1 AM; Fri. and Sat. 5 PM–4 AM
Reservations: Accepted
Handicapped Access: Yes
Special Features: Hookah lounge, take-out

Quite possibly the only restaurant in town with pillowed floor seating, belly dancers, *and* a hookah lounge, Luxor Café is also home to an extensive (if eclectic) menu featuring a variety of Middle Eastern delicacies, including Lebanese tabbouleh (a salad of finely chopped parsley, mint, tomato, scallion, and other herbs with lemon juice), Turkish kibbe (fried bulgur stuffed with chopped lamb and spices), and Greek dolmas (rice and minced beef wrapped in grape leaves). Luxor also offers *kafta* kabob, *shwarama,* gyro, and *koshari,* a traditional mixture of rice, pasta, lentils, garbanzos, and fried onions with a side of spicy tomato sauce.

SHISH KEBAB HOUSE

520-745-5308
5855 E. Broadway Blvd. #118, Tucson, AZ 85711
Price: Inexpensive
Credit Cards: AE, D, MC, V
Hours: Mon. 11–8; Tues. through Sat. 11–9; Sun. noon–8
Reservations: Not accepted
Handicapped Access: Yes
Special Features: Take-out

Shish Kebab House might make Tucson's best hummus, the perfect accompaniment to any dish on its extensive menu, including standouts like the *motabal* (a thick puree of fire-grilled eggplant), the *foul* (fava beans with lemon and garlic), the *magloubeh* (a traditional Jordanian dish of beef, chicken, or lamb with crispy fried cauliflower and potatoes), and the *kafta* (ground beef spiced with ginger). Limited seating makes this place better for meals to go, particularly on nights when it's crowded.

Peruvian
CANDELA

520-407-0111
5845 N. Oracle Rd., Tucson, AZ 85704

Price: Moderate
Credit Cards: AE, D, MC, V
Hours: Mon. through Fri. 11–2:30 and 5–9;
Sat. and Sun. 5–9
Reservations: Recommended for dinner
Handicapped Access: Yes

While Candela's location in a nondescript shopping plaza on North Oracle Road leaves a lot to be desired, the food and atmosphere at this small Latin restaurant are authentic and sure to please. The obligatory bread and butter you'll find at most restaurants has here been replaced by a basket of lightly salted plantain chips and a spicy *aji verde* dipping sauce. In keeping with traditional Peruvian cuisine, most dishes at Candela feature potatoes, beef, tropical fruits, seafood, yucca, or quinoa (a South American grain). Popular with lunch crowds is the brightly flavored seviche (citrus-marinated whitefish, onions, and parsley), while for dinner, the *pescado sudado* (steamed fish) or *picante de carne* (a stewlike dish of beef and potatoes) are both excellent choices.

Spanish
CASA VICENTE

520-884-5253
375 S. Stone Ave., Tucson, AZ 85701
Price: Moderate
Credit Cards: AE, MC, V
Hours: Lunch Thurs. and Fri. 11–2; dinner
Tues. through Thurs. 4–10, Fri. and Sat.
4–10:30
Reservations: Accepted
Handicapped Access: Limited in places by stairs
Special Features: Live Spanish guitar and flamenco music

Owner Vicente Sanchez's restaurant is known around town more for its hot and cold tapas than just about anything else on the menu—and for good reason. With most priced between $5 and $10, the tapas are an affordable way to sample Casa Vicente's Mediterranean fare. Particularly exquisite

are the *salmon ahumado con pasta de anchos* (smoked salmon on toast with anchovy paste, capers, and olives), the *chorizo palacios* (spicy Spanish chorizo with olives and greens), and the *berenjenas salteadas* (sautéed eggplant in garlic, ginger, and wine). Groups of four or more would do well to try the paella, a traditional Spanish dish of rice, seafood, chicken, and vegetables served family-style in a giant bowl. The wine list here is respectable and features a variety of Spanish reds, as well as full and half carafes of homemade sangria. While the atmosphere doesn't quite approach the feel of a Barcelona café, the sounds of live flamenco guitar and Spanish classical piano on nights and weekends make for a lively, festive air.

Thai
KARUNA'S THAI PLATE

520-325-4129
1911 E. Grant Rd., Tucson, AZ 85719
Price: Inexpensive
Credit Cards: MC, V
Hours: Tues. through Thurs. noon–9; Fri. and Sat. noon–10; Sun. 5–9
Reservations: Accepted
Handicapped Access: Yes
Special Features: Take-out

Tucson's Thai scene may be small compared to other cities, but Karuna's makes up in quality what the city lacks in quantity. While those with a penchant for heat might think the pad thai needs a bit more kick, house specialties like the *pad prig king* (chicken and crispy green beans in red curry sauce), the *koo chai* (pan-fried rice cakes with chives), and the green papaya salad with crab benefit from the kitchen's sure-handed spicing. Prices at Karuna's are more than affordable given the generosity of the portions, but don't expect the ambience here to inspire. A family-run hole-in-the-wall, Karuna's is a resolutely plain place where all of the love is reserved for the food.

Ocotillo and saguaro cacti are all over Saguaro National Park.

Vietnamese
MISS SAIGON

520-320-9511
1072 N. Campbell Ave., Tucson, AZ 85719
Price: Inexpensive
Credit Cards: AE, D, MC, V
Hours: Daily 10:30–9:30
Reservations: Not accepted
Handicapped Access: Yes
Special Features: Patio seating, take-out

This tiny restaurant in a strip mall at the corner of Campbell Avenue and Speedway Boulevard near the University of Arizona cooks up some of the most authentic Vietnamese food in town. What impresses especially is the *pho* (a warm broth with rice noodles and thinly sliced rare beef), though other traditional dishes like the *banh cuon* (steamed rice flour rolls stuffed with vegetables and shrimp) and the *nom* (salads that combine a variety of fresh vegetables) are tasty and affordable. Patio seating is an option, but with a view of an intersection and a few fast-food joints across the street, you're better off finding a seat inside, away from the noise. Avoid peak lunch hours in the early afternoon, when Miss Saigon is busy feeding university crowds.

Restaurants Outside the City

Whether it's an evening of fine dining in the foothills or a quick bite to eat at a downtown café, there's no shortage of restaurants *in* Tucson. However, for those looking to combine day tripping with destination dining, the listing that follows, while brief, promises great eats beyond the city's limits.

To the North
MOUNT LEMMON CAFÉ

520-576-1234
Mount Lemmon Hwy., Summerhaven, AZ
85619
Price: Inexpensive
Credit Cards: AE, MC, V
Hours: Mon. through Thurs. 10–4; Fri.
10–5; Sat. and Sun. 8–6
Reservations: Not accepted
Handicapped Access: Limited by stairs
Special Features: Outdoor deck, take-out

More than 8,000 feet above Tucson, at the
top of Mount Lemmon, in the small village
of Summerhaven, the no-frills Mount Lemmon Café has been serving up hearty soups,
fondues, and fresh fruit pies to the hiking,
climbing, and backpacking crowds for
decades. The café itself is a bit cramped and
has all the feeling of a weathered ski lodge
with barely enough room for a few indoor
tables, so it's likely you'll take a seat on the
large outdoor deck that is warmed in cooler
months by an enormous wood-burning
stove. Soup and pie selections change seasonally, daily, and even hourly, but if you
have the chance, try the beef barley soup
(served with an enormous hunk of French
bread) or a piece of the blackberry pie,
which arrives as a slab of warm, gooey
blackberries between two thick, flaky
crusts. If the road is closed due to inclement
weather, chances are so is the café, so be
sure call ahead.

SAFFRON INDIAN BISTRO

520-742-9100
7607 N. Oracle Rd., Tucson, AZ 85704
Price: Moderate
Credit Cards: AE, D, DC, MC, V
Hours: Mon. through Sat. 11–10; Sun. 11–9
Reservations: Accepted
Handicapped Access: Yes
Special Features: Daily lunch buffet

As it has been with other ethnic cuisines, so
it is at Saffron Indian Bistro, where classic
Indian fare has been retrofitted to accommodate a corporate model. Mellow oranges,
creams, and browns of Saffron's hip, minimalist interior complement the bright, bold
presentation of Saffron's food, which draws
inspiration from all over India. All the traditional dishes are here, including naan (a
pitalike flatbread), Samosa (crispy
turnovers stuffed with meats and spices),
and Tandoori meats, as well as a dozen
strictly vegetarian dishes, like the chef's
special *karhai paneer* (cubed cheese seasoned with exotic fenugreek leaves and
cooked in a wok). Compared with other
local, family-run Indian restaurants around
town, Saffron is a bit pricier, but portions
here also tend to be more generous.

To the South
LA ROCA

011-52-631-31-20891
91 Calle Elias, Nogales, Sonora, Mexico
Price: Moderate
Credit Cards: MC, V
Hours: Daily 11 AM–midnight
Reservations: Accepted
Handicapped Access: Limited by stairs
Special Features: Outdoor dining, live music

If you're looking for authentic upscale Mexican cuisine, Roca is a little over an hour's
drive from Tucson, just over the border, on
the Mexican side of Nogales. The setting is
an old stone boardinghouse built into the
side of a rock cliff, where the tiled rooms,
courtyards, and patios serve as an intimate
dining space. Waiters in white jackets and
black bow ties deliver classic Sonoran-style
fare like *carne tampiqueña* (an assortment of
grilled meats, chiles rellenos, and enchiladas), chicken mole, or fresh cabrilla
tacos. Thursday through Sunday, *trovadors*
stroll the restaurant in the evenings strumming traditional Spanish ballads.

To the East
CAFÉ ROKA

520-432-5153
35 Main St., Bisbee, AZ 85603
Price: Moderate
Credit Cards: AE, D, MC, V
Hours: Thurs. through Sat. 5–9 (hours change seasonally)
Reservations: Recommended
Handicapped Access: Limited to first-floor dining room
Special Features: Four-course menu

Two hours southeast of Tucson in the historic copper mining town of Bisbee, Café Roka features modern American cuisine with northern Italian accents. Think lots of fresh ingredients like seasonal fruits and vegetables, nuts, polenta, and pastas. The four-course dinner menu is short (typically featuring a list of entrées that runs only six or seven deep) but changes at least twice weekly and always includes a side salad, a brief but savory palette-cleansing sorbet, and a dessert. While more rustic meat dishes like roasted quail (stuffed with pine nuts, prosciutto, and vegetable *brunois* with an apple cider relish and a rosemary zinfandel sauce) tend to fill out most of the menu, chef-owner Rod Cass makes a point of including at least one or two vegetarian options, like sweet potato and black bean strudel (with white corn risotto cake and black bean cilantro relish). The gorgeous central bar—a well-kept relic dating back to 1875—is a sight in itself.

To the West
OCOTILLO CAFÉ

520-883-2702
2021 N. Kinney Rd., Tucson, AZ 85743
Price: Moderate
Credit Cards: AE, MC, V
Hours: Lunch Mon. through Fri. 11–3 (Dec. through Apr.); dinner 5–10 Sat. (June through Aug.) (opening and closing dates may vary)
Reservations: Accepted
Handicapped Access: Yes
Special Features: On the grounds of the Arizona-Sonora Desert Museum

While just getting to the Arizona-Sonora Desert Museum's Ocotillo Café will cost you an admission to the museum itself, a meal here is worth every penny. And not only for the setting, which is one part aviary, one part botanical garden. The seasonal menu features a short but frequently evolving selection of Southwestern-inspired fare, including dishes like a chile-cured sirloin (served with roasted garlic–chèvre polenta and red and yellow tomatoes), and *dorado con frijoles blanca* (mahimahi, white beans, smoked garlic, lemon preserve, tomatoes, and spinach). At just 14 bottles (nine available by the glass), the wine list, like the menu, is small, focusing mostly on California varieties. Nowhere else in the country can you enjoy a gourmet meal of this caliber and follow it up with a guided, nighttime scorpion hunt.

Food Purveyors

Bakeries

Beyond Bread (www.beyondbread.com; 520-322-9965, 3026 N. Campbell Ave.; 520-747-7477, 6260 E. Speedway Blvd.) While Beyond Bread has made a name for itself as a lunch and dinner destination with a vast menu of more than 30 artfully constructed, hot and cold gourmet sandwiches, including such heartier gems as Bettie's Brie (rare roast beef, warm Brie, sliced tomato, and creamy mayonnaise on a crispy baguette) and the vegetarian Mayay's Market (Havarti cheese, basil pesto, roasted red peppers, tomato, artichoke hearts, and red onion layered on thick multigrain bread), this local chain is just as well known for its breads, which, depending on the daily baking schedule, can include a local favorite like green chile and provolone bread or simpler peasant varieties like rustic, marble rye, and cracked wheat.

La Baguette Bakery (520-322-6297; 1797 E. Prince Rd.) From the same father and daughter owners of Ghini's French Café, which shares dining space with La Baguette, Norber and Coralie Satta's bakery serves more than one hundred types of bread and two hundred different kinds of pastries, all of it baked fresh daily under the watchful eye of Parisian transplant and master pastry chef Angelo Ferro.

Nadine's Bakery (520-326-0735; 4553 E. Broadway Blvd.) Nadine's covers the full spectrum of indulgence. Painstakingly hand-decorated specialty cakes, fudge by weight, and breakfast favorites like Danishes, bear claws, cinnamon rolls, and coffee cakes make this all-kosher bakery a Tucson favorite.

Small Planet Bakery (520-884-9313; www.smallplanetbakery.com; 411 N. Seventh Ave.) Tucsonans have been breaking Small Planet bread since it first began baking as a non-profit co-op in the 1970s. Today, the organic breads, rolls, and granolas made daily by owners Chris French and Lucy Mitchell grace the menus and shelves of many of Tucson's best restaurants and markets. Orders depend on what's baking that day, so calling ahead would be wise if you're hoping to score more exotic varieties like Small Planet's delicious orange-date or Balkin black pepper breads.

Village Bakehouse (520-531-0977; www.villagebakehouse.com; 7882 N. Oracle Rd.) High up on Oracle Road, close to Oro Valley, Village Bakehouse, in addition to full breakfast and lunch menus, offers fresh-baked breads and baguettes; made-from-scratch pastries, muffins, strudel, and fruit pies; as well as specialty cakes for all occasions, many of which can be made to accommodate gluten-free, diabetic, and vegan dietary restrictions.

Gelato

Frost: A Gelato Shoppe (www.frostgelato.com; 520-797-0188, 7131 N. Oracle Rd., Ste. 101; 520-886-0354, 7301 E. Tanque Verde Rd.; 520-299-0315, 2905 E. Skyline Dr. #286) With the exception of the milk and sugar, Frost's owners import all other ingredients directly from Italy. Even Frost's master gelato chef, Nazario Melchionda, hales from Bologna, where for 22 years he perfected the more than one hundred flavors that make up Frost's extraordinarily deep menu of gelato and ices. With exotic flavors like blackberry cabernet, tiramisu, and chocolate coconut, as well as classic favorites like espresso, lemon, and hazelnut, all made fresh in-shop daily, it's no surprise that Frost gelaterias are fast becoming the tastiest destinations in Tucson for dessert.

Pizza

Brooklyn Pizza Company (520-622-6868; www.brooklynpizzacompany.com; 534 N. Fourth Ave.) As the name suggests, Brooklyn's is New York–style pizza. Pies here are hand-tossed to order and come in one size (16-inch), making for wide, thin, foldable slices. Daily lunch specials (11–4:30 daily) draw downtown lunch crowds and students, while happy hour beer specials (4–7:30) and late-night to-go slices make Brooklyn a pit stop for hipsters heading to or from Tucson's downtown bar scene. While the pizza is the best thing here, hot and cold heroes, made-to-order calzones, and Italian ice round out Brooklyn's menu.

Magpies (www.magpiespizza.com; 520-628-1661, 605 N. Fourth Ave.; 520-795-5977, 4654
E. Speedway Blvd.; 520-297-2712, 7315 N. Oracle Rd.; 520-751-9949, 105 S. Houghton
Rd. #149; 520-572-4300, 8295 N. Cortaro Rd.) This local chain has been honored by
Tucsonans as the city's best gourmet pizza for 20 years, and it's been voted as one of the
top one hundred pizzerias in the country every year since 2000. Even the most cursory
glance at the menu will tell you why. With 19 specialty pies, including Southwestern-
inspired creations like the Pueblo (mozzarella and cheddar cheeses, ground beef, scal-
lions, roasted green chiles, tomatoes, and black olives) and the Juan Carlos Pesto (fresh
basil, spinach, cilantro, whole garlic, and jalapeños layered with fresh tomatoes and
piñon nuts), Magpies offers some of the most inventive gourmet pies around.

No Anchovies (520-623-3333; www.noanchoviespizza.com; 870 E. University Blvd.)
Located just beyond the western gates of the University of Arizona, No Anchovies offers
more than 30 different pizzas by the slice daily, many loaded with one combination or
another of its 46 possible toppings. The popularity of No Anchovies is due in no small
part to the daily happy-hour specials on beer (available here by the bottle, pint, or
pitcher), the full-service bar, the live music on weekends, and the collegiate atmosphere
that imbues the place with a festive, laid-back feel, particularly on the patio, where outdoor tables face bustling University Boulevard.

Zachary's (520-623-6323; 1028 E. Sixth St.) This nondescript, no-frills, hole-in-the-wall
pizza joint just south of the University of Arizona campus specializes in two things:
deep-dish, Chicago-style pizzas, slices of which approach 3 inches in thickness, and

microbrew draughts, 20 of which are available by pint or pitcher. The Big Z is the house specialty and comes weighted down with the works. Daily specials make Zachary's a favorite lunch and dinner spot for hungry university students and neighborhood folks alike.

Specialty Markets & Delis

AJ's Fine Foods (520-232-6340; www.ajsfinefoods.com; 2805 E. Skyline Dr.) This high-end supermarket at La Encantada in the Catalina foothills, while expensive, features a number of gourmet departments, including a *fromagerie* offering handcrafted farmstead and artisanal cheeses; a butcher's corner, featuring prime cuts of Kobe and dry aged beef; a *boulangerie* brimming with fresh-baked pastries and torts; and a wine shop lined floor to ceiling with more than 1,500 large batch and boutique labels, as well as 350 imported and domestic craft beers. Grab a chef-prepared meal to go or an artisanal sandwich from AJ's gourmet deli and enjoy it on the flagstone patio overlooking the city.

Aqua Vita Natural Food Market (520-293-7770; www.aquavitanaturals.com; 2801 N. Country Club Rd.) A no-frills point of purchase for organic produce and groceries, raw dairy products, free-range organic eggs, herbal remedies, nutritional supplements, vegan items, distilled water, and foods in bulk, including more than five hundred herbs.

Food Conspiracy Co-op (520-624-4821; www.foodconspiracy.org; 412 N. Fourth Ave.) Open to members and nonmembers alike, this community-owned natural foods market on Tucson's Fourth Avenue has been providing Tucsonans with certified organic produce since 1971. Here you'll find an ever-changing variety of local, fair-trade, and independent-label groceries; bulk foods; sulfite-free wine and beer; organic yogurts and cheeses; and natural candies; as well as gluten-free, dairy-free, vegetarian, macrobiotic, unrefined, low-fat, and low-sodium alternative foods.

Rincon Market (520-327-6653; www.rinconmarket.com; 2513 E. Sixth St.) A fixture of Tucson's historic Sam Hughes neighborhood since 1926, Rincon Market is both a corner grocer (featuring kosher meats and groceries, fresh fish, baked goods, and wine) and a cafeteria-style deli and grill offering everything from comfort foods (meat loaf, rotisserie chicken, macaroni) to hot and cold made-to-order sandwiches to fresh salads.

Roma Imports (520-792-3173; www.romaimports.com; 627 S. Vine Ave.) Like many of Tucson's best markets, Roma is a little harder to find, but it's well worth the effort. Located in a quiet residential neighborhood just south of Broadway Boulevard, Roma carries full lines of gourmet Italian foods, including imported stewing tomatoes, olive oils, and balsamic vinegars; traditional, gluten-free, and whole-wheat pastas; prepared sauces; homemade sausage and hand-rolled meatballs; and fresh-sliced *prosciutto de parma* and capicola. Roma's also offers an extensive all-day lunch menu that features specialty sandwiches, hot and cold pasta dishes, and salads. Eat in Roma's adjacent dining room or take it to go.

17th Street Market (520-792-2588; 840 E. 17th St.) Despite the fact that it's tucked away in Tucson's Armory Park Warehouse District, 17th Street has all the buzz of a bustling farmer's market, but indoors, making it one of the most sought out destinations in town for locally grown organic produce, seasonal fresh-cut flowers, grain-fed and free-range meats, sushi-grade fish and seafood, and a vast selection of imported foods, with special emphasis on exotic pan-Asian produce and foodstuffs, including more than 13 kinds of rice, 20 different types of fish sauce, and all other things dried and pickled.

Time Market (520-622-0761; 444 E. University Blvd.) If the hardwood floors look old,

Local Food Glossary

Albondigas. Mexican soup made with meatballs and often flavored with mint.

Barbacoa. Meat that is steamed until very tender.

Burros. Baked or fried burritos.

Carne asada. Very thin boneless steak that has been spiced and grilled.

Carne seca and machaca. Beef that has been spiced with chiles and dried, then rehydrated and tenderized. *Machaca* tends to come in larger pieces than *seca*.

Chilaquiles. Layers of corn tortillas that have been fried and layered with cheese and salsa.

Chivichangas. Fried tacos stuffed with meat, beans or cheese. (Not a misspelling of chimichangas, but a similar dish.)

Chorizo. Highly spiced sausage made from pork or beef, vinegar, red chile powder, and other spices. Often served with eggs for breakfast or in soups.

Flautas. Flour (and sometimes corn) tortillas wrapped tightly around meat, cheese, or some other filling and deep fried.

Fry bread. A Native American dish of fried flat dough often topped with honey or powdered sugar, as well as savory ingredients, such as those found on tacos.

Green Chile. Slow-cooked soup often made with pork shoulder and green chiles.

Menudo. A traditional soup with garlic, calf or pig's feet, garlic, onions, and other spices.

Mesquite pancakes. Pancakes made with the naturally sweet flour of ground mesquite pods from local trees.

Mole. A spicy, savory sauce often made with chocolate and chiles, but also made without chocolate in green or red variations. Mole dishes come in a variety of incarnations—often burritos or enchiladas are covered in a mole sauce, or chicken is simmered in it.

Posole. A traditional soup made with hominy, pork, chiles, and other ingredients.

Sonoran hot dog. A favorite street food in which a traditional hot dog is wrapped in bacon and layered with tomatoes, chiles, tomatillo salsa, and other condiments in a bun.

Sopas. Soup.

Tamales. Vegetables, cheese, or meat in cornmeal mush (or *masa*) that have been wrapped in a cornhusk and steamed. Sonoran green corn tamales are made with young corn *masa* and have an especially sweet taste.

Tortas. Pie, torte, or Mexican sandwich.

that's because they are. In one incarnation or another, Time Market has been serving the West University neighborhood since 1919, making it one of the oldest markets in town. In addition to some of the best espresso drinks in town, gourmet wood-fired pizza, generously portioned deli sandwiches, a small but discerning wine section that includes sakes and ports, and a refrigerated wall of imported and domestic craft beers, Time Market carries fair-trade coffees and teas, boutique bar chocolate, organic produce, and gourmet groceries. With two shaded patios outside and a number of tables inside, Time is a favorite neighborhood spot for Sunday lounging with coffee and a paper.

Trader Joe's (www.traderjoes.com; 520-323-4500, 4766 E. Grant Rd.; 520-325-0069, 4209 N. Campbell Ave.; 520-733-1313, 1101 N. Wilmot Rd. #147) What some of its offerings lack in freshness (produce and meats here mostly come prepackaged or frozen, and there's a conspicuous lack of bulk foods), Trader Joe's more than makes up for in low prices, particularly when compared with pricier competitors like Whole Foods and Sunflower. That's because Trader Joe's avoids name brands and, instead, carries its own high-quality, all natural lines—everything from basic staples to prepared foods to ethnic foodstuffs.

Whole Foods (www.wholefoods.com; 520-795-9844, 3360 E. Speedway Blvd.; 520-297-5394, 7133 N. Oracle Rd.) A superstore among natural-foods markets, Whole Foods offers full lines of all-natural groceries, grain-fed meats, locally grown organic fruits and vegetables, regional salsas, baked goods, and prepared foods "unadulterated by artificial additives, sweeteners, colorings, and preservatives." There's also an extensive bulk department that includes whole grains, dried fruits, granolas, flour, seeds, and herbs, as well as a comprehensive selection of wines and beers.

Wine, Beer & Liquor

While most major supermarkets in town carry selections of wine, beer, and liquor, a thoughtful sales staff is often harder to come by. Listed below are several specialty stores and brewpubs that offer both thoughtful service and unparalleled variety.

Barrio Brewing Company (520-791-2739; www.barriobrewing.com; 800 E. 16th St.) Owned and operated by the same folks who run Gentle Ben's Brewery (520-624-4177; 865 E. University Blvd.), Barrio Brewing Company is the latest addition to Tucson's burgeoning pub scene. Located in a converted warehouse set back from the railroad tracks that cut through Tucson's Warehouse District, Barrio offers 10 beers on tap (including pale ales, blonds, oatmeal stouts, ambers, porters, Hefeweizen, and a raspberry ale) and the pub fare to go with them. In addition to live music and shuffleboard, Barrio Brewing offers one of the more unusual drink specials in town—$3 pints during train crossings.

Nimbus Brewing Co. (520-745-9175; www.nimbusbeer.qwestoffice.net; 3850 E. 44th St. #138) This Tucson-based brewpub has only been operating since 1996, but it now boasts the distinction of being the largest brewery in Arizona, with an annual production capacity of 22,500 barrels (about 45,000 kegs). Nimbus beers (including its Dirty Guera Southwestern blond ale; its pale, red, and brown ales; its Old Monkey Shine English strong ale; and its oatmeal stout) are carefully crafted under the watchful eye of head brewer Scott Schwartz and have won local, regional, and national awards, including five consecutive years as Best Local Brew and Best Beer on Tap by the readers of the *Tucson Weekly,* and four consecutive years as Best Microbrewery by both the *Arizona Daily Star* and *Arizona Republic.* The brewery taproom is open for lunch and dinner and serves up traditional pub grub like beer-battered onion rings, burgers, and fish-and-chips. While the only beer to go comes in kegs and minikegs, most grocery stores and liquor markets around town carry the full line of Nimbus beers.

Pastiche Wine Shop (520-325-3333; www.pasticheme.com; 3025 N. Campbell Ave.) It should be no surprise that Pastiche Modern Eatery, the sister restaurant to this small but elegant wine shop of the same name, should be recognized by *Wine Spectator* magazine. After all, the restaurant's wine list draws from the more than six hundred bottles that line the store floor to ceiling. Much of the stock here is made up of small-batch vintages and wines from lesser-known boutique producers, many of which complement the shop's small but distinct selections of imported and domestic artisanal cheeses, gourmet chocolate, and wine jellies. Monthly wine tastings and gourmet gift baskets are also popular.

Plaza Liquors (520-327-0452; 2642 N. Campbell Ave.) Don't let the bland exterior fool you; it's what's inside Plaza Liquors that counts—like 600 varieties of beer (including porters, stouts, pale ales, and pilsners), 100 artisanal tequilas, and 75 single-malt scotches, as well as a discriminating selection of wine and ports that emphasize quality over quantity. For those hoping to sample the store's vast beer selection, mix-and-match six-packs are a popular (and affordable) option. With a polite and knowledgeable staff headed by longtime owner Mark Thomson, Plaza Liquors is unquestionably one of the best liquor stores in town.

The Rumrunner (520-326-0121; www.rumrunnertucson.com; 3131 E. First St.) The Rumrunner has been one of Tucson's finest wine and spirits emporiums for close to 40 years. The wine selection is ambitious, bringing together major labels and rare, small-batch vintages alike. Equally impressive is the selection of single-malt scotches, tequilas, and, yes, rums. Chef-prepared meals from the Dish, the Rumrunner's in-house bistro, are available to go and complement the shop's other gourmet edibles, like fine cheeses, pâtés, caviars, and jellies. Prices here are affordable, and special case discounts are available on all wine and liquor, even sale items, of which there are always plenty.

6

Recreation

Indoor & Outdoor Fun

From ballooning high above the city to horseback riding in the foothills, there is something for everyone in this southwest town. Golf is popular here, with a huge number of courses in most of the city's major parks, and there are dozens of hiking and camping opportunities. If you're willing to do a little extra driving, there are destinations farther afield, such as Colossal Cave in Vail, Kartchner Caverns, and the artist colony in Tubac. Parents can take their kids to Tucson's Children's Museum, which features galleries of hands-on exhibits and demonstrations, and to Reid Park Zoo, which is home to animals both common and exotic. Families should also check out Old Tucson Studios or Trail Dust Town for a little taste of Hollywood's vision of the Wild West.

BALLOONING

For a hawk's-eye view of the city and its surrounding natural beauty, consider coasting above it all in a hot-air balloon. Several companies offer balloon rides for small (2–4 people) and large (10–12 people) groups, complete with an in-depth description of the vegetation and wildlife you'll view along the way. It is traditional for the ride to be followed by a champagne brunch, and some companies take it a step further by specifically catering the flying experience to satisfy couples, certain holidays, and special occasions. A notable plus to the experience is the sheer beauty of your vehicle—the colorful patterns of the balloons are a sight to see in and of themselves. There are even companies that will document your journey for you. Be aware, however, that most companies limit their season to the coolest of Tucson's already toasty months, so don't plan your visit between late April and September if you plan to journey by balloon in the direction of the hot desert sun.

FLEUR DE TUCSON BALLOON TOURS

520-529-1025
www.fleurdetucson.net
4635 N. Caida Pl., Tucson, AZ 85718

You may have seen Fleur de Tucson on the Animal Planet production *Jeff Corwin's Arizona Experience.* Specializing in small-group rides, this family-run company offers a 60- to 75-minute ride over the Tucson Mountains and Saguaro National Park. The ride ends with a continental champagne breakfast, at which time you are given digital pictures from your journey and a flying certificate. Cheaper rates can be found by registering via the Internet. Ask your guides for stories about the adventures they've had in three decades of flying nationally and internationally.

SOUTHERN ARIZONA BALLOON EXCURSIONS

520-624-3599
www.tucsoncomefly.com
537 W. Grant Rd., Tucson, AZ 85705

This family-owned company, in operation for more than 20 years, provides trips above the Catalina and Tucson mountains with most of the same amenities offered by other companies. However, this company also provides special shaped balloons, motion picture projects, and programming for special events. Check out a video of one of their trips by visiting their Web site.

TUCSON BALLOON RIDES

520-235-5355
www.tucsonballoonrides.com
433 W. Rosales St., Tucson, AZ 85701

While this company offers a tour of the Tucson Mountains, discounted prices for buying online, photographs of the trip, and a post-flight brunch, they also can accommodate larger groups with advanced warning; couples must pay an additional fee.

BICYCLING

Bicycling magazine has ranked Tucson as one of the best biking cities in the country. The roads are mostly flat in the center of the city, but they become a good deal steeper around the foothills, providing a variety of levels to choose from for those visitors seeking a pleasure ride. Bikes are a great way to commute as well, providing a refreshing respite from the congested streets during rush hour. Most major roads have bike lanes, and several special bike routes make it even easier to surpass major byways in order to shoot from one end of the city to another. Just about any day of the year you can see cycling enthusiasts and commuters safely navigating the city's streets.

Several organizations around Tucson make an effort to increase education, safety, and agility for bikers. The Tucson Department of Transportation, for example, offers classes for people of all ages. BICAS, a cooperative located in the downtown arts district, not only sells used bikes and bike parts, but holds classes and accommodates drop-in customers with bike maintenance, construction, and repair. BICAS also offers a Build-A-Bike workshop popular with locals, and an annual fund-raising art auction full of bike-related art by local craftsmen. The city holds annual events like Bike Swap, Bike 2 Work Day, and Bike Fest, and even offers services such as "bicycle valet parking" for special events.

There are plenty of bike racks downtown near merchants and businesses. In several neighborhoods, like the Fourth Avenue shopping strip, there are even sculptures made from recycled bike parts that have been installed for commuters to lock their bikes to while shopping or dining.

If you are in town on a Tuesday, consider joining local biking enthusiasts for the Tuesday Night Community Bike Ride, which meets up at the flagpole near University of Arizona's

Colossal Cave   Courtesy Metropolitan Tucson Convention & Visitors Bureau

"Old Main" on the West Campus. Or, if you are in town during the month of November, consider joining the El Tour de Tucson, a scenic annual ride that attracts thousands of professional and amateur participants on a journey from Downtown Central to the perimeter of the city.

A selection of businesses and resources that cater to biking needs follow.

BICAS (BICYCLE INTER COMMUNITY ACTION AND SALVAGE)

520-628-7950
www.bicas.org
P.O. Box 1811, Tucson, AZ 85702
Hours: Tues. through Fri. noon–7; Sat. noon–6

BICAS is a community centered cooperative with used bikes for sale, as well as workshops in bike repair, construction, and art. On Sunday there is a special program called WRENCH, which offers BICAS services specifically to women and transgender customers. Check out their Web site for information on classes and new programming.

BICYCLE AND PEDESTRIAN PROGRAM

City of Tucson Department of Transportation
520-791-4371
http://dot.tucsonaz.gov/bicycle
201 N. Stone Ave., sixth floor, North Wing, P.O. Box 27210, Tucson, AZ 85726

This city program is a good resource for information on bike route maps, annual bike-related events, safety, legislation, and other information.

EL TOUR DE TUCSON

www.pbaa.com/!ETT/ETThome.html

This Web site offers information, registration, and background for the annual November bike tour, El Tour de Tucson.

ORDINARY BIKE SHOP

520-622-6488
www.ordinarybikeshop.com
311 E. Seventh St., Tucson, AZ 85705
Hours: Mon. through Fri. 9–7; Sat. 8–5

A helpful staff of avid cyclists will help customers with problems that run the gamut—from the most basic to the biking professional's specialized needs. Check out the selection of new bikes, state-of-the-art equipment, and antique bicycles that look like they could have come straight out of a Fellini film!

PERFORMANCE BICYCLE

520-327-3232
www.performancebike.com
3302 E. Speedway Blvd., Tucson, AZ 85716
Hours: Mon. through Sat. 10–8; Sun. noon–6; closed Thanksgiving and Christmas Day

This national store has two central locations in Tucson; the other location is at 7204 E. Broadway Boulevard (520-296-4715).

Biking down Mount Lemmon Highway Rick Machle © Metropolitan Tucson Convention & Visitors Bureau

TPCBAC (TUCSON-PIMA COUNTY BICYCLE ADVISORY COMMITTEE)

520-243-2453
www.biketucson.pima.gov

Get the kinds of information only locals would be privy to by contacting the TPCBAC or visiting their Web site.

BOWLING

BEDROXX BOWLING

520-744-7655
www.bedroxx.com
4385 W. Ina Rd., Tucson, AZ 85741
Hours: Mon. through Thurs. 1–10; Fri. and Sat. 1–1; Sun. 9 AM–10 PM; opens early for special events and large parties

This family-centered alley was named Best in Tucson by *Tucson Weekly* in 2008. It has 30 state-of-the-art lanes, offers special services for birthdays and other special events, and has a room full of pool tables and a "fun factory" video arcade. There are special discount nights and a kids' night including bowling and a movie.

GOLDEN PIN LANES
520-888-4272
1010 W. Miracle Mile, Tucson, AZ 85705
Hours: Daily 8:30 AM–12:30 AM

This bowling alley prides itself for being the home of the Pro-Bowlers Tour. There are 48 lanes, video games and laser tag, as well as Kosmic Bowling, with neon lights and a specialized music program. *Tucson Weekly* named it number three in Tucson in their 2008 ranking.

LUCKY STRIKE BOWL
520-327-4926
www.vantagebowlingcenters.com
4015 E. Speedway Blvd., Tucson, AZ 85715
Hours: Mon. through Thurs. 9 AM–midnight; Fri. and Sat. 9 AM–1 AM

Tucson Weekly named this the second-best bowling alley in town in 2008. Part of the Vantage Bowling Center franchise, Lucky Strike is known for fantastic food, especially cheeseburgers. They offer programs for schools, youth and adult leagues, day-care specials, and discounts during the week.

CAMPING

The climate of the Sonoran Desert offers visitors and residents the opportunity to camp year-round. But before you leave for your trip, it may be helpful to check out the equipment and employee expertise at Summit Hut (1-800-499-8696; www.summithut.com), a local retailer that specializes in hiking, camping, and travel needs. This is also a good place to gather personal testimonials on where to camp in and around Tucson. They will most likely direct you to the **Coronado National Forest** (520-388-8300), which encompasses the 12 mountain ranges surrounding metropolitan Tucson. Fires routinely shut campgrounds down, so be sure to contact the National Forest Service or your ranger district directly before visiting to make sure your destination is still in operation. A few of the sites you may want to consider within Coronado's National Forest include the following.

CATALINA STATE PARK CAMPGROUND
520-628-5798
P.O. Box 36986, Tucson, AZ 85740

This 5,493-acre park is just north of Tucson on AZ 77. It has an equestrian center, 48 campsites, and can accommodate recreational vehicles. This is a perfect destination if you are interested in hiking, horseback riding, barbecuing, and picnicking. Campers will enjoy taking off on multiple hiking trails and can refresh themselves with hot showers, drinking water, and flush toilets upon their return. Prices range from $10 to $25, and the season is year-round.

PEPPERSAUCE CAMPGROUND

520-749-8700
Santa Catalina Ranger District
5700 N. Sabino Canyon Rd., Tucson, AZ 85750

The Peppersauce Campground got its name when a prospector by the name of Alex McKay camped on the site in 1880 and found that the hot sauce he brought along with him had gone missing. Located on Mount Lemmon, 40 miles northeast of Tucson, this site has an elevation of 4,700 feet. Cactus-weary visitors who miss tall trees will find the creek lined with sycamores and walnuts especially tempting. Pets are welcome, drinking water and flush toilets are available, and group sites can be accommodated. Rates range from $8 to $35 depending on the size of your party. This site is open year-round.

ROSE CANYON CAMPGROUND

520-749-8700, 1-877-444-6777 (for reservations on a domestic line), 518-885-3639 (for reservations on an international line)
Santa Catalina Ranger District
5700 N. Sabino Canyon Rd., Tucson, AZ 85750

Rose Canyon Creek meanders through this elegant, ponderosa pine–covered campground, eventually trickling into the trout-filled Rose Canyon Lake. At 7,200 feet, Rose Canyon provides 74 units in a cool oasis that is outfitted with its own convenience store. Pets, recreational vehicles, and groups are welcome to make use of the campground's grills, picnic tables, drinking water, and flush toilets from May through the end of October for an $18 fee. However, you must make reservations before your arrival, so call in advance.

SHOWERS POINT GROUP CAMPGROUND

520-749-8700, 1-877-444-6777 (for reservations)
Santa Catalina Ranger District
5700 N. Sabino Canyon Rd., Tucson, AZ 85750

The three group sites at this campground are located at 7,940 feet, northeast of Tucson on the Catalina Highway. For those willing to hike a short distance, nearby Showers Point offers a startling view of the Santa Catalina Mountains, Mount Wrightson, and the Santa Cruz Valley. Groups of 25 or fewer and their pets are welcome to stay for up to 14 days at a cost of $50 per day and can expect amenities like flush toilets, drinking water, and picnic tables. Horses are not allowed; recreational vehicles are not easily accommodated and are therefore discouraged. The site is open from May through mid-October.

SPENCER CAMPGROUND

520-749-8700
Santa Catalina Ranger District
5700 N. Sabino Canyon Rd., Tucson, AZ 85750

At 8,000 feet, this site offers a hearty temperature decrease compared with the metropolitan basin that can, at night, be seen sparkling below. Enjoy one of 60 units outfitted with flush toilets, drinking water, grills, and picnic tables. You can bring your pet, and even your RV, but not your horse. Expect to pay around $16 per night. The site is open between May 7 and October 31.

Butterfly exhibit at the Tucson Botanical Gardens David Jewell © Metropolitan Tucson Convention & Visitors Bureau

FAMILY FUN

According to the U.S. Census Bureau, about one quarter of Tucson's population is under 18 years old, and there are a multitude of institutions and activities geared to the interests of these young people. If you're looking for a great resource to use in order to locate innovative activities for the family in Tucson, visit Tucson Kids online, a self-proclaimed "one-stop kid-friendly site" (www.tucsonkids.com). This Web site can provide information on upcoming events, educational opportunities, and even child-focused medical information and book recommendations. With or without the navigational help of this Web site, you'll find that many businesses and organizations around the city have programming that specifically targets children. The following are a few options that the entire family can enjoy.

GENE C. REID PARK ROSE GARDEN

520-791-4874
www.tucsonaz.gov/parkandrec
900 S. Randolph Way, Tucson, AZ 85716
Admission: Free
Hours: Daily sunrise–sunset

This rose garden is home to more than 100 different species of roses and 1,080 different color rose beds. A layout plan is available free at the garden, which directs visitors to the locations of different species of roses as well as listing the best varieties for Tucson's unique desert climate. At the center of the garden is a large gazebo, and it's not uncommon to see weddings and parties held there. Although always impressive, the peak times for blooms occur between March and April and October through November.

REID PARK ZOO

520-791-3204
www.tucsonzoo.org
1100 S. Randolph Way, Tucson, AZ 85716
Admission: $6 for adults, $4 seniors (ages 62 and up,) $2 for children ages 2–14, free for children 2 and under
Hours: Daily 9–4 (closes early on Thanksgiving and Christmas)

The Reid Park Zoo has more than five hundred exotic animals from all over the world. The layout is charming and surprising, with the animals nearly hidden until a visitor comes right up on the habitat. The zoo also features a full-flight aviary.

TUCSON BOTANICAL GARDENS

520-326-9686
www.tucsonbotanical.org
2150 N. Alvernon Way, Tucson, AZ 85712
Admission: $7 for adults, $4 for children 4–12
Hours: Daily 8:30–4:30

An oasis in the middle of a metropolitan desert, the Tucson Botanical Gardens sits on more than 5 acres and features 16 specialty gardens, including one dedicated to the farming styles of the Hohokam. Tours and classes are available, as is a unique gift shop with local ecofriendly products and local artwork.

TUCSON CHILDREN'S MUSEUM

520-792-9985
www.tucsonchildrensmuseum.org
200 S. Sixth Ave., Tucson, AZ 85701
Admission: $7 for adults, $5 for seniors and children 2–18; groups of 10 or more require a reservation
Hours: Tues. through Sat. 10–5; Sun. noon–5 (closed Thanksgiving and Christmas Day)

Located inside the original Carnegie Library building in Tucson's historic downtown, the Tucson Children's Museum offers exhibitions and interactive studios such as Dinosaur World, Art Studio, the Enchanted Rain Forest, Electri-City Gallery, Young Explorers Center, Musica de las Americas, Ocean Discovery Center, and more. Workshops and events at the museum sometimes run concurrently with local cultural events, such as the outdoor festival Carnaval, for which the museum offers children's courses in necklace making. Birthdays and other special events are accommodated with special rooms, and the facility even allows for museum-centered parties to be catered by local restaurants around town. The museum store, Toyastorus, may be the perfect location to find unique, child-oriented souvenirs.

TUCSON MUSEUM OF ART

520-624-2333
www.tucsonmuseumofart.org
140 N. Main Ave., Tucson, AZ 85701
Admission: $8 adults, $6 seniors, $3 students
Hours: Tues. through Sat. 10–4; Sun. noon–4; closed Mon. and major holidays

In addition to the impressive range of exhibitions that will be of interest to the budding artist of any household, the Tucson Museum of Art has family-oriented programming that caters to children. There is, for example, a Family Art Days program that includes a monthly series called Picture This! Art for Families, which utilizes tours and interactive art creation to ensure that the experience of art is more than a passive activity.

VALLEY OF THE MOON

520-323-1331
www.tucsonvalleymoon.com
2455 E. Allen Rd., Tucson, AZ 85719
Admission: Free
Hours: Vary widely; call for information

In 1967, the *Daily Star* described this gem: "Should Disneyland cover the entire State of California, not one corner would speak to childhood as does this imperfect, perfect little theater." The Valley of the Moon was built in the 1920s by George Phar Legler in attempt to appeal to the magic and imagination of children and relax the mind and spirit at the same time. The Valley of the Moon has mineralized rock cliffs, a pool, garden miniatures, caves, and more, all blended with native desert and tropical flora.

GOLF

Given Tucson's arid climate, one of the first things visitors comment on upon seeing a golf course's expanse of green has something to do with water. How does a desert support that much grass? Not to worry. Tucson's golf courses are all irrigated with reclaimed water, taking the guilt out of golfing in the desert. All of Tucson's courses are equipped with electric and pull carts, banquet facilities, lighted driving ranges, rental equipment, lessons, clubhouses, and separate putting greens. Tee times can be reserved online by visiting www.tucsoncitygolf.com. There are a few other courses in Tucson as well, but membership tends to be limited as these are attached to specific country clubs and resorts.

DELL URICH

520-791-4161
600 S. Alvernon Way, Tucson, AZ 85716

If hills entice you, consider visiting this course, located on Alvernon, near Reid Park, between Broadway and 22nd Street. Open since 1996, this 18-hole, par 70, 5,270-by-6,673-yard course will be a convenient destination for those staying in central Tucson.

EL RIO

520-791-4229
1400 W. Speedway Blvd., Tucson, AZ 85745

Golfing in the desert Courtesy Westin La Paloma

This 18-hole, par 70, 6,000-by-6,400-yard course has a reasonably flat terrain and quite a few trees. It has been around since the 1930s and was the site for the Tucson Open before it moved to its current home at the Tucson National.

FRED ENKE

520-791-2539
8251 E. Irvington Rd., Tucson, AZ 85730

For those who would prefer to golf on a terrain closer to Tucson's natural environment, Fred Enke provides an interesting challenge. Grass is limited, sand traps and hills are frequent, and native plants abound. Given the inconsistent elevation, golf carts are recommended. Golfers have the option of four teeing areas, measuring 6,800, 6,400, 5,800, and 5,000 yards.

RANDOLPH GOLF COURSE

520-791-4161
600 S. Alvernon Way, Tucson, AZ 85716

Randolph, the longest golf course in Tucson (7,000 yards from the championship tees and 6,500 yards from the regular tees), used to encompass the Dell Urich course as well, but now it has separated off on its own. With 18 holes and a par of 70, it is the present home of the PING/Welch's LPGA (Ladies Professional Golf Association) Championship. Professional golfers will appreciate the challenge provided by long fairways and water hazards, and visitors will appreciate its central location.

SILVERBELL GOLF COURSE

520-791-5235
3600 N. Silverbell Rd., Tucson, AZ 85745

Golfers who come to Silverbell are treated to a rare Tucson sight—multiple lakes. Close to the site of the Santa Cruz River, this 18-hole, par 70 course offers a 6,300-yard retreat on mostly flat terrain.

GYMS AND WORKOUT FACILITIES

Tucson's level streets, multitude of hikes, and incessantly sunny environment allow residents to jog, run, and walk their way to good health. However, the city also houses an array of workout facilities for swimming, weight training, indoor fitness, and specialized classes. No matter what your budget, there is a huge range of membership rates—and even some discounts—that will fit your financial and fitness needs.

BALLY TOTAL FITNESS

520-323-1238
www.ballyfitness.com
2475 N. Swan Rd., Tucson, AZ 85712

With one branch in the foothills and a second in central Tucson (4690 N. Oracle Rd.; 520-293-2330), Bally Total Fitness can provide members with a personalized path to "total" fitness. There are periodic discounts on the enrollment fee and low-commitment membership opportunities.

BLUE SKY FITNESS AND RECREATION

520-323-3146
www.blueskyfitrec.com
2509 N. Campbell, P.M.B. 51, Tucson, AZ 85719

Blue Sky caters specifically to children and adults with developmental, emotional, and psychiatric disabilities. Activities to promote a healthy lifestyle, personal fitness, increased energy, and heightened self-esteem all take place in community parks, neighborhoods, and national parks. Choose from a selection of programming, from vacation trips, hiking programs, and daytime programs for adults to after-school programs for children.

DESERT SPORTS AND FITNESS

520-791-7799
www.desertsportsandfitness.com
Multiple locations

If you are interested in a full-fitness center that caters solely to Tucson, visit one of the six Desert Sports and Fitness branches around the city. Open for more than 25 years, this company has regular as well as trial memberships, child care, personal training, state-of-the-art equipment, and group fitness classes that will help you tone, sweat, and meditate your way to personal health.

GOLD'S GYM

520-623-6300
www.goldsgym.com
Multiple locations

With three locations in Tucson, including a 26,000-square-foot facility downtown, Gold's Gym provides fitness resources with a national reputation. In addition to the traditional amenities like child care, up-to-date aerobic and toning equipment, a variety of classes, and personal training, Gold's Gym offers nutritional education.

LA FITNESS

520-888-4900
www.lafitness.com
Multiple locations

Outfitted with a juice bar, Kids Klub, personal trainers, basketball and racquetball leagues, pool, Jacuzzi, saunas, state-of-the-art equipment, and a range of classes, LA Fitness has been called "hands-down the one to beat" by *AVID Living Magazine.* They also offer a corporate wellness program for companies wishing to increase employee health and morale. Visit one of their three central Tucson locations.

TUCSON JEWISH COMMUNITY CENTER

520-299-3000
www.tucsonjcc.org
3800 E. River Rd., Tucson, AZ 85718

Anyone is welcome to join the JCC (Jewish Community Center) at its full fitness center for a general workout. The center also has facilities for tennis, swimming, basketball, racquetball, various fitness classes, and more. Discounted membership rates are offered for those whose income makes them eligible to apply.

YMCA

www.tucsonymca.org
Multiple locations

For perhaps the most reasonable membership and program fees available in the world of fitness, try contacting a local branch of the YMCA. Each of the four full-service branches has a room full of treadmills, stationary bikes, and other cardio equipment, in addition to basketball courts, personal fitness programming, and courses in yoga, tai chi, cycling, and other forms of fitness.

HIKING

Tucson has been described as a hiker's dream. Given the climate, outdoor activity is feasible during all seasons, and the flora and fauna that can be seen during the course of a hike will attract nature lovers of all kinds. Caution should be taken during summer months, however, at which time attention to flood warnings, proper clothing, and plenty of water are vital not only to ensure comfort but survival. Only certain trails around Tucson allow pets, so check beforehand if you'd like to bring your dog along. An indispensable hiking resource for residents and visitors alike is the newest edition of the *Tucson Hiking Guide* by Betty Leavengood. You can also get a complete list of trails by checking out the Web sites for the areas listed in this section.

ARIZONA-SONORA DESERT MUSEUM

520-883-1380
www.desertmuseum.org
2021 N. Kinney Rd., Tucson, AZ 85743
Admission: June through Aug. $9 adults, $2 children 6–12; Sept. through May $12 adults, $4 children 6–12; always free to children 5 and under
Hours: Daily 7:30–5 Mar. through Sept.; Sat. 7:30 AM–10 PM in summer; daily 8:30–5 Oct. through Feb.

An outdoor walking experience and one of Tucsonans' favorite places to take visitors, the Arizona-Sonora Desert Museum is a hands-on outdoor museum that gives guests the opportunity to witness hundreds of native desert plants and animals in their natural environment. Located 14 miles west of downtown, the museum can be reached via a lovely drive through the mountains. Some highlights include the hummingbird aviary, which holds more than a hundred of the quick-moving, brightly feathered creatures, and the landscaped habitat of javelinas and coyotes. The museum is also home to threatened and endangered species such as the Mexican wolf, thick-billed parrot, ocelot, desert pupfish, and Apache trout.

Often, museum docents give educational talks about the animals, including rattlesnakes and the many night birds that call the museum home. During the summer, special night programs are offered, featuring astrological talks and telescoped views of the night sky.

View from Pima Canyon trail

Prairie dogs at the Arizona-Sonora Desert Museum Gill Kenny © Metropolitan Tucson Convention & Visitors Bureau

CORONADO NATIONAL FOREST

520-388-8300
www.fs.fed.us/r3/coronado
300 W. Congress St., Tucson, AZ 85701
Admission: Free

The 12 mountain ranges of the Coronado National Forest get their names from when they were happened upon in 1540 by Spanish explorer Don Francisco de Coronado, who was seeking the Seven Cities of Gold. Instead, he found the mountains, which provided life to the cacti, lizards, and other flora and fauna. The 1.7 million acres of public land include such popular spots as Mount Lemmon and Sabino Canyon. There are places for camping, picnicking, hiking, rock climbing, skiing, fishing, and more.

GATE'S PASS

Gate's Pass Rd., Tucson, AZ 85743

Nestled in the heart of the Tucson Mountains is Gate's Pass, a 22-mile-long paved and gravel drive known for its breathtaking views and slightly dangerous curves. West of Tucson, the trailheads along Gate's Pass are popular spots for picnicking, hiking, and taking in one of those red, purple, and orange Southwestern sunsets that bleed across the sky.

Sabino Canyon   James Randklev © Metropolitan Tucson Convention & Visitors Bureau

MOUNT LEMMON

520-749-8700
www.fs.fed.us/r3/coronado/index.shtml
Santa Catalina Ranger District
5700 N. Sabino Canyon Rd., Tucson, AZ 85750
Admission: Free

A sight to see in all seasons, majestic Mount Lemmon is a popular spot for outdoor adventures—hiking in the summer and spring and skiing in the fall and winter. Standing 9,000 feet above sea level, the mountain is particularly enjoyable as a respite from Tucson's summer heat, as it is typically much cooler. Near the summit of Mount Lemmon is the southernmost ski area in the country. Ski runs are usually open from the middle of December until April, but this depends on winter weather and snowfall (520-576-1321; 10300 Ski Run Rd.). Equipment rentals and instruction are available, as are overnight accommodations in nearby Summerhaven. Even if skiing is not in season, you can take the chairlift up for a breathtaking view of the Santa Catalinas, the city of Tucson, and the San Pedro Valley. Open all week except Tuesday and Wednesday, sky rides are $9 for adults, $8 for seniors and members of the military, and $5 for children. You can also purchase a family ticket for $20.

SABINO CANYON

520-749-8700
www.sabinocanyon.org
Santa Catalina Ranger District
5700 N. Sabino Canyon Rd., Tucson, AZ 85750
Admission: Free
Hours: Park recreation area open 24 hours daily; visitors center open Mon. through Fri.
8–4:30, weekends and holidays 8:30–4:30; closed Thanksgiving and Christmas Day

A popular spot for both casual and serious hikers, Sabino Canyon offers scenic trails that
are backdropped by thousands of saguaros and a close-up view of the eastern foothills of
the Catalina Mountains. Trail maps are available for free at the visitors center, and helpful
rangers can assist you in finding the right trail for your interest and physical ability. Dip
your toes in Sabino Creek and take in the plants and animals that call the canyon home.

Gay-Friendly Hiking

If you are looking to enjoy a hike with your partner, or to socialize with other GLBT (gay,
lesbian, bisexual, and transgender) folk while enjoying Tucson's natural splendor, consider
contacting **Tucson Frontrunners** through their Web site, www.tucsonfrontrunners.org.
This running, walking, hiking, and social club is specifically open for GLBT people, their
friends, and their families in the Tucson area, and they meet regularly. If you are not interested in a group hike but want tips on where to go, this group could be a helpful resource for
you as well. You can also visit www.gaytucson.com for updated information on group GLBT
hikes in and around Tucson.

Hiking in Sabino Canyon   Fred Hood © Metropolitan Tucson Convention & Visitors Bureau

Clothing-Optional Hiking and Sunbathing

MIRA VISTA RESORT

520-744-2355
7501 N. Wade Rd., Tucson, AZ 85743
Before becoming a clothing-optional spa in 2006, this secluded property was visited by such far-ranging historical personalities as Geronimo, John Wayne, Judy Garland, and Suzanne Somers. Now it is a family-oriented retreat for those who wish to leave their worries, and their clothes, behind. Some amenities include heated pools, complimentary wireless Internet, a covered spa, a tennis court, a full-service restaurant, a fitness center, massage treatment, and a gift shop. Day visitors are welcome.

TANQUE VERDE FALLS

520-749-8700
Sabino Canyon Recreation Area
5700 N. Sabino Canyon Rd., Tucson, AZ 85750
Located in the Santa Catalina Mountains of Tanque Verde, Arizona, just northeast of Tucson, the majestic Tanque Verde Falls have been known for attracting nude swimmers, sunbathers, and hikers. Explicit warnings of steep conditions and flash floods should be heeded: this area can be as dangerous as it is exquisite if not navigated carefully.

HORSEBACK RIDING

You might not feel like you've truly arrived in the American West until you've glimpsed a rider on horseback with a cowboy hat on her head. If that is the case—or if you'd like to see yourself in the saddle—consider one of the many Tucson equestrian centers in the area that cater to the needs of amateur and professional riders alike.

COWAN HORSE ADVENTURES

520-883-5529
www.cowanhorseadventures.com
5552 S. Beehive Ave., Tucson, AZ 85746

This team of experts have been to rodeos and led carriage rides in addition to their years of riding experience. A family-run business, Cowan caters to groups of four or fewer who would like to venture through the trails of Saguaro National Park West. If you have never ridden or would like to experience a horse-drawn adventure without mounting a saddle, consider one of their three-person carriages.

DIAMOND PARK RANCH

520-616-7194
www.diamondpkranch.com
11265 W. Orange Grove Rd., Tucson, AZ 85743

In addition to training horses, this small operation also trains people. Whether you have a horse or not, consider visiting this 100-by-100-foot arena for on-site lessons.

PUSCH RIDGE STABLES

520-825-1664

The desert on horseback James Randklev © Metropolitan Tucson Convention & Visitors Bureau

http://puschridgestables.com
13700 N. Oracle Rd., Tucson, AZ 85739

One of the most dynamic riding companies in the area, Pusch Ridge offers a variety of unique services, including accommodations for weddings, parties, Christmas caroling, Western theme events, and other special events. They will even prepare you for a horse-accompanied overnight. Their lessons can prepare you for driving, harnessing, hitching and handling, riding on a gaited horse, or even carriage driving and navigation. There is an affordable weekly after-school program and a year-round riding club as well.

SABINO EQUESTRIAN CENTER

520-886-6672
www.sabinoequestrian.com
4825 N. Paseo, Tucson, AZ 85750

This center, located in the Tucson foothills, caters to riders of all levels. They are especially equipped to help young or inexperienced riders, offering individual lessons and summer sessions. Check out the photos on their Web site to see just how polished a rider you could become. Trainer Tara Weber and her team work primarily with American saddlebred horses, and their scheduling is flexible. Sabino Equestrian also offers boarding, horse training, and sales.

TUCSON TRAIL RIDE

520-615-9898
www.trailride-tucson.net

For the experienced rider ready to set out immediately on the sandy washes and trails of southern Arizona, Tucson Trail Ride offers customized trips on their well-trained trio of horses—Zip, Sombrero, and Jesse.

IN-LINE SKATING

Visitors who enjoy in-line skating should consider a sunny afternoon of coasting along the long, flat expanse of Tucson's desert terrain. Local in-line skaters tend to utilize the paths at Reid Park (at Alvernon and 22nd Street), Santa Cruz River Walk (Silverlake and 22nd), Rillito River (between Craycroft and I-10), and Freedom Park (5000 East 29th Street). Skates can be bought or rented at a number of area businesses, including the following.

PETER GLENN SKI AND SPORTS

520-745-4514
www.peterglen.com
5626 E. Broadway Blvd., Tucson, AZ 85711

This national sporting store will be able to fit you with new in-line skates, repair your old ones, or provide you with the appropriate accessories for a beginner or seasoned skater.

PLAY IT AGAIN SPORTS

520-296-6888
www.playitagainsportstucson.com
Multiple locations

The three branches of this national chain will buy, sell, and trade new and used sports equipment. If you are looking for a discounted pair of high-quality skates, this could be your best bet.

PARKS AND PICNICKING

If you are looking to have a picnic but aren't up to making the hike to Coronado National Park, Sabino Canyon, or Mount Lemmon, consider visiting one of Tucson's metropolitan parks. Grassy areas with playgrounds, charcoal grills, and picnic tables can be found at most of the city's parks. Ramadas are available at select locations for group parties, weddings, and picnics—so long as a reservation is made ahead of time. Beer permits can be obtained for an $18 or $23 fee, sporting fields or courts can be reserved, and live or amplified music is permitted with approval from the Parks and Recreation director. For a complete list of parks, permit information, or to make a reservation, visit the City of Tucson

Parks and Recreation Web site at www.tucsonaz.gov/parksandrec. A listing of a few of the more popular parks in the city follows.

ARMORY PARK

221 S. Sixth Ave., Tucson, AZ 85701
Hours: Daily 6 AM–10 PM

Complete with a band shell, picnic tables, and shuffleboard courts, this park is located where the military guarding the Tucson Presidio was once stationed. Now it stands along-side the Armory Senior Center and is home to many of Tucson's annual festivals.

CATALINA PARK

900 N. Fourth Ave., Tucson, AZ 85705
Hours: Daily 7 AM–dusk

Visitors who are wandering around the university may find their way to this park, one of Tucson's oldest. Often the site of candlelight vigils and memorial services, this centrally located park has a picnic area, playground, and a wading pool open during the summer.

DE ANZA PARK

1000 N. Stone Ave., Tucson, AZ 85705
Hours: Daily 7 AM–dusk

De Anza, a former cemetery, has all the amenities of a city park, in addition to a large, lit, sand volleyball court. There are traces of history lining the perimeter of this vestige of Tucson's past, as shown in the wall made from lava rock that remains standing from the park's initial opening in 1872.

HIMMEL PARK

1000 N. Tucson Blvd., Tucson, AZ 85716
Hours: Daily 6 AM–10:30 PM

If reading in the sun while children play, dogs cavort, and families barbecue in the background is your idea of a pleasant afternoon, consider visiting this centrally located park. Nestled up against a branch of the Pima Public Library that shares this park's name, the 26.36-acre area contains public art, tall palm and olive trees, soccer fields, a basketball court, an exercise course, and a children's play area. After a picnic, you may enjoy strolling down Third Street to get a taste of the surrounding historic Sam Hughes neighborhood. Beautiful homes line this broad avenue, often used by student cyclists en route to the university down the street.

LA PLACITA GAZEBO

119 W. Broadway Blvd., Tucson, AZ 85701
Hours: Daily 6 AM–10:30 PM

Weddings and ceremonies often take place in this historic area, located around a centuries-old gazebo in Tucson's downtown. If you're in town for the gem show and find yourself spending time at the Tucson Convention Center, this palm-surrounded park will be well worth the short walk.

REID PARK

520-791-4873
1030 S. Randolph Way, Tucson, AZ 85716
Hours: Daily 6 AM–10:30 PM

This is one of Tucson's largest parks, and it attracts joggers, dogs, and children, as well as those gathering to celebrate birthdays and other events, on a daily basis. You can wander through the huge eucalyptus and pine trees, over a grass-covered field, until you find the perfect picnic spot, perhaps taking in the unusual sounds of a desert waterfall flowing into the lake near the park's middle. Not unlike the Parisian Luxembourg Gardens, this park's water feature is dotted by toy boats. Ducks and other waterfowl wander the terrain. There is free programming in the DeMeester Performance Center, quite a few ramadas to reserve for private gatherings, two nearby golf courses, an enclosed dog run, and, of course, the Reid Park Zoo. (See the *Family Fun* section earlier in this chapter for information on the zoo.)

Rock Climbing

There are two ways to do it—indoors or out. Tucson has a strong, dedicated community of climbers who practice indoors during the week and set out on weekends for adventures in the wild. Experienced visitors can go straight to 9,157-foot Mount Lemmon to enjoy the 1,200 climbing routes; beginners eager to climb can venture to the foothills for less-intensive bouldering. Some area gyms and fitness centers have rock walls, but for specialized indoor, community, or professional support, contact one of the following organizations.

ASPEN EXPEDITIONS

520-721-6751
www.aspenexpeditions.com

For a guided climb on Mount Lemmon's 1,200 climbing routes or the granite crags of Cochise Stronghold, contact Aspen Expeditions for a one-day trip. No need for equipment, just bring yourself. The AMGA-trained mountain guide will help beginners and encourage advanced climbers on their daily outings and can be contacted for private or group trips as well.

BUENA VISTA CLIMBING CLUB

520-730-3337
www.buenavistaclimbingclub.com
1145 N. Craycroft #101, Tucson, AZ 85712

This family-owned business has multiple operations under way, and they are currently constructing what will be Tucson's largest indoor climbing gym on the southeast side of the city. They also have an online shop of climbing equipment, where you can order from a selection of state-of-the-art gear after getting the advice of a seasoned professional. Contact them by phone for information on their guided climbs, or for more information on the Tucson climbing scene.

ROCKS AND ROPES

520-882-5924
www.rocksandropes.com
330 S. Toole Ave. #400, Tucson, AZ 85701

Children, beginners, and professionals alike come to Rocks and Ropes to satisfy their climbing needs. An indoor climbing gym near the business sector of downtown Tucson, this center offers specials for students, military folk, children, and families. Their mission is to "unfailingly teach and practice good stewardship of the environment, positive community involvement, and development of the climbing community of the future," and you could not put yourself into more professional hands.

SOUTHWEST TREKKING

520-296-9661
http://swtrekking.com
P.O. Box 57714, Tucson, AZ 85732

In addition to bringing clients on hikes, mountain biking trips, camping trips, and trail runs, this group of professionals offers expert assistance on climbing trips in more remote areas in southern Arizona and Mexico. Climbers of all experience levels can embark on a trip that might bring them to elevations of 3,000 to 9,000 feet in the Santa Catalina Mountains. Southwest Trekking offers individual and group rates, and equipment rentals. Check out their Web site for more information on their canyoneering course and the multitude of other outdoor services available "for those who indulge in extremes."

RUNNING

Each December, visitors and residents come together for the **Tucson Marathon** (www .tucsonmarathon.com), which takes runners on a sweeping tour of the city and its surrounding areas. Not only does the terrain of Tucson make the marathon feasible for amateurs, the slight decline will likely improve running times for veterans looking for bragging rights. The 2009 marathon, for example, goes down almost 2,200 feet in elevation after its start in Oracle, just north of Tucson, at which point it follows the Santa Catalina Mountain range, descends through Catalina, and ends just north of Oro Valley. If what runners have declared "one of the prettiest courses in the country" does not entice you, however, you may enjoy running around the perimeter of Reid Park (see *Parks and Picnicking* earlier in this chapter), down the 4.9-mile Rillito River Walk (accessible at River Road and Campbell Avenue), or along a path of your own.

RUN.COM

www.run.com

Though it does not cater specifically to Tucson, Run.com has a fantastic, up-to-date listing of new routes available to runners in different areas of the world. Simply navigate to the Tucson page of this Web site to see where residents have forged new paths for their running routines, or to find out whether there is new information about construction and other potential changes on existing routes.

THE RUNNING SHOP

520-325-5097
http://runningshopaz.com
3055 N. Campbell Ave., Tucson, AZ 85719

Stone massage   Fred Hood © Metropolitan Tucson Convention & Visitors Bureau

If you are looking for a Cinderella fit for your running feet, check out the selection at the Running Shop. Employees are sensitive to the needs of runners, walkers, joggers, and marathoners. Running apparel, accessories, and other shoe-related products are also available.

SOUTHERN ARIZONA ROADRUNNERS

www.azroadrunners.org

This Web site provides information on running groups, routes, races, volunteer opportunities, and special occasions for the southern Arizona running world. New posts are constantly being added with information about upcoming events. There is a comprehensive list of links available to national running organizations, publications, and Web sites. For directions to the best places to run in Tucson, take a look at the "Places to Run in Tucson" section.

SPAS

Visitors come from afar to experience the health benefits of Tucson's arid, sunny climate. The quiet calm found just miles away from the city's center, along with breathtaking sunsets and a serene landscape, add to the medicinal effect of this Southwestern atmosphere. Resorts offer short- and long-term opportunities for visitors to regain a sense of composure through treatments, activities, and courses that cater specifically to physical and psychological well-being, while day spas give residents and vacationers a glimpse of the good life by offering a few hours of serenity. With such a naturally serene environment to work with, the city's spas have a slightly unfair advantage compared to their national competitors.

Resorts

CANYON RANCH
520-749-9000
www.canyonranch.com
8600 E. Rockliff Rd., Tucson, AZ 85750

Though it has sister spas in Massachusetts and Florida, the Canyon Ranch facility in Tucson is known for being one of a kind. Located in the northeast foothills, this resort suspends its visitors in an oasis of beauty. One-story lodgings are nestled into the landscape, decorated with a Southwestern style that blends into the surrounding colors and textures of the desert. In keeping with its mission to promote health, there are limited areas for smoking, and alcohol is not permitted in public or sold anywhere on the premises. Food served at Canyon Ranch has been prepared by a team of chefs and nutritionists to ensure that each (mostly vegetarian) dish is packed with disease-preventing ingredients and that taste meets high gourmet standards. As for day-to-day activities, a wide-ranging array of programming is available for everyone's fitness needs. Yoga, boot camp, aquatic therapy, and outdoor hikes and bike rides can help invigorate the body through cardiovascular activity, while facials, massage, tarot card readings, and counseling are available to soothe the soul. Specialists from around the world are available for consultations about diet, nutrition, and health, as well as spiritual and psychological issues. Because this is a popular destination for visitors and residents alike, you'll want to make a reservation as far in advance as possible. Spa services are available only to guests of the resort.

JW MARRIOTT STARR PASS RESORT
520-792-3500
www.jwmarriottstarrpass.com
3800 W. Starr Pass Blvd., Tucson, AZ 85745

On the Web site for the JW Marriott Starr Pass Resort, you will be welcomed with tantalizing music and a bold statement: "Something amazing has arrived." And visitors seem to agree. Everything from the hotel's welcoming lobby and Western decor to the attentive staff has been highly praised. This may be a good choice if you are in a social mood, looking for more than just a mellow respite—special occasions are specifically catered to by this award-winning destination. Weddings, corporate retreats, and other group trips are met with a variety of special rooms and resources, such as discounted rates, catering, specialized technology for lectures and events, a business center, and more. What is perhaps most impressive about Starr Pass is its commitment to environmental awareness and preservation. For example, 330 acres of the resort were donated to the Sonoran Desert for preservation in 2005, and the resort donates an impressive percentage of its profits to research initiatives that focus on maintaining Tucson's desert environment. Starr Pass has also partnered with the local Tohono O'odham Nation in an initiative to encourage organic farming and reduce Tucson's carbon footprint. The golf course attached to this resort utilizes reclaimed water,

Red Door Spa, Westin La Paloma

seafood is line caught, recycling is encouraged, and an organic garden supplies food to the on-site Primo Restaurant. Other amenities include the Hashani Spa, open to the public, which offers massage, facials, body treatments, Ayurvedic treatments, and a spa store; a fitness center; and a salon. In addition to Primo, an Italian eatery helmed by James Beard Award–winning chef Melissa Kelly, there are multiple options for dining, including the Salud bar, which is a tequila aficionado's dream.

MIRAVAL RESORT
1-800-232-3969
www.miravalresort.com
5000 E. Via Estancia Miraval, Tucson, AZ 85739

This 400-acre resort has been voted number one in the world by a most judicious panel of critics at *Travel + Leisure* magazine, SpaFinder, and *Condé Nast Traveler*. You have the option of staying in one of 118 exquisitely decorated rooms located in the foothills of the Catalina Mountains, at the center of which you'll find a sleep-inducing bed with a plush feather mattress. After bathing with the signature line of Cactus Cream bath products, you'll be tempted to stay in your room, where you can put on a velour bathrobe to lounge in while you watch an LCD television, utilize the complimentary Internet, or listen to the radio through state-of-the-art Bose speakers. But leaving will do you good. You have the option of relaxing in one of the outdoor treatment rooms, baking in a sauna, or sweating out toxins in a steam room at the resort's world-class spa. The Olympic lap pool, Pilates studio, and standard array of gym equipment will keep your blood flowing, as will the outdoor challenge course. For the less aerobic, there are pools equipped for a peaceful float, with waterfalls and acupressure stone walks underfoot. Spiritual needs can be met at the Agave yoga center, or in the Zen and desert gardens. Customer service at Miraval is key, so rest assured that the conscientious staff will help you to remain "in the moment" during your stay. You'll dine on seasonal, locally grown, organic produce and naturally raised meats, all cooked to perfection by an expert culinary team. Corporate retreats and other group trips are happily accommodated. Spa services are available only to guests of the resort.

WESTIN LA PALOMA RESORT & SPA

520-742-6000
www.westinlapalomaresort.com
3800 E. Sunrise Dr., Tucson, AZ 85718

Every room at La Paloma is seeped in luxury. All guests will enjoy a private balcony or patio, wireless Internet, an oversize closet, and a "Heavenly Bed." Some suites also include a fireplace for those cool Tucson winter nights, a sunken spa tub, and a conference table. Wedding ceremonies and receptions are easily accommodated by the expansive property, and indoor and outdoor banquet facilities are available for parties that range in size from 10 to 650. Guests will enjoy the privacy of La Paloma's country club, as well as the Jack Nicklaus signature 27-hole golf course. The Red Door Spa, open to the public, is equipped with Elizabeth Arden products and offers unique services like a shea butter body melt, antiaging facial, eucalyptus sauna, and European steam rooms. This resort has been proclaimed the best Westin in the entire world, winning awards from AAA, *Condé Nast Traveler,* and *Golf Digest* and other magazines. Magazines that cater specifically to a corporate readership have praised La Paloma for its accommodations for conferences, conventions, and meetings. Check out their Web site for special discounts and reservations.

Day Spas

While some of the aforementioned resorts have spas that are open for day visits, there are other locations around town that cater solely to individual appointments for massage, facials, and other spa services.

ELEMENTS IN BALANCE

520-623-3804
www.elementsinbalance.com
614 N. Fourth Ave., Tucson, AZ 85705
Hours: Mon. and Sat. 9–5; Tues. through Fri. 9–7

Voted Tucson's best day spa and hair salon by *Tucson Weekly* readers in 2008, this centrally located facility specializes in "total tranquility." This is the place to come if you need some physical rejuvenation, to heal from an injury, or an uplifting new look. A host of trained massage therapists will morph your body back into balance with specialized massages including deep tissue, hot stone, ancient Hawaiian, chakra balancing, fusion stone, prenatal, and foot reflexology. Enjoy lavender, mint, and herbal body wraps as well. Hair, skin, and nail services are available, ranging from the simplest shampoo or trim to a full-body, prewedding makeover.

GADABOUT SALON SPAS

520-325-0000
www.gadabout.com
Multiple locations
Hours: Wed. and Sat. 7–6; Tues., Thurs., and Fri. 7 AM–8 PM

The Gadabout spa corporation has six locations in Tucson and one in Italy. The emphasis here is on beauty, with a 20-page list of services for men and women including skin hydration, eyelash extensions, hair coloring, waxing, massage, manicures, pedicures, and facials. This company is not all about looks, however. Gadabout also participates with local organizations like the Boys and Girls Club, SAAF, the United Way, the Humane Society, and the American Cancer Society to make the community of Tucson and the world beyond it a better place.

TOUCH OF TRANQUILITY SPA

520-615-9608
http://touchoftranquility.com
6884 E. Sunrise, Ste. 150, Tucson, AZ 85750

If you wish you could feel the sense of escape offered by a resort but don't have the time or money, drive up to the foothills to visit this day spa for a procedure and for the breathtaking view. Nestled close to the Catalina Mountains, this spa specializes in treatments for men and women that include brine light therapy, water therapy, alpine herbal steam therapy, massage, facials, hand and foot therapy, body wraps, and waxing. While some focus may be on the beauty of the body, for the most part Touch of Tranquility concentrates on improving the soul. By using "the magic of touch and crystal clear waters," the folks at this day spa seek to offer "a perspective of vigor and joy."

TENNIS

Whether you're interested in watching the women's team at the University of Arizona or seeking to improve your backhand, Tucson is a good place for tennis lovers. There are stores specifically geared toward racquet sports, academies aimed at crafting future champions, and public centers for casual games among friends. Except for a few weeks in the height of summer, when you may wish to wait for evening to start shouting "love," weather is no enemy to sports in this city. Outdoor courts can be used all year long.

EL TENISTA SOCCER AND TENNIS

520-323-6070
4817 E. Speedway Blvd., Tucson, AZ 85712
Hours: Mon. through Sat. 9–6; Sun. 10–3

This centrally located store is a good place to stop for tennis footwear, accessories, equipment, and, for the seasoned player, racquet repair.

FORT LOWELL TENNIS CENTER

520-791-2584
www.tucsontennis.com
2900 N. Craycroft Rd., Tucson, AZ 85712

This center is the place to call for tennis-themed birthday parties for children, junior and adult classes, city tennis leagues, tournaments, senior programs, and even just a few rounds with the ball machine. Costs are reasonable, and the service is professional and comprehensive.

HIMMEL PARK TENNIS CENTER

520-791-3276
1000 N. Tucson Blvd., Tucson, AZ 85716

Himmel is one of the nicest parks in Tucson, and tennis players come at all hours of the day to enjoy the camaraderie at the eight courts and the family-friendly setting. You'll find Himmel Park to be consistently populated with dogs frolicking on the hills and children playing in the nearby playground, and it's a safe environment even at night. Nonresidents are welcome to use the tennis facilities, but rates are cheaper for Tucsonans. You can reserve a court for two or three hours; call ahead of time.

RANDOLPH TENNIS CENTER

520-791-4896
www.randolphtenniscenter.com
50 S. Alvernon Way, Tucson, AZ 85711

Playing tennis in the desert Gill Kenny
© Metropolitan Tucson Convention & Visitors Bureau

With 25 lighted tennis courts and 10 lighted racquetball courts, this public tennis facility boasts that is the Southwest's largest, and it has won the U.S. Tennis Association's Outstanding Tennis Facility Award. There are clinics and private lessons, tournaments, leagues, and periodic charity events such as the Gooter Grand Slam of 2009. Check out their Web site for information on area services and resources, and also for articles about the national tennis community.

TUCSON RACQUET AND FITNESS CLUB

520-795-6960
www.tucsonracquetclub.com
4001 N. Country Club, Tucson, AZ 85716

Since 1967, the Tucson Racquet and Fitness Club has offered its services to families and pros alike. They are open 24 hours a day and have a 20-acre riverside area for members. There are 33 lighted tennis courts and numerous other services for fans of other racquet sports. There are also all the amenities of a great gym, including Jacuzzis, a steam room, a weight room, massage and skin care services, and child care. Summer camp programming is also available.

UNIVERSITY OF ARIZONA ATHLETICS

www.arizonaathletics.com

Visit this Web site for information on home-game tennis matches and other university sporting events.

Yoga, Pilates, and Personal Training

Whether it's baseball teams in town for training or college students who have come to play for the university team, Tucson tends to attract athletes, but the city also helps to create new athletes by offering an environment so accommodating to physical activity. For those seeking to stay in shape or to get into shape, there are centers that specialize in Pilates, personal training, and yoga.

Personal Training

The gyms in this city all have staff members who are oriented toward personal training; however, there are a few stand-alone organizations that specialize in one-on-one physical fitness.

BETTER BODIES

520-318-3488
www.betterbodiestucson.com
Multiple locations

This training facility will tailor your personal fitness program to your ultimate goals, so if you are interested in improving your golf skills, for example, they will gear your exercises to fit the golfer's necessary skill set. There are traditional elements of the common gym to utilize as well.

FITNESS BOOT CAMP

520-323-3488
www.ppttucson.com
Multiple locations

The Precision Personal Training centers dispense with the frills of a gym and focus in on the main objective: "accountability, motivation, structure, nutrition." Not only will you be forced into shape by your personal trainer, you will be given the tools to continue your fitness regime long after the relationship with your trainer has ended.

SWAT PERSONAL TRAINING

520-579-6791
www.swatfitness.com
Multiple locations

The team at Strength Wellness Athletic Training (SWAT) is led by personal trainers Ron and Jana Holland. You can choose from one-on-one, small group, and 12-week transformation programs, depending on your individual goals. Information on nutrition and even fitness journals all contribute to the phenomenal degree of success attained by most SWAT clients. Check out the testimonials on their Web site for inspiration.

URBAN ATHLETICS BOOT CAMP

520-235-6006

www.urbanathleticsbootcamp.com
1740 E. Hendrick, Tucson, AZ 85719

Paul Rose and Naomi Reed boast almost three decades of fitness experience, and they are knowledgeable not only about cardiovascular exercise and aerobics, but nutrition as well. Their small-group classes bring you out into the desert for training, ensuring one-on-one assistance as well as a team of comrades to encourage you.

Pilates

As with personal training, Pilates is offered at numerous gyms around town, but if you are searching for a more concentrated approach to the philosophies and practices of Pilates, you may want to visit a studio that specializes in its unique movements. Consider some of the following options.

ANDERSON PILATES

520-886-4843
www.andersonpilates.com
5989 E. Grant Rd., Ste 102, Tucson, AZ 85712

An accomplished ballet dancer, director Tracie Munn brings decades of Pilates and dance experience to the classes she teaches in this centrally located studio. Her team of teachers all work in tandem to create a loving environment for all who wish to join.

CORWORX STUDIO

520-344-9494
www.corworxstudio.com
3505 S. Desert Lantern Rd., Tucson, AZ 85735

The staff at Corworx teaches more than five hundred exercises on unique equipment. They offer periodic discounts and, at times, a complimentary orientation session to initiate newcomers to their Pilates philosophy.

TUCSON PILATES BODY STUDIO

520-834-2399
www.thepilatesbodystudio.com
11115 N. La Canada Dr., Ste. 201, Oro Valley, AZ 85737

This studio, written up by the *Arizona Daily Star,* specializes in both classical and contemporary Pilates. Their studio is meant to provide "a serene mind-body destination for the overall health and well-being of your body." They offer both group and private sessions at a beautiful location just north of Tucson.

Yoga

Internationally renowned yoga instructors teach at Tucson's many yoga studios, making this southwestern city a great place to practice yoga. You can even train at the Providence Institute to become a teacher. While you can find yoga classes at local gyms that are oriented toward fitness, these yoga studios will help educate you on the meditation, chanting, and spiritual aspects of this centuries-old lifestyle that offers much more than flexibility and strength.

BIKRAM'S YOGA COLLEGE OF INDIA NORTHWEST TUCSON

520-229-9642
www.bikramyogatucson.com
6261 N. Oracle, Tucson, AZ 85704

According to his Web site, when Bikram Choudhury was 12 years old, he became the youngest national yoga champion of India. After a crippling accident at age 20, he was able to regain his mobility through a series of yoga poses. Based on the series that Choudhury designed for himself at that time, the Bikram Yoga College of India Northwest specializes in working in and creating heat. During one of the 90-minute classes, students perform 26 postures and two breathing exercises in a heated room to improve joint, muscle, tendon, organ, gland, and ligament function. While this asana practice introduces new students to the fundamentals of yoga, it's also a nice workout for those looking to transition to a cardio-heavy yoga regime.

PROVIDENCE INSTITUTE

520-323-0203
www.providenceinstitute.com
3400 E. Speedway, Ste. 114, Tucson, AZ 85716

In addition to services in massage, personal training, and body therapy, this institute holds well-regarded classes in yoga. Students can choose from a variety of methods, including Anusara, Hatha, hot room, prenatal, restorative, Vinyasa, Yin, and Taoist classes. Some teachers have areas of expertise in certain methods, providing specialized classes for women, seniors, and certain parts of the body. Memberships of various levels of commitment are available, and discounts are offered periodically. Visit their Web site for more information.

TUCSON YOGA

520-988-1832
www.tucsonyoga.com
150 S. Fourth Ave., Tucson, AZ 85701

Ranked the best in the city by *Tucson Weekly* every year since 2005, Tucson Yoga offers bare-bones practice minus too many bells and whistles but with experienced teachers. Come here to practice Yin, Vinyasa, mindfulness, and gentle yoga or participate in some of the weekend retreats or seminars in meditation and other facets of yoga. Prices here are exceptionally reasonable, all levels are welcome, and membership opportunities are various.

YOGA FLOW

520-321-9648
www.yogaflowtucson.com
3131 N. Cherry Ave., Tucson, AZ 85719

Courses at Yoga Flow blend conventional yoga stretches and breathing exercises with spirituality, Thai massage, and acrobatics. Choose from classes in AcroYoga, Ashtanga, Hatha, Mysore, and Shakti. Yoga practitioners of various ages and ability levels are welcome, discounts are offered for students, and various membership opportunities are available.

YOGA OASIS

520-322-6142
www.yogaoasis.com
Multiple locations

Yoga Oasis has a modern atmosphere, with discounted rates during "happy hour" at lunch or in the evening. All instructors are expertly trained and certified according to the most rigorous standards in the world of yoga. Courses for beginners and experienced practitioners are available at the two branches in eastern and central Tucson. Classes focused specifically on meditation, devotional chants, and song are offered in addition to a range of conventional yoga methods.

2 HOUR PARKING 8AM-6PM

Fourth Avenue shopping

7

Shopping

Fab Finds

When it comes to shopping, there are more shops and stores awaiting discovery in Tucson than any one guidebook can cover—and that's as it should be. After all, Tucson is a thriving community made up of dozens of distinct neighborhoods and historic barrios, many of which are home to offbeat shops, intimate boutiques, working artist studios, and artisan showrooms. Old Town Artisans, tucked away in the El Presidio Historic District near downtown Tucson, is a wonderful example of this kind of neighborhood-specific shopping experience. This 150-year-old adobe building, once the site of an 18th-century Spanish fort, now houses a small but unique collection of shops and galleries, each offering traditional pottery, glass, Native American jewelry, and Southwest-inspired clothing. All of this in what is Tucson's oldest neighborhood—12 blocks of Mexican adobe row houses, many dating between the mid-19th century and 1912, the year of Arizona's statehood.

While the majority of the marketplaces in and around Tucson can't boast the historical significance of El Presidio, over the years many neighborhoods around the city have become distinct shopping districts in their own right. On and around Congress Street is the Downtown Arts District, home to dozens of galleries and museums, artist studios, and co-ops, while just a few blocks away, along Tucson's funky Fourth Avenue, vintage clothing boutiques and secondhand bookstores stand side by side with bars, coffeehouses, and restaurants, many of them local favorites. South of the university, shoppers looking for imports would do well to check out one of the city's hidden gems, Tucson's Lost Barrio. This 3-block row of old brick and adobe warehouses on South Park Avenue once housed fruits and vegetables coming from Mexico until the buildings were converted into 11 distinct shops, each specializing in imported antiques, rustic furniture, architectural elements, folk art, and home furnishings from Mexico and around the world. There is also a concentration of showrooms on the northeast side of town (between Tucson and Dodge boulevards) that makes up Tucson's Fort Lowell furniture district, as well as dozens of smaller antiques stores peddling collectibles and memorabilia along Grant Avenue between Campbell Avenue and Craycroft Road.

Spanish- and Mexican-inspired courtyards, shaded breezeways, and tiled fountains characterize the ambience of many of Tucson's ritzier shopping plazas. For those with more expensive tastes, St. Philip's Plaza, Plaza Palomino, and Casas Adobes Plaza mingle fine-dining restaurants beside art galleries, salons, and custom boutiques offering everything from original couture for men and women to artisanal jewelry to Southwestern crafts and

Wares for sale in the border town of Nogales, Mexico David Jewell © Metropolitan Tucson Convention & Visitors Bureau

stylish home furnishings. Or take the scenic drive up through the foothills of the Santa Catalinas to one of Tucson's newest shopping destinations, La Encantada. Designed to invoke the traditional open-air *mercados* (Spanish for "market") of Mexico, La Encantada is a gorgeous outdoor mall featuring stunning views of Tucson, an enormous outdoor stone fireplace, and an eclectic mix of locally owned boutiques and upscale retailers.

Like all cities, Tucson is also home to its share of outlet malls on the northern and southern edges of town. While care has been taken in this section to pay more attention to those businesses that are independent and locally owned—the kind shops and stores unique only to Tucson—a few chain stores have been thrown into the mix, too. In the *Malls, Plazas, and Shopping Centers* section in this chapter you'll find information about the Tucson Mall, Park Place Mall, and Catalina Foothills Mall, each of which is filled with literally hundreds of smaller outlets, big-box chains, and such major department stores as Sears, Macy's, and JCPenney.

This section merely begins to highlight those shops and stores around town that make Tucson exceptional among cities of the Southwest. Sometimes silly, sometimes sophisticated, the businesses listed in this chapter distinguish themselves through the thoughtfulness of their service and the quality and uniqueness of their merchandise. If there's any advice a guidebook like this can offer, it is, above all, this—explore Tucson for yourself. Don't be shy; ask around. And never fear the advice that takes you off the beaten trail.

ANTIQUES

Throughout Tucson's storied history, all kinds of people have come and gone, leaving behind a rich, complicated cultural heritage, the fruits of which can be seen in the studios and showrooms of the dozens of antiques stores in and around the city. When it comes to fine antiques, Tucson boasts galleries and showrooms second to none, many of which offer exquisite Native American arts, crafts, and relics, as well as centuries-old Spanish Colonial and Mexican furnishings and architectural elements, many of which combine simple, solid construction with the more baroque ornamentation exported from Europe. More modest collectors of memorabilia, kitsch, and Southwestern collectibles won't be disappointed either. Dozens of smaller shops across Tucson and along Grant Avenue's "antiques row" carry everything from vintage postcards to Depression glass.

American Antiques Mall (520-326-3070; www.americanantiquemall.com; 3130 E. Grant Rd.) More than one hundred consignors under one roof, showcasing a wide variety of collectibles and memorabilia, including costume jewelry, carnival glassware, fine porcelain, sterling silverware, as well as first-edition books and furniture.

Copper Country Antiques (520-326-0167; www.coppercountryantiques.com; 5055 E. Speedway Blvd.) This sprawling, 32,000-square-foot multidealer emporium has all the feel of the best indoor flea market—meaning with a keen eye and a little leg work, you can find just about anything you're looking for. It's also the only antiques store in Tucson with its own "bistro."

Designers Craft (520-629-9711; www.designerscraft.com; 3006 E. Grant Rd.) This small shop features all manner of architectural elements, such as teak doors, panels, sideboards, gates, panels, benches, and writing desks—each piece hand selected by owner Michael Midkiff during his buying trips to India, China, and Thailand.

Eric Firestone Gallery (520-577-7711; www.ericfirestonegallery.com; 4425 N. Campbell Ave.) Specializes in 20th-century American paintings; American Arts and Crafts furniture by Stickley, Limbert, and Roycroft; and metalware, pottery, and works from Arizona artists of the early 20th century.

La Buhardilla (520-622-5200; www.buhardilla.com; 2360 E. Broadway Blvd.) Spanish for "attic," Buhardilla is packed with Mexican and Latin American antiques, some dating as far back as the 16th century.

Morning Star Antiques (520-881-2121; www.morningstartraders.com; 2020 E. Speedway Blvd.) Showcases 17th- and 18th-century Spanish Colonial antiques and rustic Mexican furniture, including trasteros, butcher's tables, Mennonite hutches, and mesquite doors and chests. An adjacent second store, **Morning Star Traders** specializes in exquisite Native American arts and crafts, including Pueblo pottery, hand-dyed Navajo rugs, kachinas, and finely crafted Zuni and Hopi jewelry.

Tom's Fine Furniture & Collectibles (520-795-5210; 5454 E. Pima Rd.) Offering high-end Mexican and Spanish Colonial antiques and home furnishings, Tom's also purchases the best estate sale items, like lamps and lighting fixtures, china, crystal, and silver. Because wares here are always changing, there's always something new at this local favorite.

Books & Music

Tucson has always been home to writers and musicians, and a home away from home to those artists just passing through—as well as to the dedicated audiences who appreciate both at the many readings and concerts that take place throughout the city. As such, Tucsonans take great pride in supporting locally owned book and music stores—many of them small, secondhand shops—which, despite the rise of the Internet and the big chain stores, continue to thrive. Among the following are a number of local favorites, as well as a couple of the more, well, usual suspects.

Books

Antigone Books (520-792-3715; www.antigonebooks.com; 411 N. Fourth Ave.) Don't let its self-described "feminist slant" fool you. Yes, Antigone has a wide selection of books by, for, and about women, but it also features thoughtfully selected gay, lesbian, and transgender titles; mainstream fiction and nonfiction; and children's titles; as well as books by local writers and presses. An eclectic (and often whimsical) selection of cards, bumper stickers, coffee mugs, buttons, and T-shirts rounds out the offerings. Antigone also hosts readings and signings by local and national writers throughout the year.

Barnes & Noble (www.bn.com; 520-742-6402, 7325 N. La Cholla Blvd. #100; 520-512-1166, 5130 E. Broadway Blvd.) Though Tucsonans favor their independent bookstores, sometimes an in-house coffee bar and a plush, overstuffed reading chair is what serious book browsing demands.

Bookmans Entertainment Exchange (www.bookmans.com; 520-325-5767, 1930 E. Grant Rd.; 520-579-0303, 3733 W. Ina Rd.; 520-748-9555, 6230 E. Speedway Blvd.) If Barnes & Noble or Borders bought, sold, and traded used books, magazines, DVDs, CDs, and video games, they'd call the place Bookmans, by far the biggest and best store for secondhand books and entertainment in Tucson. This store has excellent selections in affordable paperback classics, cooking, poetry, biography, and science fiction, among others.

The Book Stop (520-326-6661; www.bookstoptucson.com; 214 N. Fourth Ave.) A casual browser's dream, the Book Stop offers the quintessential secondhand-bookstore experience—handwritten signs, makeshift shelving, the sweet smell of aging paperbacks, and always the chance that you'll find that book you never knew you were looking for until you've found it. A great source for rare first and out-of-print editions.

Borders Books & Music (www.borders.com; 520-584-0111, 5870 E. Broadway Blvd. #448; 520-292-1331, 4235 N. Oracle Rd.) Like discounts on *New York Times* best sellers, there's something about mile after mile of brand new, unspoiled books that never gets old. Unlike Barnes & Noble, Borders also sells music.

Clues Unlimited (520-326-8533; www.cluesunlimited.com; 123 S. Eastbourne) With more than 15,000 titles in stock and all of them in the mystery and detective genres, at Clues Unlimited there's no limit to where you can seek the latest page-turner. Whether it's a recent release, a hard-to-find collectible, or a rare import from afar, if Clues doesn't have it, they'll track it down for you.

Crescent Tobacco Shop & Newsstand (520-622-1559, 200 E. Congress St.; 520-296-3102, 7037 E. Tanque Verde Rd.) Pay no mind to the unremarkable exterior. With more than eight thousand titles, this shop is one of the best places in town to find the widest selection of local, national, and foreign newspapers; mainstream and niche magazines; as well as more obscure journals of art and culture.

University of Arizona Bookstore (520-621-2426; 1209 E. University Blvd.) In addition to college textbooks, popular and classic fiction, the latest nonfiction, and university para-phernalia like T-shirts, jackets, and shorts, the U of A Bookstore distinguishes itself from other bookstores around town by devoting generous shelf space to faculty publica-tions, as well as to the work (much of it signed) of the many guest writers, speakers, and scholars who visit the university every year.

Music

Chicago Music Store (520-622-3341; www.chicagomusicstore.com; 130 E. Congress St.) A favorite of local bands and touring acts alike, this landmark of Tucson's downtown is more emporium than store, and it's been buying, selling, trading, and repairing all manner of musical instruments since 1919.

Rainbow Guitars (520-325-3376; www.rainbowguitars.com; 2550 N. Campbell Ave.) For more than 30 years, Rainbow has been Tucson's best vintage guitar shop. Rainbow deals in everything from classic Fender and Gibson guitars to more recent models, both elec-tric and acoustic, new and used. It also offers brand-name amps, basses, keyboards, and drum kits. There's something here in every price range.

Toxic Ranch Records (520-623-2008; www.toxicranchrecords.com; 424 E. Sixth St.) Looking for an album by that obscure, underground punk band you once slammed to at CBGB's? Visit the record store "too tough to die." Toxic Ranch Records is the only place in Tucson devoted to all things hard-core, punk, industrial, and psychobilly, most of it on vinyl, some on CD.

Zia Record Exchange (www.ziarecords.com; 520-327-3340, 3370 E. Speedway Blvd.; 520-887-6898, 3655 N. Oracle Rd. #107) If you're unwilling to forsake a well-scuffed, well-stocked record store staffed by music savants for the anonymous online ease of downloading, Zia's the place for you. Indie rock, hip-hop, R&B, blues, jazz, classical—whatever your taste, Zia has it new and gently used.

CLOTHING

Women's

Butz (520-299-4220; 4330 N. Campbell Ave. #48) If you're on the hunt for the perfect jeans, this is the place for high-end denim. Butz features Citizens of Humanity, Gold-sign, and 575, as well as tops by Grail and Yvette Mandell.

Chico's (www.chicos.com; 520-797-1200, 7003 N. Oracle Rd.; 520-325-2422, 4811 E. Grant Rd. #107) Chico's offers elegant, moderately priced Southwestern fashions for women, including vibrant, ethnic-inspired prints and natural fabrics that are appropri-ate for work and casual wear.

Maya Palace (www.mayapalacetucson.com; 520-748-0817, 6332 E. Broadway Blvd.; 520-325-6411, 2960 N. Swan Rd. #133; 520-575-8028, 7057 N. Oracle Rd.) Consistently rated one of Tucson's best stores for sophisticated women's Southwestern chic, Maya Palace showcases vibrant clothing by Tianello, Anna Konya, Sole Ballare, and others. Maya also carries handbags, belts, shoes, and jewelry to complement any ensemble.

Piece by Piece (520-577-6392; www.piecebypiecewear.com; 4330 N. Campbell Ave., Ste. 54) Offers European street fashions that are ahead of the curve, including dresses, skirts, and separates by designers such as France's Cop Copine and Save The Queen.

Rochelle K Fine Women's Apparel (520-797-2279; 7039 N. Oracle Rd.) An upscale boutique where the emphasis is on youth and moxie. Whether you're looking for a little black dress or more sassy sundresses and separates, Rochelle K offers something for all ages.

W Boutique (520-577-3470; 4340 N. Campbell Ave. #185) Designer denim, short A-line silhouette dresses, cropped pants, stacks of tees, and the entire line of Trina Turk's latest designs—all of it available in a spare, no-frills setting.

Zoe Boutique (520-740-1201; www.zoestyle.com; 735 N. Fourth Ave.) This small women's boutique next to Epic Café would go unseen if not for the sassed-up mannequins in its display windows. One of Tucson's trendsetters, Zoe carries mostly skirts, separates, and blouses by designer lines like Plum, Rojas, Blue Marlin, and Juicy Couture.

Men's

Franklin Men's Store (520-747-0680; 5420 E. Broadway Blvd. #210) Franklin offers fine clothing and shoes for men, everything from suits and formal wear by Hugo Boss, Canali, and Zegna to a plentiful selection of casuals from Cole Haan and Tommy Bahama. On-site tailoring and wardrobe consulting are available.

The Landmark (520-623-3706; 876 E. University Blvd.) Sometimes a name says it all. A university landmark for more than 40 years, this shop does California cool at reasonable prices. Though there's a small section for women's clothing, most of items here (including jeans, shorts, polo shirts, button-downs, and T-shirts) are for men. Expect to find clothing brands like Polo, Lucky, and Quicksilver, and footwear by Vans, Reef, and Rainbow.

Men's Warehouse (www.menswarehouse.com; 520-696-9846, 90 W. River Rd.; 520-571-8231, 5628 E. Broadway Blvd.) In addition to suits, slacks, dress shirts, and ties from a broad range of popular lines, Men's Warehouse has expanded its offerings to include graphic tees, designer jeans, and athletic wear that should appeal to a younger, hipper clientele.

Alternative

Blaze Threads (520-882-6564; 317 N. Fourth Ave.) If it's sarcastic, obnoxious, ironic, or offensive, Blaze has it on T-shirts, hats, belt buckles, and baby's clothes. Located right next door to Majestic Tattoo Shop, Blaze also carries an extensive selection of body jewelry.

Firenze Boutique (520-299-2992; 2951 N. Swan Rd.) For the most discerning fashionistas, this foothills boutique offers an extensive selection of classic men's and women's haute couture, including Italian fashions by Zanella, Mondi, and Luciano Moresco.

Hydra (520-791-3711; 145 E. Congress St.) Fetish fashion at its best. In the market for something leather, rubber, or spiked? Nurturing a penchant for bondage or drag? Whatever your fetish, this downtown shop has it for both men and women, including club wear, camisoles, fringed chaps, corsets, biker jackets, and lingerie.

Southwestern

Arizona Hatters (520-292-1320; 2790 N. Campbell Ave.) Custom-fitted hats for both men and women by major label outfitters like Stetson, Resistol, and Milano, as well as full lines of Western shirts and belts. Cleaning, blocking, and restoring of new and used hats done on premises.

Dark Star Leather (520-881-4700; www.darkstarleather.com; 2940 N. Swan Rd.) This locally owned shop in Plaza Palomino features distinctive leatherwork for men and women, including one-of-a-kind jackets, belts, and purses.

Western Warehouse (520-327-8005; www.bootbarn.com; 4640 E. Broadway Blvd.) The largest store for Western wear in Tucson offers more than just boots. This place is a one-stop shop for Wrangler jeans, Sedona West and Carhartt button-downs, and Outback hats for both sexes.

Children

For those visiting Tucson with kids, or for those with a special child in their lives, no trip to Tucson would be complete without a stop at one of the many independently owned toy stores tucked away in the shopping centers and plazas around town. The following shops carry toys for kids of every age, from traditional hand-carved wood figurines to plush animals to offbeat novelties, electronics, and board games.

Kid Center (520-322-5437; www.e-kidscenter.com; 1725 N. Swan Rd.) From electronics to action figures, handmade to brand name, the Kid Center stocks toys of every kind for every age group.

Lil' Traders (520-881-8438; www.liltraders.com; 6216 E. Speedway Blvd.) Formerly Buffalo Kids, Lil' Traders buys, sells, and trades new and used children's clothes, toys, strollers, car seats, and cribs. Stock here tends to rotate with the seasons, but the styles are always hip, the condition of the clothing is always good, and the prices are always far below what you'd pay for new. Consistently rated one of Tucson's top resale stores for kids.

Mildred and Dildred (520-615-6266; www.mildredanddildred.com; 2905 E. Skyline Dr. #186) This small, upscale specialty boutique in the Tucson foothills, while expensive, carries collectible dolls, miniature figurines, tops, puppets, wooden toys, and books. Child-height play tables encourage parents and children to be hands-on in the store.

Mrs. Tiggy-Winkle's (520-326-0188; www.tiggytoysonline.com; 4811 E. Grant Road #151) In addition to playing host to in-store puppet shows, sing-alongs, and story times, this locally owned favorite is brimming with out-of-the-box board games, plush animals, hand-carved wooden toys, and everything in between. Trying toys out in the store is a must before taking something home.

Mudpies and Pigtails (520-319-7888; 2559 N. Campbell Ave.) The result of one artist's need to go public with her obsession of all things handmade, Monique Green's boutique has hair bows and barrettes, tutus, ribbons, onesies, blankets, and finger puppets, all hand sewn, much of it by the owner herself. Custom orders are also encouraged.

Yikes! Toys (520-320-5669; 2930 E. Broadway Blvd.) If there's no on-off switch, chances are you'll find it at Yikes! Shelves here are packed with more traditional toys, stuff like puppets, kites, pull toys, model kits, and sillier novelty items like whoopee cushions and potato guns.

GIFTS

You'd be remiss to visit Tucson and not bring back something for friends and family. Whether its ethnically inspired wares like traditional hand-painted *retablos* and Mexican

Chocolate Iguana is a great Fourth Avenue coffee shop.

crosses, more exotic gifts like endangered heirloom seeds and indigenous cacti, or edible gifts like wines or custom-made spice blends, there are gift ideas here to meet every whim and budget. The following are just a few of the Old Pueblo's more interesting shopping destinations.

Anthony's Cigar Emporium (www.anthonyscigar.com; 520-324-0303, 4811 E. Grant Rd.; 520-531-9155, 7866 N. Oracle Rd.) Leather lounge chairs and private lockers keep locals coming back to Anthony's year after year, so if it's the gift of fine tobacco you're after, step inside Anthony's walk-in humidor. From small-batch blends to more premium lines, individual cigars to whole boxes, Anthony's offers one of the widest selections of cigars in Tucson.

B & B Cactus Farm (520-721-4687; www.bandbcactus.com; 11550 E. Speedway Blvd.) This 2-acre nursery and greenhouse on the eastern outskirts of Tucson carries a stunning variety of cacti and succulents, many of which are cold-hardy and packed and shipped easily by B & B to anywhere in the country. In addition, the farm carries a selection of handmade Mexican pottery, desert gardening kits, hanging baskets, and garden art.

Blue Willow Gift Shop (520-327-7577; www.bluewillowtucson.com; 2616 N. Campbell Ave.) The gift shop that's really the lobby to a restaurant. Or is it the restaurant that's really a gift shop? Whatever it is, this small shop adjoins the Blue Willow restaurant and carries gifts that range from the silly to the saucy. The shelves here brim with offbeat greeting cards, whimsical figurines, kitschy trinkets, keepsakes, seasonal items, and locally made crafts.

Bohemia (520-882-0800; www.bohemiatucson.com; 2920 E. Broadway Blvd.) Bohemia calls itself an artisan's emporium, and for good reason. This shop is funky in the best sense of the word and showcases an eclectic mix of handmade perfume, artisanal jewelry, woodblock prints, and one-of-a-kind knickknacks.

Bon (520-795-2272, 3022 E. Broadway Blvd.; 520-615-7690, 4419 N. Campbell Ave.) A locally owned designer boutique featuring the latest trends in home decor, gardening, and fashion—all of it elegant, all of it hand selected by the mother-daughter team of Bonny and Crystal. Looking for a children's history of rock 'n' roll or that perfect gardening trowel? This store has a little bit of everything, making it one of the most popular stores of its kind in town.

Chocolate Iguana (520-798-1211; www.chocolateiguanaon4th.com; 500 N. Fourth Ave.) An espresso bar, a candy store, and a gourmet sandwich and sweets shop, the Chocolate Iguana also carries nostalgic children's toys and irreverent greeting cards for every occasion.

Flavorbank Spice Market (520-747-5431; www.flavorbank.com; 6372 E. Broadway Blvd.) Flavorbank is an epicure's dream. Exotic salts, spices, and aromatics from around the world are artfully arranged on wooden tables and sideboards and are sold by the pinch or the pound. Create your own custom mix, or consult the owners about one of their signature spice blends made in-shop with mortar and pestle.

Native Seeds SEARCH (520-622-5561; www.nativeseeds.org; 526 N. Fourth Ave.) If you're a gardener—or are looking for a gift for one—this local nonprofit conservation organization offers 350 varieties of heirloom seeds (many of them endangered) for a wide variety of Southwestern and Native American crops, as well as handmade prickly pear soaps, lavender salves, brazilwood dyes, and mole gift baskets.

Paper Paper Paper (520-326-3830; www.p3onlinecom; 3130 E. Fort Lowell Rd.) Found your gifts and now need to wrap them? Paper, Paper, Paper carries paper of every texture, pattern, and color imaginable. Unconventional gift wrap, letterpress stationary, origami paper, bookbinding materials, and wax letter-seal stamps are just some of the items you'll find here.

Pastiche Wine Shop (520-325-3333; www.pasticheme.com; 3025 N. Campbell Ave.) Adjacent to a restaurant of the same name, this gourmet shop carries imported cheeses, chocolates, wine jellies, personalized gift baskets, and more than six hundred different wines from around the world, many of them small-batch vintages from lesser-known vineyards.

Picante Boutique (520-320-5699; 2932 E. Broadway Blvd.) Specializes in folk art of the American Southwest and Mexico, featuring a fine collection of *retablos* (small images of Mexican-Catholic saints painted on tin or tile), *milagros* (small amulets used as votive offerings), Day of the Dead skeletons, and Mexican crosses.

The Rustic Candle Company (520-623-2880; www.rusticcandlecompany.com; 324 N. Fourth Ave.) The candles here are hand poured in-store every day and come in a variety sizes and one-of-a-kind scents like Boyfriend's Jacket, Sun-Dried Laundry, and Sugar Cookie. Southwest-inspired votive cups, candelabras, and sconces round out Rustic's offerings.

Santa Theresa Tile Works (520-623-1856; www.santatheresatileworks.com; 440 N. Sixth Ave.) A working ceramics studio and one of the best shops in town for hand-cut, hand-glazed mosaic-style tiles, inserts, borders, and solid-colored and decorative field tiles. Santa Theresa also offers do-it-yourself home and garden kits and how-to workshops.

Sarnoff Art and Writing (520-795-1229; www.sarnoffart.com; 2524 N. Campbell Ave.) "Staffed by artists, for artists." A favorite of local artists of every medium, this family-owned store carries everything from specialty pens and paints to architectural and graphic arts equipment.

Wilko (520-792-6684; www.wilkotucson.com; 943 E. University Blvd. #171) Part fair-trade coffee shop, part grocer, part wine shop, part jeweler, Wilko is a hip general store that carries a full line of ecofriendly products, including hip political T-shirts, organic beauty products, and letter-pressed greeting cards for every occasion.

HOME FURNISHINGS

Ask anyone where you can find home furnishings in Tucson, and inevitably you'll be urged to visit the Fort Lowell furniture district. And it's true, along this 3-block stretch of Fort Lowell Road, between Tucson and Dodge boulevards, you'll find a number of furniture showrooms, including Contents Interiors, Sunset Interiors, and Illuminations. But some of the most compelling home furnishing stores are smaller, more out-of-the-way operations run by local, globe-trotting entrepreneurs who travel the world, hand selecting the pieces that end up in their shops. The following are the best of the best.

Alexander's (520-323-0747; www.alexandersfurniture.net; 3525 E. Fort Lowell Rd.) This family-owned furniture showroom has been in business for more than 40 years and carries full lines of furniture for every room by such contemporary designers as Todd Oldham, Wesley Allan, and Sam Moore.

Asian Trade Rug Company (520-326-7828; www.gabbeh.com; 2623 N. Campbell Ave.) This company has more than 30 years' experience buying and selling new and antique handmade rugs, kilims, and other collectibles from around the world, including authentic Persian gabbeh. Cleaning, repair, and appraisals are also available.

Colonial Frontiers (520-622-7400; www.colonialfrontiers.com; 244 S. Park Ave., in the Lost Barrio) One of the must-see showrooms in the Lost Barrio, Colonial Frontiers has 13,000 square feet of antiques, including architectural elements, enormous armoires, unusual tables, long hardwood benches, and hand-carved folk art. On-site craftsmen restore or modify pieces to your specifications.

Copenhagen (www.copenhagentucson.com; 520-795-0316, 3660 E. Fort Lowell Rd.; 520-326-6491, 3648 E. Ajo Way) Located in the heart of Tucson's furniture district, Copenhagen features modern and contemporary designs that are sleek, efficient, and functional. There are furnishings here for every home or office.

Crate & Barrel (520-299-7100; www.crateandbarrel.com; 2905 E. Skyline Dr. #120) Among chain stores, this one has one of the largest selections of home furnishings and housewares around. From patterned flatware to writing desks, martini glasses to daybeds, Crate & Barrel's clean, contemporary aesthetics have made it a proven favorite for nearly two decades.

Eastern Living (520-299-3889; 212 S. Park Ave., in the Lost Barrio) Offerings include hand-selected pieces from China and the Far East, such as Ming Dynasty altars, 19th-century Chinese armoires, painted Mongolian chests, and a wide selection of brass and stone Buddhas.

Corner of Fourth Avenue and University Boulevard

Magellan Trading (520-622-4968; www.magellantraders.com; 1441 E. 17th St.) One of the most extensive stores of its kind in Tucson, Magellan carries furniture, crafts, and housewares imported from more than 35 countries, many bought by the owner, Kevan Daniel, during buying trips to Africa, Asia, New Guinea, Mexico, Central and South America, and Italy. Magellan also boasts the largest selection of mouth-blown Mexican glass in Arizona.

Pottery Barn (520-615-3470; www.potterybarn.com; 2905 E. Skyline Dr.) This high-end chain store in the Tucson foothills offers reliably tasteful furniture and furnishings.

Table Talk (www.tabletalk.com; 520-881-3322, 2936 E. Broadway Blvd.; 520-886-8433, 6842 E. Tanque Verde Rd.; 520-219-8232, 7876 N. Oracle Rd.; 520-733-6052, 7707 E. Broadway Blvd.) Locally owned and operated for more than 30 years, this store carries hand-crafted, solid hardwood furniture like buffets and cabinets, decorative home accents like mirrors and wall clocks, and one of the best collections of gourmet cookware this side of Williams-Sonoma.

Tres Amigos World Imports (www.tresamigosworldimports.com; 520-751-9776, 5975 E. Broadway Blvd.; 520-531-0090, 6431 N. Thornydale Rd.; 520-547-3247, 3616 E. Fort Lowell Rd.) If you're looking for rustic Mexican, Tuscan, Southwestern, or Spanish Colonial—style furniture and home furnishings, Tres Amigos has one of Tucson's largest selections, and at reasonable prices.

Fourth Avenue storefront window

Walter Gaby's Rug Resource (520-321-4272; www.rugresourcetucson.com; 3010 E. Broadway Blvd.) A rolling inventory of Southwestern, contemporary, and traditional area rugs for all price ranges.

Zocalo (520-320-1236; www.zocalonyc.com; 3016 E. Broadway Blvd.) Fine Spanish Colonial and Mexican furniture, Talavera pottery, hand-carved mirrors, chandeliers, and glassware, as well as pressed tin, pewter, and Mexican-styled religious art.

MALLS, PLAZAS, AND SHOPPING CENTERS

Casas Adobes Plaza (520-299-2610; www.casasadobesplaza.com; 7001–7153 N. Oracle Rd.) Spanish-style tile, shaded brick breezeways, and blooming bougainvillea complement the upscale ambience of Casas Adobes merchants. Here you'll find men's and women's fashion boutiques side by side with salons, jewelry galleries, a day spa, fine-dining restaurants, and Frost, Tucson's only gelato shop.

Catalina Foothills Mall (520-219-2444; www.shopfoothillsmall.com; 7401 N. La Cholla Blvd.) A high-end factory-outlet mall and shopping center with more than 90 retailers, among them a Nike Factory Store, a Saks Fifth Avenue Outlet, and a Haggar Clothing store, as well as a 15-screen multiplex theater, several restaurants, and the Thunder Canyon Brewery.

Fourth Avenue Historic Shopping District (between University Blvd. and Ninth St.) Tucson doesn't get any more Tucson than this 6-block stretch of Fourth Avenue. If you like to window-shop and people-watch, a leisurely stroll past Fourth Avenue's more than one hundred shops, bars, and restaurants (many of them local favorites) is a must. Here you'll find stores selling everything from vintage clothing to jewelry to Southwestern souvenirs. Twice a year (in the fall and spring), avenue merchants bring together local and national vendors of arts and crafts to fill the street with booths and exhibits for a three-day street fair—one of Tucson's premier events.

Kaibab Courtyard Shops (520-795-6905; 2837 N. Campbell Ave.) This collection of stores focuses on Southwestern design, everything from Native American art and jewelry to Mexican folk art Nambé, Talavera, Zapotec rugs, and rustic furniture.

La Encantada (520-299-3556; www.laencantadashoppingcenter.com; 2905 E. Skyline Dr. #279) High in the foothills overlooking the city perches one of Tucson's newest plazas, featuring a variety of upscale retailers such as Apple, Talbot's, Pottery Barn, and Williams-Sonoma mingled in an open-air setting beside a range of fine-dining options, including Ra Sushi, Blanco, and North, each with outdoor patio settings.

Lost Barrio (www.lostbarrioartists.com; 141–299 S. Park Ave.) There may be no better concentration of quality imports than those located on South Park Avenue, just south of East Broadway Boulevard. Originally built in the 1920s, this old 3-block row of brick and adobe warehouses has been reclaimed and converted to house 11 different retailers selling everything from handmade Southwestern home furnishings to architectural and decorative elements imported from Mexico, Guatemala, Africa, and Indonesia. It's the definitive stop for the lover of ethnic and exotic styles.

Main Gate Square (520-622-8613; www.maingatesquare.com; 814 E. University Blvd.) Located west of the University of Arizona, on a short strip of University Boulevard between Euclid and Park avenues, Main Gate Square is a 2-block mix of pubs, restaurants, salons, and stores, many of which, like Urban Outfitters and American Apparel, cater to the area's more collegiate clientele.

Old Town Artisans (520-623-6024; www.oldtownartisans.com; 201 N. Court Ave.) Located in the historic El Presidio neighborhood and comprising an entire city block, Old Town Artisans is as charming as it is impressive. Local, regional, and Latin American artisans sell everything from world imports to chile *ristras*.

Park Place Mall (520-748-1222; www.parkplacemall.com; 5870 E. Broadway Blvd.) With 120 stores, 22 eateries, and a 20-screen movie theater, this midtown mall is only 10 minutes from downtown (depending on the traffic) and features a wide range of retailers, everything from Godiva and Ann Taylor to Abercrombie and Borders.

Plaza Palomino (520-795-1177; www.plazapalomino.com; 2970 N. Swan Rd.) Elegant fashion boutiques, arts and crafts galleries, and upscale restaurants in a tranquil hacienda-style setting. Throughout the year, special artist and farmer's markets fill the courtyards here every Saturday. Courtesy shuttle service and group shopping tours are available from major hotels and resorts in the area.

St. Philip's Plaza (520-529-2775; www.stphilipsplaza.com; 4280 N. Campbell Ave.) High-end clothing and health boutiques, small cafés, fine-art galleries, jewelry stores, and restaurants are what you'll find tucked away among tiled fountains in this shaded courtyard setting. A farmer's market featuring everything from organic produce and meats to baked goods, honey, and soap—all of it from area growers—is a local favorite on weekends.

Tucson Mall (520-293-7330; www.tucsonmall.com; 4500 N. Oracle Rd.) Two hundred vendors, six major department stores (including Sears, JCPenney, and Macy's), several family-friendly play areas, and an indoor carousel make this two-level mall the biggest (and busiest!) in Tucson.

Sporting Goods

With five mountain ranges for hiking, backpacking, and climbing; dozens of private and municipal golf courses (two of which host annual PGA tournaments); El Tour de Tucson (considered the oldest and largest perimeter cycling event in the United States); Sidewinders minor league baseball; and any number of perennially ranked university teams, Tucson makes no secret that it's an active city. Highlighted here are a number of stores where you can score your outdoor and athletic gear.

Baum's Sporting Goods (www.baumssportinggoods.com; 520-881-1100, 2845 E. Speedway Blvd.; 520-797-7779, 6446 N. Oracle Rd.) Baum's has everything baseball—bats, gloves, helmets, masks, uniforms, and padding by name brands like Easton, Rawlings, and Wilson—everything you'd need to outfit yourself or an entire team.

Big 5 Sporting Goods (www.big5sportinggoods.com; 520-573-4135, 6441 S. Midvale Park Rd.; 520-296-3326, 5695 E. Speedway Blvd.; 520-292-2778, 4901 N. Stone Ave.) Gear for the usual sports (baseball, football, and basketball), as well as camping supplies, fitness equipment, hunting gear, and accessories for water sports. There is also an enormous selection of outdoor and athletic clothing for both men and women.

Fleet Feet (520-886-7800; www.fleetfeettucson.com; 6538 E. Tanque Verde Rd.) Voted one of the top 50 running and walking specialty stores in the country annually since 2006, Fleet Feet offers a full line of footwear and running-related apparel and accessories, as well as professional fitting, fitness assessments, in-store and off-site seminars, and year-round training groups.

Miller's Surplus (520-622-4777; www.millerssurplus.com; 406 N. Sixth Ave.) Whether you're after the latest military-issue digital camouflage fatigues, big and tall Carhartt and Dickies outdoor clothing, construction boots, knives, or camping or hunting gear, Miller's is a one-stop shop.

Ordinary Bike Shop (520-622-6488; www.ordinarybikeshop.com; 311 E. Seventh St.) This full-service shop is consistently rated the top bike shop in Tucson, and for good reason. You'd be hard-pressed to find a more knowledgeable sales or repair staff ready to answer

Old Town Artisans David Jewell © Metropolitan Tucson Convention & Visitors Bureau

questions about everything from their Fuji road bikes to Electra cruisers. Test rides are not only encouraged, they're expected.

Performance Bicycle (www.performancebike.com; 520-327-3232, 3302 E. Speedway Blvd.; 520-296-4715, 7204 E. Broadway Blvd.) All things biking and cycling, including cruisers, mountain bikes, top-of-the-line racing cycles, parts, tires, and the widest selection of bike-related gear in Tucson. Riding assessments and repairs also done on the premises.

Play It Again Sports (www.playitagainsportstucson.com; 520-293-2010, 4128 N. Oracle Rd.; 520-296-6888, 7280 E. Broadway Blvd.; 520-795-0363, 5015 E. Speedway Blvd.) From treadmills to golf clubs, helmets to in-line skates, Play It Again Sports has secondhand sports equipment in every condition for every sport, game, or exercise, and at drastically reduced prices.

The Running Shop (520-325-5097; www.runningshopaz.com; 3055 N. Campbell Ave., Ste. 153) Walkers, joggers, runners, and marathoners will find a wide selection of shoes, insoles, shorts, sports bras, water bottles, and packs at reasonable prices. Stock changes seasonally.

Summit Hut (www.summithut.com; 520-325-1554, 5045 E. Speedway Blvd.; 520-888-1000, 605 E. Wetmore Rd.) A local favorite for climbing, camping, and backpacking supplies, served by a staff with decades of cumulative experience in Arizona's mountaineering scene. Expect to find full lines of car racks, tents, sleeping bags and pads, backpacks, dehydrated food, knives, binoculars, maps, compasses, and GPS receivers.

VINTAGE

Step into one Tucson's many offbeat stores selling secondhand clothing and furnishings, and the irreverence of the Old Pueblo immediately strikes you. For those cultivating a shabby chic sensibility, Tucson offers a number of vintage shops, many of which are clustered in and around Tucson's historic Fourth Avenue shopping district. Here your inner bohemian will glory in one after another of funky shops, each with an unusual something to complement your wardrobe or home.

Wearable

Buffalo Exchange (www.buffaloexchange.com; 520-795-0508, 2001 E. Speedway Blvd.; 520-885-8392, 6170 E. Speedway Blvd.) The buyers at Buffalo Exchange know fashion, which is why the clothing here, while secondhand, is always cool. Ralph Lauren shirts mingle on the same rack with one-of-a-kind vintage tees. The store is packed with designer jeans, tees, skirts, dresses, sweaters, jackets, and shoes. Equal portions of the store's stock are designated men's and women's, though the store farthest east on Speedway carries only women's clothing. Belt buckles, jewelry, flasks, sunglasses, and cigarette cases are also available.

Desert Vintage & Costume (520-620-1570; 636 N. Fourth Ave.) If it's specific to the period between the 1920s and the 1970s, Desert Vintage probably carries it. Seventies leisure suits, '50s poodle skirts, '20s flapper get-ups, as well as purses and costume jewelry—all of it for sale, much of it for rent.

How Sweet It Was (520-623-9854; www.howsweetitwas.com; 419 N. Fourth Ave.) This is one of Tucson's oldest and largest vintage stores, but until you've browsed the racks here, you never quite know what you'll find. This store is brimming with an eclectic collection of items dating from Victorian high fashion to polyester and disco.

The Other Side (520-623-8736; 321 N. Fourth Ave.) An emporium for new and used vintage fashions from the 1950s to 1970s, as well as sterling silver jewelry, Native American spreads, and platform shoes.

Preen (520-628-2991; www.myspace.com/preentucson; 272 E. Congress St.) This shop is packed with an ever-changing selection of old-fashioned hats, purses, patent leather shoes, hair brooches, capes, and costume jewelry, as well as local music, Swarovski crystals, and art on consignment. An on-site sewing station makes custom alterations easy and quick.

Tucson Thrift Shop (520-623-8736; www.tucsonthriftshop.com; 319 N. Fourth Ave.) From Levis to tuxedos, an eclectic, funky, fashionable blend of '50s to '80s vintage clothing, as well as body jewelry, sunglasses, and hats. New and used costumes, props, wigs, and masks are also available for sale or rent.

Wares

Annabell's Attic (520-571-8400; www.annabellsatticinc.com; 6178 E. Speedway Blvd.) The popularity of Annabell's Attic ensures a high turnover of recycled furniture and housewares. Aisle after aisle of furniture, antiques, collectible glassware, and figurines.

The Myriad (520-275-1419; www.myspace.com/themyriadgallery; 118 N. Hoff Ave.) This tiny resale shop buys and sells anything that "seems cool," everything from tchotchkes to local art on consignment. One-of-a-kind handmade items, like a notebook made from scrap paper, make for strange (but interesting) gifts.

Paris Flea Market (520-327-1161; www.parisfleamarketaz; 2855 E. Grant Rd.) While the owners of this inconspicuous little store have yet to visit Paris, calling the store a flea market is more than apt when it comes to describing the sheer eclecticism of the merchandise you'll stumble across here. Offering architectural finds and kitschy curios to trinkets and antique Victorian furniture, this place is for serious browsers.

Cacti in Saguaro National Monument West

8

INFORMATION

Practical Matters

Ambulance, Fire & Police
Area Codes and Town Government
Banks
Books
Climate, Weather Report & What to Wear
Guided Tours
Handicapped Services
Hospitals
Late-Night Food
Late-Night Fuel
Media
Real Estate
Religious Services and Organizations
Road Service
Schools
Tourist Information

AMBULANCE, FIRE & POLICE

Tucson's **Police Department** offers a comprehensive Web site with information about job opportunities, crime prevention tips, services for teens and seniors, crime statistics, reporting, and other areas of concern. The **Fire Department**'s Web page has information on everything from fire prevention and news on recent emergencies to hazardous waste removal. There are also links to individual fire station Web sites for local information. In case of emergency for fire, police, or medical reasons, call 911. The contact information that follows is for nonemergency use.

Fire Department (520-791-4511; www.tucsonaz.gov/fire; 265 S. Fire Central Pl.)
Police Department (520-791-4444; www.tpdinternet.tucsonaz.gov; 270 S. Stone Ave.)
   Call listed number 8 AM–10 PM; after 10 PM call 911 for both emergency and nonemer-
   gency complaints.

AREA CODES AND TOWN GOVERNMENT

Area Codes
Tucson's area code is 520.

Town Government
The city's mayor, Bob Walkup, was elected for his third term in May 2007, and his term expires in 2010. In addition to council-elected City Manager Mike Hein, there is an elected city council member for each of Tucson's six wards. Mayor and council usually meet at 5:30 PM on the first four Tuesdays of the month at City Hall, excluding holidays and summer months. You will find evidence of an active and ongoing community discourse if you drop in on these discussions of city development, education, and other pertinent issues. City Hall is located at 255 West Alameda in downtown Tucson. For questions call 520-791-4700 or visit www.tucsonaz.gov/index.php.

BANKS

Tucson is home to quite a few national banks and even more ATMs, which are located at grocery stores and other common destinations. It may be a good idea to contact your local bank and check to see whether or not they have locations in Tucson before visiting, and if they do, what ATMs to utilize. The centrally located branch of some frequently used local and national banks include the following.

Bank of America (520-903-3332; www.bankofamerica.com; 33 N. Stone Ave., Ste 600)
Bank of Tucson (520-321-4500; www.bankoftucson.com; 4400 E. Broadway Blvd.)
Chase (520-792-7431; www.chasebank.com; 2 E. Congress St.)
Compass Bank (520-620-3270; www.compassbank.com; 120 N. Stone Ave.)
National Bank of Arizona (520-884-1500; www.nbarizona.com; 136 N. Stone Ave.)
US Bank (520-205-8880; www.usbank.com; 1 E. Congress St.)
Wells Fargo (520-792-5436; www.wellsfargo.com; 150 N. Stone Ave.)

BOOKS

Tucson is not just a hotbed when it comes to the weather—there are energetic national and even global discussions about the city's climate, development, native populations, border issues, and history. The following collection of fiction and nonfiction texts will lend a bit of ethnographic background (*Yaqui Deer Songs*), scientific data (*A Natural History of the Sonoran Desert*), biographical detail (*Don't Look at Me Different*), and culinary know-how (*Tucson Cooks!*) to your visit. If you are a true literature lover, it may be a good idea to stop by the University of Arizona's Poetry Center when you arrive in Tucson. It houses a library of poetry and rare books, has multimedia features, and periodically hosts readings and workshops that are open to the public.

Bowden, Charles, and Michael Berman. *Inferno*. Austin: University of Texas Press, 2006.
Carranza, Arcely, et al. *Don't Look at Me Different/No Me Veas Diferente: Voices from the Projects/Voces de los Proyectos, Tucson, Arizona, 1943–2000*. Tucson: Tucson Voices Press, 2000.

Childs, Craig. *Secret Knowledge of Water.* New York: Back Bay Books, 2001.

Evers, Larry, and Felipe S. Molina. *Yaqui Deer Songs/Maso Bwikam: A Native American Poetry.* Tucson: University of Arizona Press, 1987.

Farley, Stephen, ed., et al. *Snapped on the Street: A Community Archive of Photos and Memories from Downtown Tucson 1937–1963.* Tucson: Tucson Voices Press, 1999.

Flores, Carlotta D. *El Charro Café: The Tastes and Traditions of Tucson.* Philadelphia: Running Press, 1998.

Harte, John Bret. *Tucson: Portrait of a Desert Pueblo.* Sun Valley, CA: American Historical Press, 2001.

Kingsolver, Barbara. *High Tide in Tucson: Essays from Now or Never.* New York: Harper Perennial, 1996.

———. *The Bean Trees.* New York: Harper Collins, 2001.

Lawton, Paul A. *Old Tucson Studios (Images of America: Arizona).* Charleston: Arcadia Publishing, 2008.

Leavengood, Betty. *Tucson Hiking Guide.* Boulder: Pruett Publishing Company, 2004.

Nequette, Anne M. *A Guide to Tucson Architecture.* Tucson: University of Arizona Press, 2002.

Petersen, David, ed. *Confessions of a Barbarian: Selections from the Journals of Edward Abbey, 1951–1989.* Boulder: Johnson Books, 2003.

Phillips, Steven J., ed., et al. *A Natural History of the Sonoran Desert: Arizona-Sonora Desert Museum.* Berkeley: University of California Press, 1999.

Primavera Foundation. *Tucson Cooks! An Extraordinary Culinary Adventure.* Tucson: Primavera Foundation, 2005.

Rosenthal, Gerald A. *Sonoran Desert Life: Understanding, Insights and Enjoyment.* Tucson: University of Arizona Press, 2008.

Shelton, Richard. *Going Back to Bisbee.* Tucson: University of Arizona Press, 1992.

Silko, Leslie Marmon. *Almanac of the Dead.* New York: Penguin Books, 1992.

Urrea, Alberto. *Devil's Highway: A True Story.* New York: Back Bay Books, 2005.

Wittig, Susan Albert, ed., et al. *What Wildness Is This: Women Write about the Southwest.* Austin: University of Texas Press, 2007.

CHILD CARE

So long as your child is enrolled, many schools provide before- and after-school care to their students. Outside school walls, a good place to look for structured recreational activities is the **Tucson Parks and Recreation Department.** After-school and summer classes in acting, visual arts, sports, martial arts, swimming, and other fields of interest are available to older kids, while programming like the Busy-Bodies Play and Learn Preschool Program is available for younger children. To get more details, you can pick up a booklet at a local park or at a branch of the public library. It may also be a good idea to check out one of the local branches of the **YMCA,** where they offer affordable after-school and summer classes in activities as wide ranging as baseball, skateboarding, aquatics, dance, digital photography, and gymnastics. For a list of other child-care centers, contact the **Department of Health Services, Office of Child Care Licensing.**

Department of Health Services (520-628-6540; www.azdhs.gov/als/childcare; Office of Child Care Licensing, 400 W. Congress St., Ste. 100)

Tucson Parks and Recreation Department (520-791-4873; www.tucsonaz.gov/parks andrec)

YMCA of Metropolitan Tucson (520-623-5511; www.tucsonymca.org; Administrative Offices, 60 W. Alameda)

Climate, Weather Report & What to Wear

Tucson's desert climate is typically dry and hot, though the city has somewhat cooler temperatures in the winter, as well as afternoon and evening monsoons in the summer and early fall. However, irregularities do occur, so it may be prudent to get an up-to-date, detailed weather report at the **National Weather Service Forecast Office**'s Web site, www.weather.gov.

Seasonal Overview

Cooler temperatures tend to begin in **late October** and extend until the end of January, with nights in December getting as low as 30 degrees and days as cool as 40. It's advisable to layer with close-toed shoes, sweaters, jackets, and long pants as well as short-sleeved shirts during this time. When traveling during the **spring**, one can expect warm and sunny days that reach up into the 80s and 90s, so a lighter wardrobe is appropriate. By **June**, it's wise to have a hat, sunglasses, lots of sunscreen, light-colored clothing, and sandals, because temperatures often exceed 100 degrees. In fact, it can be a good idea to stay out of the sun during midday to avoid overexposure and potential illness. One of Tucson's greatest features, but also its most dangerous, are its summer monsoons. Typically beginning in **July** and extending into the fall, these afternoon showers are brief and extreme. Many areas of the city, such as underpasses and washes, have explicit warnings to steer clear of low ground should a flood occur. It is possible for a person or a car to be uprooted by these daily high-water levels, so travel is ill advised if rain seems likely. Rain gear is a necessary accessory for summer travelers. The **fall** is a favorite season for locals and visitors alike. Sunsets tend to be dramatic and colorful at this time of year. Hot afternoons are still periodically punctuated by a brief storm, followed by the sweet smell of desert creosote, which permeates the city after rain falls. Evenings are still reasonably warm, so only a light sweater or jacket will be necessary to keep warm during the day's cooler hours.

Guided Tours

There are a number of touring options for visitors to the Sonoran Desert. If you are an urban traveler, you might enjoy taking a short, quaint tour of the neighborhood just west of the main university campus with **Old Pueblo Trolley, Inc.** After visiting the Southern Arizona Transportation Museum, you have the option of riding a historic bus or authentic trolley along an electric track. The trolley will guide you past the houses, restaurants, cafés, and boutiques on University and Fourth avenues, letting you off to shop and dine as you please. If you plan to venture outside Tucson's city limits but want a bit of direction, there are other resources to consider. Anyone with an interest in archaeology should consider making a reservation with the **Old Pueblo Archaeology Center,** to arrange for an ancient discovery tour to see sites like the Ventana Cave of the Tohono O'odham Nation, the rock art of the Mimbres Ruins, or the Hopi and Zuni Pueblo areas. Families with young children might enjoy an off-road jeep tour with **Southwest Off-Road Tours,** where a cowboy-clad guide will simulate an old-time Western adventure through the geological and archaeological phenomena of the region. Those who'd like to see the desert from above can arrange a trip to Sedona, where they can arrange a flight with **Redrock Biplane Tours.** Nature lovers who come to Tucson with an interest in learning more about the Sonoran Desert can explore the region with a team of highly trained outdoor educators from **Sonoran Adventures,** who will provide a more rugged interaction with Tucson's natural world and offer information about ecology and conservation on their hikes, backpacking tours, skills training, youth trips, and more. If Tucson is only the beginning of your journey south, consider taking a train with **Argonaut Tours** from central Tucson into Mexico's *Sierra Tarahumara* (Copper Canyon).

Argonaut Tours (520-325-4321; www.argonaut-tours.com; 110 S. Church Ave., Ste. 4290, La Placita Village)

Old Pueblo Archaeology Center (520-798-1201; www.oldpueblo.org; P.O. Box 40577, Tucson, AZ 85717)

Old Pueblo Trolley, Inc. (520-792-1802; www.oldpueblotrolley.org; P.O. Box 1373, Tucson, AZ 85702)

Redrock Biplane Tours (1-888-TOO-RIDE; www.sedonaairtours.com)

Sonoran Adventures LLC (520-780-6994; www.sonoran-adventures.com; 4729 E. Sunrise Dr. #428)

Southwest Off-Road Tours (520-579-9330; 1220 S. Alvernon Way)

HANDICAPPED SERVICES

Tucson is outfitted with a number of resources for individuals with physical disabilities. Taxis and public buses are equipped with wheelchair accessibility, and local businesses and retail outlets are often equipped with wheelchair ramps and some automated doors. For those with hearing or speech impairments, Tucson's pay phones are equipped with TTY/TDD devices to make communication feasible. The **Arizona Office of Tourism** has more information about services for visitors with disabilities and can be reached toll-free at 1-800-842-8257. Another highly acclaimed source of detailed information and research on disability services in the Tucson area is the University of Arizona's **Disability Resource Center,** which can be reached at 520-621-3268.

HOSPITALS

Tucson has more than 40 hospitals to choose from for general and specialty health care. One of the most prominent health care organizations in the city is the **University Medical Center,** a nonprofit hospital near the University of Arizona campus. Because it is a research and teaching hospital, this facility can offer state-of-the-art treatment for rare, general, and emergency medical needs. Among other well-regarded facilities in the city, **Carondelet Health Network** has several highly ranking hospitals and health services, including **St. Joseph's Hospital,** the **Tucson Heart Hospital,** and the **Carondelet Hospice.** In fact, in December 2008, Carondelet Hospice and Palliative Care was given a Distinguished Service Award for its efforts to educate residents of southern Arizona on how to "preplan for their future health care needs."

Certain populations will find that there are hospitals and medical facilities specifically

Otherworldly giant saguaros in Saguaro National Park L.S. Warhol

oriented toward their needs. Affordable health care for underserved populations can be accessed at **El-Rio Community Health Center.** Students and employees affiliated with the University of Arizona can contact **Campus Health Service.** Citizens who have served in the U.S. armed forces can find treatment through the **Southern Arizona VA Healthcare System.** Those seeking psychological treatment can visit the **Palo Verde Mental Health Service.** Individuals seeking assistance with HIV- and AIDS-related concerns might wish to contact the **Southern Arizona AIDS Foundation (SAAF).** As always, in the case of an emergency, it is recommended that you call 911.

Carondelet Health Network (www.carondelet.org; St. Joseph's Hospital, 520-873-3918; St. Mary's Hospital, 520-872-1052; Tucson Heart Hospital, 520-696-2328; Carondelet Hospice, 520-205-7700)

El-Rio Community Health Center (520-792-9890; www.elrio.org; 839 W. Congress St.)

Palo Verde Mental Health Service (520-324-4340; 2695 N. Craycroft Rd.)

Southern Arizona AIDS Foundation (SAAF) (520-628-7223; www.saaf.org; 375 S. Euclid Ave.)

Southern Arizona VA Healthcare System (520-792-1450; www.tucson.va.gov; 3601 S. Sixth Ave.)

University Campus Health Services (520-621-6490; www.health.arizona.edu; Highland Commons, 1224 E. Lowell St.)

University Medical Center (520-694-0111; www.umcarizona.org; 1501 N. Campbell Ave.)

Animal Hospitals

If your pet needs medical attention, consider contacting the centrally located **Speedway Veterinary Hospital.** Emergency services are offered by **Pima Pet Clinic Animal Emergency.**

Pima Pet Clinic (520-327-5624; 4832 E. Speedway Blvd.)

Speedway Veterinary Hospital (520-321-4235; www.speedwayvet.com; 3736 E. Speedway Blvd.)

LATE-NIGHT FOOD

Late-night hunger pangs can be relieved at many of the national fast-food chains in the area, but there are also some great local options. Diners with a few extra dollars to spare have until midnight to enjoy the **Kingfisher American Bar and Grill,** which offers renowned seafood dishes, an award-winning wine list, and weekly jazz and blues performances. If you are looking for a classic atmosphere and want to venture into the foothills, you'll be able to enjoy a view of metropolitan Tucson while eating northern Italian cuisine at **North,** open until midnight on Friday and Saturday. Young clubgoers with less cash and more gumption can top off their night of dancing with a late-night meal of tater tots at the **Grill,** which is located in the city's historic downtown. This all-night diner, with a variety of international and microbrewed beers on tap, also hosts daily performances by local musicians in its Red Room. If you are looking for stimulation to help you write the next great American novel, you'll find coffee, free Internet, and a hearty meal at the 24-hour **Shot in the Dark Café**—though this downtown neighborhood is not one you'll want to wander around looking lost in. For a quick snack to tide you over, stop in at **Brooklyn Pizza Com-**

pany, located on the always-busy Fourth Avenue. In addition to a selection of authentic gelato, this pizzeria has "late night slices" every Friday and Saturday until 2:30 AM. Another Fourth Avenue favorite is **Bison Witches Bar and Deli,** which serves soups and sandwiches, and features from their full bar, until 1 AM Monday through Saturday. The **Waffle House,** with several Tucson locations, serves breakfast all night long. Grocery stores like **Safeway** are open until midnight.

Bison Witches Bar and Deli (520-740-1541; www.bisonwitches.com; 326 N. Fourth Ave.)
Brooklyn Pizza Company (520-622-6868; www.brooklynpizzacompany.com; 534 N. Fourth Ave.)
The Grill (520-623-7621; www.myspace.com/redroomatthegrill; 100 E. Congress St.)
Kingfisher American Bar and Grill (520-323-7739; www.kingfishertucson.com; 2564 E. Grant Rd.)
North (520-299-1600; www.foxrestaurantconcepts.com/north; 2995 E. Skyline Dr.)
Safeway Grocery Store (520-546-3929; www.safeway.com; 10380 E. Broadway Blvd.)
Shot in the Dark Café (520-882-5544; www.shotinthedarkcafe.com; 121 E. Broadway)
Waffle House (520-573-1551; www.wafflehouse.com; 2710 E. Valencia Rd.)

LATE-NIGHT FUEL

Certain gas stations like **Circle K** are open 24 hours a day. In addition to this, some stations have automated pumps that can service your filling needs after the convenience store has closed. For cars that run on biodiesel, select **Safeway** grocery store filling stations have biofuel pumps, some open until 1 AM. A 24-hour biofuel pump can be found at **Arizona Petroleum Products.**

Arizona Petroleum Products (520-623-4721; 1015 S. Cherry)
Circle K (520-624-0919; www.circlek.com; 130 E. Speedway Blvd.)
Safeway PowerPump (520-206-9052; 1940 E. Broadway Blvd.)

MEDIA

Newspapers

For daily national as well as local news, purchase a copy of the *Tucson Citizen* or *Arizona Daily Star.* These papers, jointly operated, complement one another rather than compete. These papers hold themselves to a high level of journalistic inquiry and integrity—in fact, the *Star* reached acclaim in 1981 when reporters Clark Hallas and Robert B. Lowe won a Pulitzer Prize for a story about a controversy involving the University of Arizona's football team. If you are looking for a copy of the *New York Times,* try visiting one of the many Starbucks locations, or drop by **Time Market** at 444 East University Avenue (520-622-0761).
Arizona Daily Star (1-800-695-4492; www.azstarnet.com; 4850 S. Park Ave.)
Tucson Citizen (520-573-4561; www.tucsoncitizen.com; P.O. Box 26767, Tucson, AZ 85726)

Magazines

If you prefer the quirky voice of an independent press, pick up a free copy of the *Tucson Weekly.* Like many city papers, the *Weekly* has nationally syndicated columns like "Free Will

Astrology" and "Savage Love," but it also features restaurant, book, and film reviews; articles on current events; and a comprehensive listing of upcoming art and music events. *Tucson Lifestyle* deems itself "the magazine Tucson lives by," and if you are interested in
learning about Tucson's latest trends in fashion, golf, architecture, and fine dining, this
may indeed be the magazine for you. Their "Best Of" section offers up-to-date rankings of
the crème de la crème of the city's chefs, lawyers, doctors, and more, while the events listings can help you fill your calendar with art walks, plays, public parties, tours, and other
cultural occasions. For the green traveler, a free copy of *Green Times* will provide information on local news and events that relates to conservation and the environment. If you are
thinking of making your stay in Tucson long-term, you might find the decorating tips in
Tucson Home Magazine inspiring. Families seeking to get their children involved with local
sports teams can pick up a copy of *Tucson Sport Magazine* at one of the three hundred locations distributing it around town. And for couples and families looking to orchestrate a
wedding in the area, *Tucson Bride and Groom Magazine* will help with a multitude of nup-
tial-planning needs.

Green Times (520-751-7926; www.tucsongreenzine.com; P.O. Box 18331, Tucson, AZ 85731)
Tucson Bride and Groom Magazine (www.tucsonbrideandgroom.com)
Tucson Home Magazine (520-322-0895; www.tucsonhomemagazine.com; 1650 E. Fort
    Lowell Rd.)
Tucson Lifestyle (520-721-7994; www.tucsonlifestyle.com; 7000 E. Tanque Verde Rd. #11)
Tucson Sport Magazine (520-360-8485; www.tucsonsport.net; 8340 N. Thornydale
    #110–222)
Tucson Weekly (520-792-3630; www.tucsonweekly.com; P.O. Box 27087, Tucson, AZ 85726)

Radio

Tucson has a number of music and talk show stations, but for national and local news, tune
into the **Arizona Public Media** (520-621-5828; www.azpm.org; 1423 E. University Blvd.)
station **KUAZ** (AM 1550 and FM 89.1 in Tucson, FM 91.7 in Sierra Vista). This station features NPR favorites like "Morning Edition," "Science Fridays" and "This American Life," as
well as local programming such as "Arizona Spotlight." A selection of other stations follows.

AM
530 KSAV (adult standards)
690 KVOI The Voice (conservative talk)
790 KNST (news, talk, and sports)
830 FLT (Christian ministry)
1210 KQTL Radio Unica (Spanish talk, news, sports, and entertainment)
1290 KCUB Fox (sports)
1330 KJLL The Jolt (talk radio)
1450 KWFM (cool oldies)
1550 KUAZ (jazz and news)

FM
89.1 KUAZ-FM (jazz and National Public Radio)
89.7 and 90.5 KUAT-FM (classical)
91.3 KXCI (community radio)
92.9 KWMT The Mountain (adult album alternative)

96.1 KLPX (rock)
97.1 KTZR-FM Que Suave (Spanish)
98.3 KOHT Hot (hip-hop and R&B)
98.9 KJZZ Rio Salado College (public radio)
99.5 KIIM (country favorites)
100.9 KLVA-FM (Christian contemporary)
102.7 KNOG Nogales (Spanish)
104.1 KZPT The Truth (FM news and talk radio)
106.3 KGMG Mega (oldies)

Television

Amid the many cable channels familiar to all TV watchers, there are some locally produced shows worth watching for local news and human-interest stories. In addition to the above-mentioned radio station, **Arizona Public Media** also hosts a television station on **channel 6, KUAT.** This station features popular PBS programming like *World Focus,* as well as the celebrated show *Arizona Illustrated.*

NBC: Channel 4, KVOA
PBS: Channel 6, KUAZ
ABC: Channel 9, KGUN
FOX: Channel 11, KMSB
Government Access: Channel 12
CBS: Channel 13, KOLD
Telenoticias: Channel 14, KQBN
Telemundo: Channel 40, KHRR
Univision: Channel 52, KUVE

REAL ESTATE

As far as temporary dwellings are concerned, the Web site **www.craigslist.org** has become a frequently used resource for both landlords and apartment seekers. But those looking to purchase may want to start by contacting **Long Realty**, an Arizona company with a monopoly on local Tucson listings and 80 years of experience. Another resource to consider is the **Pepper Group,** a "boutique" real estate company that boasts of high national rankings and friendly brokers.

Long Realty (520-918-1616; www.longrealty.com; 900 E. River Rd.)
Pepper Group (520-977-0003; www.thepepper.com; 1873 N. Kolb Rd.)

RELIGIOUS SERVICES AND ORGANIZATIONS

Tucson has a diverse population, and visitors of multiple faiths are likely to find support, services, volunteer opportunities, and educational facilities nearby. For those of Orthodox Jewish faith, the **Congregation Young Israel of Tucson,** served by Rabbi Yossie Shemtov, is open year-round. Visitors of all ages who practice Islam can visit the **Islamic Center of Tucson** for prayer, interfaith education, and volunteering. There is a **Roman Catholic Diocese** led by Bishop Kicanas, affiliated with a multitude of historic churches in the Tucson metropolitan area. A Franciscan mass can be heard at the famed **Mission San Xavier del Bac,** one of the most outstanding examples of mission architecture in the country. Those seeking Buddhist meditation can visit the **Tara Mahayana Buddhist Center** and even one of the many yoga studios around town. A small sampling of various religious centers follow.

Catalina United Methodist Church (520-327-4296; www.catumc.org; 2700 E. Speedway Blvd.)

Church of Jesus Christ of Latter-day Saints (520-622-8866; www.lds.org; 1333 E. Second St.)

Congregation Young Israel of Tucson (520-326-8362; www.chabadoftucson.com; 2443 E. Fourth St.)

Diocese of Tucson (520-792-3410, ext. 1012; www.diocesetucson.org; 111 S. Church Ave.)

Emmanuel Baptist Church (520-323-9379; www.ebc-tucson.org; 1825 N. Alvernon Way)

Grace St. Paul's Episcopal Church (520-327-6857; www.gsptucson.org; 2331 E. Adams St.)

Islamic Center of Tucson Inc. (520-624-3233; www.ictucson.info; 901 E. First St.)

St. Mark's Presbyterian Church (520-325-1001; www.stmarkspresbyterian.org; 3809 E. Third St.)

Tara Mahayana Buddhist Center (520-296-8626; www.meditationintucsion.org; 1701 E. Miles St.)

Unitarian Universalist Church (520-748-1551; www.uuctucson.org; 4931 E. 22nd St.)

ROAD SERVICE

Many areas in Tucson have been undergoing reconstruction, including the interstate. After you've gotten directions for travel, you may want to be sure that the route you've chosen is operable. While information about open freeway exits are updated and posted on the relevant routes, traffic reports can be found by calling **Road Condition Information** at 520-547-7510 or visiting www.transview.org.

SCHOOLS

Primary and Secondary Schools

The city has a wide-ranging assortment of schools for children and teenagers, including public, charter, Waldorf, Christian, Montessori, Hebrew, and international institutions. While the city's public school system suffers from major challenges, there are some dynamic diamonds in the rough. For example, the secondary school **BASIS Charter,** which stands for Builds Academic Success in School, was ranked the best public school in the nation by *Newsweek* magazine in May 2008. Founded by two economists who were dissatisfied by their own child's education, this free school's mission is to combine "the depth and rigor of European and Asian college prep schools with the expansiveness of the American curriculum." Both the middle and high school campuses are centrally located. Another school with national accolades is the **Civano Community Charter School.** Part of the Vail District, this school is located in the community-oriented and conservation-minded Civano neighborhood, but it is open to all Tucson residents. A primary school with a child-initiated approach to learning, Civano was awarded the title of Greenest Grade School in America in January 2008.

Beyond select outstanding schools, however, there are nonprofit organizations in Tucson that help to augment the efforts of already established public schools with retention, achievement, and college preparation. Since 1999, the community-based organization **VOICES** has mentored low-income youth in the Tucson community in writing and photography, with the aim of creating polished storytelling projects. Though the central focus is to help young learners "strengthen their cognitive, artistic, emotional, leadership, and higher education skills," several publications have emerged for the public to enjoy (see the *Books* section earlier in this chapter). Another organization called **GEAR UP** (or Gaining Early Awareness and Readiness for Undergraduate Programs) brings some of the brightest graduate students and alumni from the University of Arizona to schools serving low-income communities.

For parents interested in exploring alternative approaches to their child's education, there are programs modeled on a diversity of educational philosophies all over the city. Since the list of elementary, middle, and high schools is quite long, it may be wise to start by contacting the district that will be serving your area. Most Tucson schools have a Web site, and in order to navigate among the many scholastic options, it may be valuable to check out a resource like **GreatSchools.net,** which offers a ranking system as well as student and parent feedback on area schools.

School Districts

Amphitheater School District (520-696-5000; www.amphi.com; 701. W. Wetmore)
Catalina Foothills School District (520-299-6446; www.cfsd16org; 2101 E. River Rd.)
Flowing Wells School District (520-690-2201; www.flowingwellschools.org; 1556 W. Prince Rd.)
Sunnyside School District (520-545-2000; www.sunnyside.ud.k12.az.us; 238 E. Ginter Rd.)
Tanque Verde School District (520-760-6884; www.tanqueverdeschools.org; 2300 N. Tanque Verde Loop)
Tucson Unified School District (520-617-7233; www.tusdk12az.us; 1010 E. 10th St.)

Outstanding Secondary Schools and Educational Organizations

Academy of Math & Science (520-293-2676; www.amstucson.org; 1557 W. Prince Rd.)
BASIS Charter School (520-326-3444; www.basistucson.org; 3825 E. Second St.)
Civano Community School (520-879-1700; www.vail.k12az.us/~civano; 10673 E. Mira Lane)
GEAR UP (520-626-3082; www.dreamscometrueaz.org)
VOICES Community Stories (520-622-7458; www.voicesinc.org; 48 E. Pennington St.)

Higher Education

As for higher education, **Pima Community College,** the **University of Arizona,** and a host of other schools have campuses all over the city. The U of A is home to highly ranked programs for undergraduate and graduate study, such as the Eller College of Management, which was ranked the fifth-strongest program in the world by London's *Financial Times* in January 2009. Pima Community College provides affordable opportunities for young students looking to transfer to a university, adult learners hoping to finish their degree, and community members interested in buffing up their language or cooking skills. For those looking to acquire a less-conventional degree, there are programs in acupuncture, massage therapy, and yoga teacher certification as well, offered at schools such as the **Providence Institute** and the **Arizona School of Acupuncture and Oriental Medicine.**

Given the large educational community in Tucson, impressive programming—from football games and Broadway shows to prize-winning author lectures—can be found at local bookstores, the university's sports centers, and institutions like the newly renovated **Poetry Center** at the University of Arizona.

Colleges and Universities

Cochise College (1-800-966-7943; www.cochihse.edu; Douglas Campus, 4190 W. AZ 80)

Northern Arizona University, Tucson (520-879-7900; www.nau.edu; 401 N. Bonita Ave., Ste. A140)

Park University, Davis-Monthan Air Force Base (520-748-8266; www.park.edu/DAVI; 5355 E. Granite St.)

Pima Community College (520-206-4500; www.pima.edu; District Office, 4905 E. Broadway Blvd.)

Prescott College (520-206-4500; www.pima.edu; 2233 E. Speedway Blvd.)

University of Arizona (520-621-4608; www.arizona.edu; External Relations, 1401 E. University Blvd., P.O. Box 21006, Tucson, AZ 85721)

Select Business, Technical & Trade Schools

Arizona School of Acupuncture and Oriental Medicine (520-795-0787; www.asaom.edu; 4626 E. Ft. Lowell Rd., Ste. 104)

The Art Center Design College (520-325-0123; www.theartcenter.edu; 2525 N. Country Club Rd.)

Pima Medical Institute (1-888-635-5219; www.pmi.edu; 3350 E. Grant Rd., Ste. 200)

The Providence Institute (520-323-0203; www.providenceinstitute.com; 3400 E. Speedway Blvd., Ste. 114)

TOURIST INFORMATION

More information for visitors can be found at a number of organizations, some of which include the following.

Arizona Office of Tourism (1-866-275-5816; www.arizonaguide.com; 1110 W. Washington St., Ste. 155, Phoenix, AZ 85007)

Fourth Avenue Merchant's Association (520-624-5004; www.fourthavenue.org; 329 E. Seventh St., Tucson, AZ 85705)

Metropolitan Tucson Convention and Visitors Bureau (1-800-638-8350; www.visit tucson.org; 100 S. Church Ave., Tucson, AZ 85701)

Tall palms swaying in the wind

9

If Time Is Short

Best of Tucson

Ideally, a visit to Tucson should be long enough to explore at least a few venues in each chapter of the book. A week is probably a good starting point, but if you only have a few days and want to make the most of every minute, this chapter is tailored to your needs. Think of it as a "best of" list, a highly subjective accounting of the top restaurants, hotels, shops, museums, and activities—things you absolutely shouldn't miss on a visit to the Old Pueblo.

CULTURE

The Center for Creative Photography (520-621-7968; www.creativephotography.org; 1030 N. Olive Rd.) A destination photography museum on the campus of the University of Arizona, the CCP houses a world-class collection of images, as well as rotating exhibits from internationally acclaimed artists.

Mission San Xavier del Bac (520-294-2624; www.sanxaviermission.org; 1950 W. San Xavier Rd., San Xavier District) San Xavier is the parish church on the Tohono O'odham settlement south of the city. Known as the "white dove of the desert," it is the most compelling example of mission architecture in the area. Don't miss the fry bread stands in the parking lot.

RECREATION

Sabino Canyon (520-749-8700; www.sabinocanyon.org; 5700 N. Sabino Canyon Rd.) Whether you're looking for a serious hike or a casual stroll through the desert, Sabino Canyon is the local hiking headquarters.

RESORTS & SPAS

Arizona Inn (520-325-1541 or 1-800-933-1093; www.arizonainn.com; 2200 E. Elm St.) This elegant, understated hotel perfectly combines historic beauty with modern luxury. And it's smack in the center of town!

Canyon Ranch (520-749-9000 or 1-800-749-9000; www.canyonranch.com; 8600 E. Rockcliff Rd.) For an all-out splurge, nothing beats Canyon Ranch, the destination resort and spa whose legendary health and healing programs are internationally renowned.

RESTAURANTS

Janos and **J Bar** (520-615-6100; www.janos.com; 3770 E. Sunrise Dr.) Tucson's best fine dining and upscale, moderately priced dining are under one roof. James Beard Award winner Janos Wilder helms the kitchen at his namesake restaurant, Janos—where he perpetually reinvents Southwestern cuisine—and next door at J BAR, where he serves casual regional Mexican food with some Latin American and Caribbean undertones.

Mariscos Chihuahua (520-623-3563; 1009 N. Grande Ave.) Though there are now four locations of this family-run place that originated across the border in Nogales, Mexico, this original Tucson location remains the top choice. It is a destination for seviche, shrimp *culichi,* seafood cocktails, and whole fried fish.

Taqueria Pico de Gallo (520-623-8775; 2618 S. Sixth Ave.) This is the best place in town for tacos (especially fish and carne asada) and has a laid-back, local vibe.

General Index

A

AAA Airport Taxi, 32
Acacia, 112
Academy of Math & Science, 214
activities. *see also* festivals; fitness; indoor
   recreation; outdoor recreation; parks; shop-
   ping
      art classes, 68–69
      books and bookstores, 83–85, 188–89,
        204–5
      botanical gardens, 158–59
      cinemas, 71–72
      cultural, 217
      dance, 74–78, 98, 108–9
      karaoke singing, 98–99
      libraries, 83–85
      live theater, 101–5
      museums, 66, 85–94, 159, 160
      music, 94–95, 189
      seasonal events, 105–9
      theaters, 71–72
      zoos, 159
AJ's Fine Foods, 146
Akimel O'odham Nation, 16, 17, 18–20
Alamo car rental, 32
Alexander's, 194
Ali Baba, 139
All Souls Procession, 105
Allstate Cab, 32
alternative clothing, 190
ambulance service, 203
AMC Loews Foothills theater, 72
American Antiques Mall, 187
The Amerind Foundation: A Museum of Native
   American Archaeology, Art, History, and
   Culture, 93
Amphitheater School District, 214
AMTRAK, 31
Anderson Pilates, 181
animal hospitals, 209
Annabell's Attic, 201
Annual Waila Festival, 106
Anthony's Cigar Emporium, 192
Anthony's in the Catalinas, 112
Antigone Books, 83–84, 107, 188
Antigua de Mexico, Inc., 78
antiques, 187
Aqua Vita Natural Food Market, 146
archaeology, 206
architecture and historic sites, 61–68
area code, 204

Argonaut Tours, 207
Arizona Daily Star, 210
Arizona Friends of Chamber Music, 96
Arizona Hatters, 190
Arizona Historical Society, 62
Arizona Historical Society Downtown Museum,
   86, 88
Arizona History Museum, 86–87
Arizona Inn, 52, 53, 112–13, 217
The Arizona Inn, 100
Arizona International Film Festival, 73–74
Arizona map, 6
The Arizona Media Arts Center, 70–71
Arizona Office of Tourism, 207, 215
Arizona Onstage Productions, 101
Arizona Opera, 96
Arizona Petroleum Products, 210
Arizona Repertory Theatre, 101
Arizona Rose Theater Company, 101–2
Arizona School of Acupuncture and Oriental
   Medicine, 215
Arizona-Sonora Desert Museum, 22, 25, 98, 99,
   164, 165
Arizona State Museum, 10, 66, 87
Arizona Theatre Company, 102
Armitage Wine Lounge and Café, 123
Armory Park, 65, 171
The Art Center Design College, 215
art classes, 68–69
art councils, 70–71
art galleries, 78–83
arts, literary, 83–85
Asian Trade Rug Company, 194
Aspen Expeditions, 172
Athens on 4th Avenue, 129
Avis car rental, 32

B

bakeries, 143–44
Ballet Folklórico Tapatío, 74–75
ballooning, 151–52
Bally Total Fitness, 162
Bank of America, 204
Bank of Tucson, 204
banks, 204
Barnes & Noble, 188
Barrio Brewing Company, 148
Barrio Grill, 113
Barrio Historico, 63
barrios, 22
Basin and Range, 12–14

BASIS Charter School, 213, 214
Baum's Sporting Goods, 198
B & B Cactus Farm, 192
bed & breakfasts, 35–40
Bedroxx Bowling, 155–56
beer, wine & liquor, 148–49
Bentley's Coffee and Tea, 107
Beowulf Alley Theatre Company, 102–3
Best Western Brisas Hotel–Tucson Airport,
    42–43
Best Western Inn Suites, 42
Better Bodies, 180
Beyond Bread, 143–44
BICAS, 33, 154
Bicas Art, 69
Bicycle and Pedestrian Program, 154
Bicycle Inter Community Action and Salvage
    (BICAS), 33, 154
bicycles, 33, 152–55
Big 5 Sporting Goods, 198
Bikram's Yoga College of India Northwest
    Tucson, 182
Biosphere 2, 24
Bisbee, 24, 143
Bison Witches Bar and Deli, 210
The Biz, 107
BJ's Restaurant and Brewhouse, 101
BK Hot Dogs, 133–34
Blanco, 134–35
Blaze Threads, 190
B Line, 113–14
Bluefin restaurant, 114
Blue Sky Fitness and Recreation, 162
Blue Willow Gift Shop, 192–93
Blue Willow restaurant, 123–24
Bob Dobbs', 100
Bohemia, 193
Bon, 193
Bookmans Entertainment Exchange, 188
books and bookstores, 83–85, 188–89, 204–5
The Book Stop, 188
Borderlands Theater, 103
Borders Books & Music, 188
botanical gardens, 158–59
bowling, 155–56
Broadway in Tucson, 103
Brooklyn Pizza Company, 144, 145, 209–10
Brown House, Charles O., 65
Budget car rental, 32
Buena Vista Climbing Club, 172
Buffalo Exchange, 200
bus travel, 30–31, 31–32
Butz, 189

C
Cactus Moon Café, 98

cafés. see also dining
    Armitage Wine Lounge and Café, 123
    Blue Willow, 123–24
    Cactus Moon Café, 98
    Café 54, 124–25
    Café Poca Cosa, 137
    Café Roka, 143
    The Cup Café, 125
    Delectables, 125
    El Charro Café, 124, 134, 135
    Epic Café, 125–26
    Ghini's French Café, 127–28
    The Grill, 126, 209, 210
    Laffs Comedy Club and Café, 99
    Le Delice Bakery & Café, 128
    Luxor Café, 139
    Mi Nidito Café, 136
    Mount Lemmon Café, 24, 142
    Ocotillo Café Restaurant, 98, 143
    Shot in the Dark Café, 209, 210
    Teresa's Mosaic Café, 138–39
camping, 156–57
Candela, 139–40
Canyon Ranch, 52–53, 175, 217
Capoeira Malandragem, 75
Carondelet Health Network, 207, 209
Carondelet Hospice, 207
car rentals, 32
car travel, 27–29
Casa Grande, 93–94
Casa Grande Valley Historical Society &
    Museum, 93–94
Casa Libre en la Solana, 84
Casas Adobes Plaza, 197
Casa Tierra Adobe, 35–36, 36, 37
Casa Vicente, 140
Casa Video, 74
Cascade Bar, 100
Casino Del Sol, 99
Catalina Foothills Mall, 197
Catalina Foothills School District, 214
Catalina Park, 171
Catalina Park Inn, 36
Catalina Players' Theatre, 103–4
Catalina State Park Campground, 156
Catalina United Methodist Church, 213
Centennial Hall, 66
Center for Creative Photography, 66, 87, 102, 217
Central Tucson Gallery Association, 71
Century 20 El Con theater, 72
Century 20 Park Place theater, 72
Charles O. Brown House, 65
Chase Bank, 204
Chavez, Cesar, 30
Checker Cab, 32
Cheyney House, 65
Chicago Music Store, 189

Chico's, 189
child care, 205–6
children's clothing, 191
Chiricahua National Monument, 13, 14, 24
Chocolate Iguana, 192, 193
churches, 62–63, 66, 107, 212–13
Church of Jesus Christ of Latter-day Saints, 213
Cinco de Mayo, 106
Cinema La Placita, 98
cinemas, 71–72
Circle K, 210
Civano Community Charter School, 213, 214
Clarion Hotel–Tucson Airport, 43
Click Billiards, 100
climate, 206
clothing, 189–91, 200–201, 206
clothing-optional hiking and sunbathing, 168
Club Congress, 94, 99
Clues Unlimited, 188
Cochise College, 215
colleges, 215
Colonial Frontiers, 194
Colossal Cave, 153
Comfort Suites at Sabino Canyon, 43
Comfort Suites Tucson Mall, 43
Compass Bank, 204
Congregation Young Israel of Tucson, 212, 213
Copenhagen, 194
Copper Country Antiques, 187
Copper Queen Hotel, 24
Copper Queen Mine, 24
Corbett House, J. Knox, 64, 64
Coronado National Forest, 23–24, 165
Corworx Studio, 181
Courtyard by Marriott–Tucson Airport, 43–44
Courtyard by Marriott–Williams Centre, 44
Cowan Horse Adventures, 168
Crate & Barrel, 194
Crescent Tobacco Shop & Newsstand, 188
Crossroads Festival Cinemas 6, 71
cultural activities, 217
The Cup Café, 125
Cushing Street Bar and Restaurant, 22, 100, 114

D
dance, 74–78, 98, 108–9
Dark Star Leather, 191
Davis Dominguez Gallery, 78–79
daycare, 205–6
day spas, 177–78
De Anza Drive-In Theatres, 72
De Anza Park, 171
DeGrazia Gallery in the Sun, 60, 79
Delectables, 125
delis, 146–48
Dell Ulrich golf, 160

de Niza, Marcos, 18
Department of Health Services, 205–6
Desert Artisans' Gallery, 79
Desert Diamond Casino Resort Hotel, 44, 99
Desert Sports and Fitness, 162
Desert Vintage & Costume, 200
Designers Craft, 187
Diamond Park Ranch, 168
dining. see also cafés; food purveyors
    best of Tucson, 218
    ethnic restaurants, 126–41
    late-night food, 209–10
    nightlife, 98–101
    restaurants (outside Tucson), 141–43
    restaurants (Tucson proper), 112–23
    wine, beer & liquor, 148–49
Dinnerware Artspace, 79–80
Diocese of Tucson, 213
Disability Resource, 207
The Dish, 114–15
Dominguez Gallery, Davis, 78–79
Doubletree Hotel–Reid Park, 44–45
Dragoon, 93
The Drawing Studio, 69

E
Eastern Living, 194
El Charro Café, 124, 134, 135
El Cubanito, 127
Elements in Balance, 177
El Fronterizo newspaper, 63
El Guero Canelo, 135
El Minuto, 135–36
El Nacimiento, 106
El Parador Restaurant, 98
El Paso & SW Depot, 63
El Presidio B&B, 37
El Presidio Park, 64
El-Rio Community Health Center, 209
El Rio golf, 160–61
El Tenista Soccer and Tennis, 178
El Tiradito, 22, 63
El Torero, 136
El Tour de Tucson, 106, 154
Embassy Suites-Tucson Paloma Village, 45
Embassy Suites-Williams Centre, 45
emergency services, 203, 207–9
Emmanuel Baptist Church, 213
Enoteca, 130
Enterprise car rental, 32
Epic Café, 125–26
Eric Firestone Gallery, 80, 187
Etherton Gallery, 80
events, seasonal, 105–9
exercise facilities and gyms, 162–63, 180–83
Expressions Art Glass, 70

F

Fairfield Inn by Marriott—I-10/Butterfield Business Park, 45
family activities, 158–60
Family Arts Festival, 106
Feast restaurant, 115–16
Fenderskirts, 98
festivals
    Annual Waila Festival, 106
    Arizona International Film Festival, 73–74
    Family Arts Festival, 106
    film, 73–74
    Nuestras Raíces Literary Arts Festival, 84
    Tucson Film and Music Festival, 74
    tucsonfilm.com Short Fest, 74
    Tucson Meet Yourself festival, 108
    Tucson Poetry Festival, 85
Fiesta de San Augustin, 107
film festivals, 73–74
fire department, 203
Firenze Boutique, 190
Firestone Gallery, Eric, 80, 187
fitness
    exercise facilities and gyms, 162–63
    personal training, 180–81
    pilates, 181
    yoga, 181–83
Fitness Boot Camp, 180
Flam Chen Pyrotechnic Theatre Company, 75
Flavorbank Spice Market, 193
Fleet Feet, 198
Fleming's Prime Steakhouse, 116
Fleur de Tucson Balloon Tours, 151–52
Flowing Wells School District, 214
Folk Festival, 107
Food Conspiracy Co-op, 146
food glossary, 147
food purveyors. see also dining
    bakeries, 143–44
    delis, 146–48
    gelato, 144
    pizza, 144–46
    Safeway Grocery Store, 210
    specialty food markets, 146–48
    wine, beer & liquor, 148–49
Fort Lowell furniture district, 194
Fort Lowell Museum, 87–89
Fort Lowell Tennis Center, 178–79
fossils, 15
Four Points by Sheraton-University Plaza, 45–46
Fourth Avenue Historic Shopping District, 195, 196, 197
Fourth Avenue Merchant's Association, 215
Fourth Avenue Street Fair, 107
Fox Theatre, 72, 73, 94
Franklin Men's Store, 190
Fred Enke golf, 161

French Quarter of Tucson, 99
Frost: A Gelato Shoppe, 144
fuel, 210

G

Gaby's Rug Resource, Walter, 196
Gadabout Salon Spas, 178
galleries, art, 78–83
Gandhi restaurant, 129
gardens, botanical, 158–59
The Gaslight Theatre, 104
gasoline, 210
Gate's Pass, 24, 165
GEAR UP, 214
gelato, 144
Gene C. Reid Park Rose Garden, 158–59
Gentle Ben's, 100
geography, 23–24
geologic activity, 15
getting around, 31–33
getting there, 27–31
Ghini's French Café, 127–28
gifts, 191–94
Gila River Indian Community, 18
GLBT Tucson, 107, 167
Glenn Ski and Sports, Peter, 170
glossary, food, 147
Golden Pin Lanes, 156
Gold's Gym, 163
golf, 160–62, 161
government, town, 204
Grace St. Paul's Episcopal Church, 213
Grand Cinemas theater, 73
Green Times, 211
Greyhound Lines, Inc., 30–31
The Grill at Hacienda del Sol, 116
The Grill, 126, 209, 210
Grogan Gallery of Fine Art, 80–81
Gross Gallery, Joseph, 81
groups and associations, 96–98
Guadalajara Grill, 137
guest ranches, 40–42
guided tours, 206–7
Guilin Healthy Chinese Restaurant, 126
gyms and workout facilities, 162–63, 180–83

H

Hacienda del Desierto, 37–38, 38, 39
Hacienda del Sol Guest Ranch Resort, 40–41
handicapped services, 207
Hertz car rental, 32
hiking, 163–68
hiking, clothing-optional, 168
Hilton Tucson East, 46
Hilton Tucson El Conquistador Golf & Tennis Resort, 53–54, 54

Himmel Park, 171
Himmel Park Tennis Center, 179
Historic Depot, 63
The Historic Rialto Theatre, 95
historic sites, 61–68
Historic Stone Avenue Temple, 63
history, 12–15, 16–21, 20–24
Hohokam Chronological Sequence (HCS), 18
Hohokam people, 16–17
Holiday Inn and Suites—Tucson Airport North,
    46
Holiday Inn Express Hotel and Suites-Tucson
    Airport, 46
home furnishings, 194–96, 201
horseback riding, 168–70
hospitals, 207–9
Hotel Congress, 47, 47–48
hotels & motels, 42–52
The Hotel Arizona, 46–47
Hotel Tucson City Center Conference Suite
    Resort, 48
How Sweet It Was, 200–201
Hyatt Place Tucson Airport, 48
Hydra clothing, 190

I

India Oven restaurant, 130
indoor recreation. *see also* outdoor recreation;
    sports
        bowling, 155–56
        family activities, 159–60
        gyms and workout facilities, 162–63, 181–83
in-line skating, 170
The Invisible Theatre, 104
Islamic Center of Tucson, Inc., 212, 213

J

J. Knox Corbett House, 64, 64
James A. Walsh Federal Courthouse, 64
Janos Restaurant, 110, 116–17, 218
Jax Kitchen, 117
J Bar, 110, 117–18, 218
Jeff's Pub, 99–100
Jonathan's Cork, 118
Joseph Gross Gallery, 81
JW Marriott Starr Pass Resort & Spa, 54–55,
    175–76

K

Kaibab Courtyard Shops, 197
karaoke singing, 98–99
Karuna's Thai Plate, 140–41
Kid Center, 191
Kingfisher American Bar and Grill, 209, 210
Kingfisher restaurant, 101, 118

Kino, Eusebio, 19
Kitt Peak National Observatory, 24, 98
Kitt Peak Night Visitor Program, 98

L

La Baguette Bakery, 144
La Buhardilla, 187
La Casa Cordova, 64
La Encantada, 197
Laffs Comedy Club and Café, 99
La Fitness, 163
The Landmark, 190
La Placita Gazebo, 171
La Posada del Valle, 34, 38
La Roca, 142
late-night food, 209–10
Le Delice Bakery & Café, 128
Le Rendez-Vous, 129
libraries, 83–85
Lil' Traders, 191
Lionel Rombach Gallery, 81
liquor, beer & wine, 148–49
literary arts, 83–85
literature, 204–5
live theater, 101–5
Live Theatre Workshop, 104–5
Lodge on the Desert, 48
The Lodge at Ventana Canyon, 55–56
lodging
        bed & breakfasts, 35–40
        guest ranches, 40–42
        hotels & motels, 42–52
        resorts & spas, 52–59, 174–78, 217
Loews Ventana Canyon Resort, 55, 56, 56
The Loft, 72
Long Realty, 212
Lost Barrio, 197
Lucky Strike Bowl, 156
Luxor Café, 139

M

magazines, 210–11
Magellan Trading, 195
Magpie's, 145
Main Gate Square, 197
malls, plazas, and shopping centers, 197–98
Mariscos Chihuahua, 137, 218
markets, food, 146–48
Marriott University Park, 48–49
massage, stone, 174
Maverick nightclub, 98
Maya Palace, 189
McClintock's, 119
McMahon's Prime Steak House, 101, 119
medical centers, 207–9

Medicine Man Gallery, 81
The Memorial Fountain, 66
men's clothing, 190
Men's Warehouse, 190
Metropolitan Tucson Convention and Visitors Bureau, 215
Mildred and Dildred, 191
Miller's Surplus, 198
Mi Nidito Café, 136
Miraval Resort, 176–77
Miraval Tucson, 56–57
Mira Vista Resort, 168
Mission San Xavier del Bac, 19, 20, 24, 67–68, 68, 69, 213, 217
Miss Saigon, 141
MOCA on the Plaza (Museum of Contemporary Art), 89
Montana Avenue, 119–20
Morning Star Antiques, 187
Mount Lemmon, 23–24, 26, 166
Mount Lemmon Café, 24, 142
Mount Lemmon Highway, 155
Mount Lemmon Ski Valley, 24
Mrs. Tiggy-Winkle's, 191
Mudpies and Pigtails, 191
Museum of Contemporary Art (MOCA on the Plaza), 89
museums, 66, 85–94, 159, 160
music, 94–95, 189
The Myriad, 201

N

Nadine's Bakery, 144
National Bank of Arizona, 204
National car rental, 32
National Weather Service Forecast Office, 206
Native Seeds SEARCH, 193
natural history, 12–15
Neo of Melaka, 133
New Architecture Dance Theatre, 75–76
newspapers, 210
New York Times, 210
nightlife, 98–101
Nimbus Brewing and Tap Room, 100
Nimbus Brewing Co., 148
No Anchovies, 145
Nogales, 24, 142, 186
Northern Arizona University, Tucson, 215
North restaurant, 130–31, 209, 210
Nuestras Raíces Literary Arts Festival, 84

O

O'Connor, Hugh, 20
Ocotillo Café Restaurant, 98, 143
off-roading, 207
Old Main, 66

Old Pima County Courthouse, 64
Old Pueblo Archaeology Center, 206
The Old Pueblo Playwrights, 105
Old Pueblo Trolley, Inc., 32, 206, 207
Old Town Artisans, 81–83, 197, 199
Old Tucson Studios, 25
O'Malley's on Fourth, 99
Omni National Tucson Resort, 57–58
Oracle State Park, 24
Oracle View theater, 73
Ordinary Bike Shop, 154, 198
The Other Side, 201
outdoor recreation. *see also* parks; parks; sports
　　ballooning, 151–52
　　bicycles, 33, 152–55
　　camping, 156–57
　　family activities, 158–60
　　guided tours, 206–7
　　hiking, 163–68, 217
　　horseback riding, 168–70
　　in-line skating, 170
　　off-roading, 207
　　picnicking, 170–72
　　rock climbing, 172–73
　　rodeos, 42, 91–92, 108
　　walking tours, 62

P

Paca de Paja B&B, 39
Paleo-Indians, 16
Palo Verde Mental Health Service, 209
Paper Paper Paper, 193
Paris Flea Market, 201
Park Place Mall, 197–98
parks. *see also* outdoor recreation
　　Armory Park, 65, 171
　　Catalina Park, 171
　　El Presidio Park, 64
　　Himmel Park, 171
　　Oracle State Park, 24
　　Picacho Peak State Park, 24
　　Reid Park, 158–59, 172
　　Saguaro National Park, 22, 141, 202, 208
　　Tucson Mountain Park, 24
　　Tumacácori National Historical Park, 66
Park University, Davis-Monthan Air Force Base, 215
Pastiche, 120
Pastiche Wine Shop, 148, 193
Pepper Group, 212
Peppersauce Campground, 157
Performance Bicycle, 154, 200
personal training, 180–81
Peter Glenn Ski and Sports, 170
pet hospitals, 209
P.F. Chang's, 126–27

Philabaum Glass Gallery, 83
Picacho Peak State Park, 24
Picante Boutique, 193
picnicking, 170–72
Piece by Piece, 189
pilates, 181
Pima Air & Space Museum, 89–90
Pima Canyon, 164
Pima Community College, 215
Pima County Public Library, 84–85
Pima Medical Institute, 215
Pima people, 16, 18–20
Pima Pet Clinic Animal Emergency, 209
Pinacate field, 15
Pioneer Memorial, 65
pizza, 144–46
plane travel, 31
Play It Again Sports, 170, 200
Plaza Liquors, 149
Plaza Palomino, 198
plazas, malls, and shopping centers, 197–98
Plush bar & club, 95, 97
police department, 203
The Postal History Foundation, 90
pottery, ancient, 18
Pottery Barn, 195
Preen, 201
Prescott College, 215
Presidio of San Augustin de Tucson, 20
Presidio Trail Historic Walking Tour, 62
prickly pear cactus, 115
primary schools, 213–14
Pro Baseball Spring Training, 107–8
Providence Institute, 182
The Providence Institute, 215
Pusch Ridge Stables, 168–69

R
radio stations, 211–12
Radisson Suites, 49
Rainbow Guitars, 189
Ramada Inn and Suites Foothills Resort, 49
ranches, guest, 40–42
Randolph Golf Course, 161
Randolph Park Hotel and Suites, 49
Randolph Tennis Center, 179
Ra Sushi, 131–32
real estate companies, 212
recreation. see indoor recreation; outdoor
   recreation
Red Door Spa, 176
Redrock Biplane Tours, 207
Reid Park, 172
Reid Park Rose Garden, Gene C., 158–59
Reid Park Zoo, 159
religious services and organizations, 212–13

rental cars, 32
Residence Inn by Marriott, 49–50
Residence Inn by Marriott—Tucson Airport, 50
Residence Inn by Marriott—Williams Center, 50
resorts & spas, 52–59, 174–78, 217
restaurants. see dining
Rillito River Bike Trail, 33
Rincon Market, 146
Riverpark Inn, 50–51
Riverside Suites, 51
Road Condition Information, 213
A Roadrunner's Hostel, 42
road service, 213
road travel, 27–29
Rochelle K Fine Women's Apparel, 190
rock climbing, 172–73
Rocks and Ropes, 172–73
rodeos, 42, 91–92, 108
The Rogue Theatre, 105
Roma Imports, 146
Roman Catholic Diocese, 212–13
Rombach Gallery, Lionel, 81
Romero House, 64
Roosevelt Dam, 21
Rosa's, 136
Rose Canyon Campground, 157
Royal Elizabeth Bed & Breakfast, 40, 107
The Rumrunner, 149
Run.com, 173
running, 173–74
The Running Shop, 173–74, 200
The Rustic Candle Company, 193

S
Sabino Canyon, 166, 167, 167, 217
Sabino Equestrian Center, 169–70
Safeway Grocery Store, 210
Safeway PowerPump, 210
Saffron Indian Bistro, 142
Saguaro National Park, 22, 24, 141, 202, 208
Sam Hughes Inn, 40
Santa Catalina Mountains, 23–24
Santa Theresa Tile Works, 193–94
San Xavier Indian Reservation, 19
Sarnoff Art and Writing, 194
School of Dance at the University of Arizona, 76
schools, 213–15
The Screening Room, 72
seasonal events, 105–9
secondary schools, 213–14
Sentinel Peak, 67
Settlers West Galleries, 83
17th Street Market, 146
Shall We Dance, 76
The Shelter, 100
Sheraton Tucson Hotel and Suites, 51

Sher-E Punjab, 130
Shish Kebab House, 139
shopping. *see also* food purveyors
    antiques, 187
    bookstores, 188–89
    clothing, 189–91
    gifts, 191–94
    home furnishings, 194–96
    malls, plazas, and shopping centers, 197–98
    music, 189
    sporting goods, 198–200
    vintage, 200–201
Shot in the Dark Café, 209, 210
Showers Point Group Campground, 157
Silverbell Golf Course, 162
skating, in-line, 170
Sky Blue Wasabi, 132
Small Planet Bakery, 144
social history, 16–21
Solar Culture performing arts, 95
Sonoran Adventures, 207
Sonoran Desert, 12–15
The Sonoran Glass Art Academy, 70
Sosa-Carrillo-Freemon House, 90
Southern Arizona AIDS Foundation (SAAF), 209
Southern Arizona Balloon Excursions, 152
Southern Arizona Roadrunners, 174
Southern Arizona Transportation Museum, 90
Southern Arizona VA Healthcare System, 209
Southern Pacific Depot, 31
Southwestern Arizona Transportation Museum, 206
southwestern clothing, 190–91
Southwest Off-Road Tours, 207
Southwest Trekking, 173
spas, 174–78
specialty food markets, 146–48
Speedway Veterinary Hospital, 209
Spencer Campground, 157
sporting goods, 198–200
sports. *see also* outdoor recreation
    events, 99–100, 106
    golf, 160–62, 161
    running, 173–74
    tennis, 178–80, 179
St. Augustine Cathedral, 62–63
St. Joseph's Hospital, 207
St. Mark's Presbyterian Church, 213
St. Philip's in the Hills, 66
Steinfeld Mansion, 65
Stevens House, 65
Stevie Eller Dance Theatre, 66
stone massage, 174
Stork's Nest, 64
Summerhaven, 142

Summit Hut, 200
sunbathing, clothing-optional, 168
Sun Tran, 31–32
Superstition mountains, 13
Swat Personal Training, 180

T
Table Talk, 195
Takamatsu, 132
Tanque Verde Falls, 168
Tanque Verde Ranch, 41, 41
Tanque Verde School District, 214
Taqueria Pico de Gallo, 4, 137–38, 218
Tara Mahayana Buddhist Center, 213
Tavolino, 131
taxi travel, 32
Teatro Carmen, 63
television stations, 212
Temple of Music and Art, 65
tennis, 178–80, 179
Teresa's Mosaic Café, 138–39
theater, live, 101–5
theaters, 71–72
Thrifty care rental, 32
Thunder Canyon Brewery, 101
Time Market, 146–47, 210
Tohono Chul Park Tea Room, 120, 121
Tohono O'odlam Nation, 17, 18–20, 206
Tombstone, 24
Tom's Fine Furniture & Collectibles, 187
topography, 12–14
Touch of Tranquility Spa, 178
tourist information, 215
tours, guided, 206–7
town government, 204
Toxic Ranch Records, 189
TPCBAC (Tucson-Pima County Bicycle Advisory Committee), 155
Trader Joe's, 147–48
trade schools, 215
train travel, 31
transportation
    bicycles, 33
    bus travel, 30–32
    car travel, 27–29
    getting around, 31–33
    getting there, 27–31
    plane travel, 31
    rental cars, 32
    taxi travel, 32
    train travel, 31
    trolley, 32–33
Tres Amigos World Imports, 195
Trident Grill & Bar, 100
trolley, 32–33

Trophies Bar and Grill, 100
Tubac, 24, 66
Tucson
    maps, 6, 28, 62
    scenery, 17, 23, 33, 77, 82, 128, 150, 169, 216
Tucson Balloon Rides, 152
Tucson Botanical Gardens, 158, 159
Tucson Children's Museum, 91, 159
Tucson Citizen, 210
Tucson Clay Co-Op, 70
Tucson Creative Dance Center, 76
Tucson Film and Music Festival, 74
tucsonfilm.com Short Fest, 74
Tucson Gem & Mineral Show, 108
Tucson Heart Hospital, 207
Tucson Home Magazine, 211
Tucson Inner City Express Transit (T.I.C.E.T), 32
Tucson International Airport, 31
Tucson International Mariachi Conference, 108
Tucson Jazz Society, 96
Tucson Jewish Community Center, 163
Tucson Lifestyle, 211
Tucson Meet Yourself festival, 108
Tucson Mountain Park, 24
Tucson Museum of Art & Historic Block, 64, 91, 92, 160
Tucson Parks and Recreation Department, 206
Tucson Pilates Body Studio, 181
Tucson Pima Arts Council (TPAC), 71
Tucson Poetry Festival, 85
Tucson Pride Week, 107
Tucson Racquet and Fitness Club, 179
Tucson Regional Ballet, 76–78
Tucson Rodeo Parade Museum, 91–92
Tucson Stained Glass, 70
Tucson Symphony Orchestra, 97
Tucson Thrift Shop, 201
Tucson Trail Ride, 170
Tucson Unified School District, 214
Tucson Weekly, 210–11
Tucson Yoga, 182
Tumacácori, 66
Tumacácori National Historical Park, 66

U
Unitarian Universalist Church, 213
universities, 215
University Boulevard, 195
University Campus Health Services, 209
University Medical Center, 207, 209
University Museum of Art, 66
University of Arizona
    about, 21, 215
    Athletics, 179–80
    Bookstore, 189
    campus, 65–66

Center for Creative Photography, 66, 87, 102, 217
    map, 67
    Mineral Museum, 92
    Museum of Art and Archive of Visual Arts, 92–93
    Poetry Center, 85, 86
    School of Music, 97
Urban Athletics Boot Camp, 180–81
US Bank, 204

V
Valley of the Moon, 160
Varsity Clubs of America Suites Hotel, 51
Ventana Cave, 206
The Ventana Room, 120–21, 122
veterinarians, 209
video stores, 74
Village Bakehouse, 144
Vin Tabla, 121–22
vintage shopping, 200–201
Viscount Suites Hotel, 51
Vivace, 131
VOICES Community Stories, 214
Voyager Inn at Voyager RV Resort, 52

W
Waffle House, 210
walking tours, 62
Walsh Federal Courthouse, James A., 64
Walter Gaby's Rug Resource, 196
Water of Life Metropolitan Community Church, 107
W Boutique, 190
weather, 206
Wells Fargo, 204
Western Warehouse, 191
Westin La Paloma, 57, 58, 58–59, 176
Westin La Paloma Resort & Spa, 177
Westward Look Resort, 59, 59
what to wear, 206
White Stallion Ranch, 41–42
Whole Foods, 148
Wilder, Janos, 110
Wildflower Grill, 122–23
Wilko, 194
Windmill Suites at St. Philip's Plaza, 52
wine, beer & liquor, 148–49
Wingspan, 107
women's clothing, 189–90
workout facilities and gyms, 162–63, 180–83
World Famous Tucson Rodeo, 108

Y
Yaqui Deer Dances, 108–9

Yellow Cab, 32
Yikes! Toys, 191
YMCA, 163, 206
yoga, 181–83
Yoga Flow, 182
Yoga Oasis, 183
Yoshimatsu, 132–33
Yuki Sushi, 133

Z
Zachary's, 145–46
Zemam's, 127
Zia Record Exchange, 189
Zocalo, 196
Zoe Boutique, 190
zoos, 159
Zuzi! Dance Company, 78

Lodging by Price

Inexpensive: up to $100
Moderate: $100-$200
Expensive: $200-$300
Very Expensive: over $300

Inexpensive
Clarion Hotel—Tucson Airport, 43
A Roadrunner's Hostel, 42

Inexpensive-Moderate
Best Western Brisas Hotel—Tucson Airport, 42–43
Fairfield Inn by Marriott—I-10/Butterfield Business Park, 45
Hotel Congress, 47–48
La Posada del Valle, 38
Sam Hughes Inn, 40
Viscount Suites Hotel, 51

Moderate
Catalina Park Inn, 36
Comfort Suites at Sabino Canyon, 43
Comfort Suites Tucson Mall, 43
Courtyard by Marriott—Tucson Airport, 43–44
Courtyard by Marriott—Williams Centre, 44
Doubletree Hotel—Reid Park, 44–45
El Presidio B&B, 37
Embassy Suites-Tucson Paloma Village, 45
The Hotel Arizona, 46–47
Paca de Paja B&B, 39
Radisson Suites, 49
Ramada Inn and Suites Foothills Resort, 49
Randolph Park Hotel and Suites, 49
Voyager Inn at Voyager RV Resort, 52
Windmill Suites at St. Philip's Plaza, 52

Moderate-Expensive
Best Western Inn Suites, 42
Desert Diamond Casino Resort Hotel, 44
Embassy Suites-Williams Centre, 45
Four Points by Sheraton—University Plaza, 45–46

Hacienda Del Desierto, 37–38
Hilton Tucson East, 46
Holiday Inn and Suites-Tucson Airport North, 46
Holiday Inn Express Hotel and Suites-Tucson Airport, 46
Hotel Tucson City Center Conference Suite Resort, 48
Hyatt Place Tucson Airport, 48
The Lodge at Ventana Canyon, 55–56
Residence Inn by Marriott—Tucson Airport, 50
Riverpark Inn, 50–51
The Royal Elizabeth B&B, 40
Sheraton Tucson Hotel and Suites, 51
Varsity Clubs of America Suites Hotel, 51

Moderate-Very Expensive
Casa Tierra Adobe, 35–36
Hacienda del Sol Guest Ranch Resort, 40–41
Hilton Tucson El Conquistador Golf & Tennis Resort, 53–54
Lodge on the Desert, 48
Loews Ventana Canyon Resort, 56
Riverside Suites, 51
White Stallion Ranch, 41–42

Expensive
Marriott University Park, 48–49
Residence Inn by Marriott, 49–50
Westward Look Resort, 59

Expensive-Very Expensive
Omni National Tucson Resort, 57–58
Residence Inn by Marriott—Williams Center, 50
Tanque Verde Ranch, 41
Westin La Paloma, 58–59

Very Expensive
Arizona Inn, 52
Canyon Ranch, 52–53
JW Marriott Starr Pass Resort & Spa, 54–55
Miraval Tucson, 56–57

Dining by Price

Inexpensive: up to $15
Moderate: $15-$30
Expensive: $30-$65
Very Expensive: $65 or more

Inexpensive
Ali Baba, 139
BK Hot Dogs, 133–134
B Line, 113–114
Blue Willow, 123–124
Café 54, 124–125
Delectables, 125
El Charro Café, 135
El Cubanito, 127
El Guero Canelo, 135
El Minuto, 135–136
El Torero, 136
Epic Café, 125–126
Gandhi, 129
Ghini's French Café, 127–128
The Grill, 126
Guadalajara Grill, 137
Guilin Healthy Chinese Restaurant, 126
India Oven, 130
Karuna's Thai Plate, 140–141
Luxor Café, 139
Mi Nidito Café, 136
Miss Saigon, 141
Mount Lemmon Café, 142
Rosa's, 136
Sher-E Punjab, 130
Shish Kebab House, 139
Taqueria Pico de Gallo, 137–138
Teresa's Mosaic Café, 138–139
Tohono Chul Park Tea Room, 120
Yoshimatsu, 132–133
Zemam's, 127
Zinburger, 123

Moderate
Acacia, 112
Armitage Wine Lounge and Café, 123
Athens on 4th Avenue, 129
Barrio Grill, 113
Blanco, 134–135
Bluefin, 114
Café Poca Cosa, 137
Café Roka, 143
Candela, 139–140
Casa Vicente, 140
The Cup Café, 125
Cushing Street Bar and Restaurant, 114
The Dish, 114–115
Enoteca, 130
Feast, 115–116
Jax Kitchen, 117
J Bar, 117–118
Jonathan's Cork, 118
Kingfisher, 118
La Roca, 142
Le Delice Bakery & Café, 128
Le Rendez-Vous, 129
Mariscos Chihuahua, 137
Montana Avenue, 119–120
Neo of Melaka, 133
North, 130–131
Ocotillo Café Restaurant, 143
Pastiche, 120
P.F. Chang's, 126–127
Ra Sushi, 131–132
Saffron Indian Bistro, 142
Sky Blue Wasabi, 132
Takamatsu, 132
Tavolino, 131
Vin Tabla, 121–122
Vivace, 131
Wildflower Grill, 122–123
Yuki Sushi, 133

Expensive
Anthony's in the Catalinas, 112
Arizona Inn, 112–113
Fleming's Prime Steakhouse, 116
The Grill at Hacienda del Sol, 116
Janos Restaurant, 116–117
McClintock's, 119
McMahon's Prime Steak House, 119

Very Expensive
The Ventana Room, 120–121

Dining by Cuisine

American
Acacia, 112
Armitage Wine Lounge and Café, 123
Barrio Grill, 113
Blue Willow, 123–124
Café 54, 124–125
Café Roka, 143
The Cup Café, 125
Cushing Street Bar and Restaurant, 114
The Dish, 114–115
Epic Café, 125–126
Feast, 115–116
The Grill, 126
Jax Kitchen, 117
Jonathan's Cork, 118
McClintock's, 119
Montana Avenue, 119–120
Mount Lemmon Café, 142
Pastiche, 120
The Ventana Room, 120–121
Wildflower Grill, 122–123
Zinburger, 123

Chinese
Guilin Healthy Chinese Restaurant, 126
P.F. Chang's, 126–127

Continental
Anthony's in the Catalinas, 112

Cuban
El Cubanito, 127

Ethiopian
Zemam's, 127

French
Ghini's French Café, 127–128
Le Delice Bakery & Café, 128
Le Rendez-Vous, 129

French/Southwestern
Janos Restaurant, 116–117

Greek
Athens on 4th Avenue, 129

Indian
Gandhi, 129
India Oven, 130
Saffron Indian Bistro, 142
Sher-E Punjab, 130

Italian
Enoteca, 130
North, 130–131
Tavolino, 131
Vivace, 131

Japanese
Ra Sushi, 131–132
Sky Blue Wasabi, 132
Takamatsu, 132
Yoshimatsu, 132–133
Yuki Sushi, 133

Malaysian
Neo of Melaka, 133

Mediterranean/Californian
Delectables, 125

Mexican
Café Poca Cosa, 137
Guadalajara Grill, 137
La Roca, 142
Mariscos Chihuahua, 137
Taqueria Pico de Gallo, 137–138
Teresa's Mosaic Café, 138–139

Mexican/Latin American/Caribbean
J Bar, 117–118

Mexican (Sonoran)
BK Hot Dogs, 133–134
Blanco, 134–135
El Charro Café, 135
El Guero Canelo, 135
El Minuto, 135–136
El Torero, 136
Mi Nidito Café, 136
Rosa's, 136

Middle Eastern
Ali Baba, 139
Luxor Café, 139
Shish Kebab House, 139

Peruvian
Candela, 139–140

Regional/International
Arizona Inn, 112–113

Seafood
Bluefin, 114
Kingfisher, 118
Vin Tabla, 121–122

Southwestern
B Line, 113–114
Ocotillo Café Restaurant, 143

Spanish
Casa Vicente, 140
The Grill at Hacienda del Sol, 116
Tohono Chul Park Tea Room, 120

Steak and Seafood
Fleming's Prime Steakhouse, 116
McMahon's Prime Steak House, 119

Thai
Karuna's Thai Plate, 140–141

Vietnamese
Miss Saigon, 141